MEDIA AND SOCIETY

MEDIA AND SOCIETY

A Critical Perspective

Third Edition

ARTHUR ASA BERGER

with illustrations by the author

ROWMAN & LITTLEFIELD PUBLISHERS, INC.
Lanham • Boulder • New York • Toronto • Plymouth, UK

Published by Rowman & Littlefield Publishers, Inc.
A wholly owned subsidiary of The Rowman & Littlefield Publishing Group, Inc.
4501 Forbes Boulevard, Suite 200, Lanham, Maryland 20706
www.rowman.com

10 Thornbury Road, Plymouth PL6 7PP, United Kingdom

British Library Cataloguing in Publication Information Available

Library of Congress Cataloging-in-Publication Data

Berger, Arthur Asa, 1933–
    Media and society : a critical perspective / Arthur Asa Berger.—3rd ed.
        p. cm.
    Includes bibliographical references and indexes.
    ISBN 978-1-4422-1779-9 (cloth : alk. paper)— ISBN 978-1-4422-1780-5
(pbk. : alk. paper)—ISBN 978-1-4422-1781-2 (electronic)
    1. Mass media—Social aspects. I. Title.
    HM1206.B47 2012
    302.23—dc23
                                                        2012014723

⊗™ The paper used in this publication meets the minimum requirements of
American National Standard for Information Sciences—Permanence of Paper
for Printed Library Materials, ANSI/NISO Z39.48-1992.

Printed in the United States of America

To my pal, Tom Maxon. Tai Chi master, excellent barista,
imaginative chef, and friend.

CONTENTS

ACKNOWLEDGMENTS FOR
THE THIRD EDITION

I'm pleased to offer this third edition of *Media and Society* to my readers. I was asked to write this new edition because the first two editions of this book had enough readers to warrant an updating and expansion of the book. I hope that you will find this new edition provides you with a number of ideas that will enhance and expand your understanding of the relation that exists between media and society.

In the third edition of this book, I decided to deal with a number of new aspects of the media and to offer enhanced discussions of topics found in previous editions of the book. In this third edition of *Media and Society* you will find I have:

revised the order of the chapters to make the book flow better
updated the statistics
expanded the analysis of cell phone use and texting
discussed the impact of Facebook on young people
added to my discussion of social media
offered a list of things to do to analyze commercials
added new drawings
discussed the scandal involving the Murdoch media empire
added new material on modernism and postmodernism

and made numerous other changes, major and minor, in the book.

I've had the benefit of a number of useful suggestions from professors who have used *Media and Society*, for which I am grateful. I have incorporated many of these suggestions in the book. I want to thank Marissa Park for her continued support and encouragement, and a reader whose name I do not know for ideas about how the book might be reorganized. Things move so rapidly in the media that it is impossible to keep up with them, but by focusing on concepts that can be used to understand the media, I believe I have provided you with a number of ideas and theories that will enable you to make sense of them yourselves.

I hope you will like this book and that you will learn something interesting about the role the media play in society and also—and this is of particular importance—in your lives. If you are typical students, you spend a great deal of time with the media. The question we must ask is—you use the media, but how do the media use you? You might be interested in how the media might be affecting your life, your friends, the members of your family, and society in general.

INTRODUCTION: YOU AND THE MEDIA—A CONSIDERATION

There have been incredible changes in the media world since I wrote the second edition of this book in 2007. The use of cell phones has exploded, the iPad (and hundreds of other so-called "iPad-killer" tablets) has revolutionized the computer world, and more than 750 million people now spend time on Facebook and millions of others send off tweets and participate in other social media. I will deal with many of these new developments in this third edition of *Media and Society*.

Let me begin with a typical student and a television program she is watching. One night in 2013 a young college student—let's call her Emily Greatgal—turned on her television set to watch a rerun episode of *CSI: Crime Scene Investigation*. This action is similar to what millions of us do every day when we "watch television." We can look upon Emily's watching this show from a number of different points of view, which I call focal points involving media and society. We have:

1. An **art work or text**. In this case, the text is the show *Crime Scene Investigation*. I will adapt the convention used in academic discourse and call television programs, films, print advertisements, commercials, and the like *texts*.
2. An **audience**. Here the audience is Emily Greatgal and everyone else watching the show.
3. The many different kinds of **artists** such as actors, actresses, producers, directors, camera-persons, and script writers who are responsible for creating and performing the text.
4. The larger entity of which the CSI audience is a part, namely a country such as **America**.
5. The **medium** (television in this case) that carries the program.

Let's assume that Emily Greatgal is a citizen of the United States of America—that is, she's an American. (I will generally use the term *American* in this book to stand for the *United States* so I don't have to keep writing *the United States* all the time. And when I write "society" I will be discussing American society, unless otherwise noted.) Audiences are parts of a larger entity, namely society—not everyone in a given society watches the same program on television at any given time during the day or night (and not everyone watching a television program in America is a citizen).

This discussion of focal points builds upon a framework originated by a literary scholar, M. H. Abrams. In his book *The Mirror and the Lamp: Romantic Theory and the Critical Tradition*, he suggests there are four relationship to be considered when dealing with literary works in print form: the *universe* refers to the world at large, the *work* is what we call a "text" in academic jargon, the *artist* refers to the creator of the text, and the *audience* refers to the people who read the text.

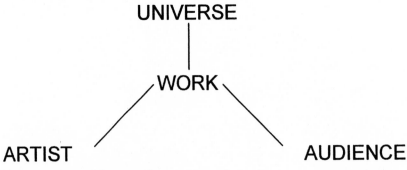

Figure I.1.   M. H. Abrams's Diagram

In my work on focal points, what I did was add "media" to the mix and change "universe" to "society." Abrams was writing about literary works, so the medium (print) was not an important consideration for him. In my analysis, however, there are many different media, and they play varying roles in the creation and dissemination of texts.

FOCAL POINTS IN THE STUDY OF THE MASS MEDIA

What we have, then, are what I call the focal points that can be used in dealing with the media in a given society. For the sake of alliteration to help you remember these focal points, I will use words that begin with an "A" for four of them. We have, then,

Art works (texts in various genres),
Audiences (of varying sizes),
Artists (of all kinds),
America (the United States of), and
Media (such as television, film, video, and print).

All of these are, or can be, connected to each other. For example, there are interrelationships that exist between a text carried on television, the artists who are involved in creating and performing the text, the medium in which the text is carried, the audience for whom the text is created, and the society in which the audience lives. Depending on our interests, we can focus on one or more of these focal points in studying the media.

Since this book deals with the social aspects of the mass media, it will focus on media, audiences, and society—but it will also have a good deal to say about mass-mediated texts and media artists. We must always keep in mind that the media carry texts or works of popular art (for the most part) and not neglect aesthetic aspects of these texts due to our fascination with social, political, economic, and cultural matters related to the media. We also must remember that the media affect the texts they carry. In some cases audiences are global, which means "society" expands from, say, the United States to other countries and in some cases—such as in the broadcast of the Super Bowl football game—much of the world.

CSI: CRIME SCENE INVESTIGATION
AND THE FOCAL POINTS

Let's take an episode of the show *Crime Scene Investigation* and plug it into the focal points chart. This may help you see more clearly what I'm talking about.

Art Work: *Crime Scene Investigation* (an episode of)
Audience: General public
Medium: Television
Artist: Writers, production staff, directors, and performers
America: (and other countries in many cases)

Writers (and artists of all kinds) always must think about their audiences. For example, my most immediate audience for this book is college students taking courses dealing with media in the United States, but I hope the book might be adopted in other countries as well. When I wrote this book I had a specific audience in mind—people like you, my reader—whom I assume are undergraduates taking courses on media, popular culture, or **communication** in colleges and universities. If I had a different audience I was trying to reach—for example, Ph.D. candidates in communication—I would have written it in a much different manner. So the potential audience affects the way books are written and, by extension, the way all texts carried by the mass media are created.

I think you can see from this example that there are many different topics to consider when dealing with media and society. There is a logical problem involved with writing about the media and society—where do you best deal with a particular topic, since some topics could be put in any number of different places? For example, where do you write about media ethics—in a chapter on media, on society, or on media artists and creators?

In this book, I put my discussion of media ethics in the chapter on artists and creators, since they are the people who most directly face ethical problems in creating their texts. Is it ethical to make a print advertisement for cigarettes? Is it ethical to make a television commercial that slanders and lies about a political figure? Is it ethical to write a television script or make a movie or video game full of gratuitous violence? That is a problem that artists and creators face, even though there may be other people and other factors involved—such as the people who work for the networks that carry violent shows. I have tried to place the topics where I thought they best fit. In July 2011, there was a scandal involving Rupert Murdoch's newspapers that I deal with. It seems that some people who worked for Rupert Murdoch's publications hacked into people's cell phones looking for information that could lead to "scoops." That provoked a series of investigations that all deal with ethical responsibilities of editors, reporters, and news organizations.

After reading *Media and Society*, Third Edition, I hope you will have a better understanding of the role that the media and the texts they carry have played (and continue to play) in your life, in the lives of your friends and the members of your family, and in the society in which you find yourself. Although you may make individual choices of what media to consume (and what other products and services to consume), your decisions are affected by demographic factors such as your age, socio-economic class, gender, educational level, and zip code, among other things.

You may not realize it, but you fit into certain marketing categories and thus your behavior is, in a certain sense, predictable. For example, if

you are 18 to 34, live in an upscale area, are college-educated, and are white, you are a typical member of the audience of *CSI: Crime Scene Investigation*, according to the Nielsen ratings. (There is some question, I might add, about how reliable the Nielsen ratings are.)

TWO ANECDOTES ON CHOICE

This matter of our behavior being predictable is quite interesting and extends to realms other than choosing films to see or television programs to watch. In the summer of 2002 my wife and I took a cruise from San Francisco to Alaska and back. During the cruise we were given a tour of the ship's galley. The *maitre d'* who was leading the tour told us that the cruise line was able to predict, with remarkable accuracy, what people would choose to eat at every meal. Long experience had taught them what to expect.

Thus, at a given dinner, while there may have been five main courses, the ships cooks knew that 80 percent of the diners would order a certain main course, such as lobster, 10 percent would order a different main course, and so on. This anecdote serves as a metaphor for our understanding media

usage. We can choose anything we like (given what is available, that is), but we tend to like certain programs depending upon our demographic and psychographic profiles and other variables.

The Puritan preacher Jonathan Edwards raised this matter of choice and action many years ago. He was trying to figure out how human beings could be free if God was all-powerful. His solution was to suggest there were two realms to be considered—the realm of choice, where God was all-powerful, and the realm of action, in which people could do whatever they wanted. The problem with this notion is that if God determines what choices we will make and then allows us to choose whatever we want, in reality we only have the illusion of freedom, since our choices have already been determined.

Age is a very important factor. In 1984 I was a visiting professor at the Annenberg School for Communication at the University of Southern California. I had a large class of 200 students taking a course in popular culture. I brought a number of visitors from the media world to speak to my students. One visitor was a vice president of an easy-listening light rock station. When I introduced him and mentioned the station where he worked, my students all laughed.

"That's all right," he said. "You're laughing now, but when you're 40 years old you'll be listening to my station. And I've got statistics to prove it." So the music we like when we are 20 may not be the music we like when we are 30 or 40, and the same applies to our preferences for texts in all the media.

Scenes with alcohol, tobacco, and/or illicit drugs are present in seven out of ten prime-time network dramatic programs. Scenes of drinking alcoholic beverages are seen an average of every twenty minutes . . . More major characters in prime-time television drink alcoholic beverages than anything else . . . Female smokers now outnumber male smokers among major characters in prime-time television . . . In a sample of the 40 highest-grossing movie titles for the years 1994 through 1995, 39 (97.5 percent) contain portrayals of alcohol, smoking and/or illicit drugs. Those who view the most popular music video channel see alcohol use an average of every fourteen minutes, tobacco use every twenty-five minutes, and illicit drugs every forty minutes . . . The use of addictive substances is shown as generally risk-free. More than nine out of ten drinkers, more than eight out of ten smokers, and six out of ten illicit drug users experience positive health effects or no health effects . . . . Addictive substances appear much more frequently in movies and music videos than on prime-time television. Only one of the forty movies surveyed does not have scenes involving alcohol, tobacco, and/or illegal drugs . . . Two titles do not include any portrayal of alcohol, and six titles do not have any smoking. Illicit drug scenes are present in over one-third of the movies, more than twice their presence on prime-time television . . . . A child who grows up watching only three hours of prime-time television a day on one channel will have watched 32,000 characters who demonstrate tobacco as a part of their lives. Over 2,500 tobacco smokers will have been playing central roles in the stories being told. Yet the story of the negative health affects and addiction is not one of them. The child will have to view 2,200 smokers on television before seeing one who experiences negative health effect.

George Gerbner, "Drugs in Television, Movies, and
Music Videos," in Y. R. Kamalipour and K. R. Rampal,
Media, Sex, Violence and Drugs in the Global Village
(2001:69–70, 73,75)

1

MEDIA IN OUR THOUGHTS AND LIVES

A Psycho-Social Perspective on Individuals, Society, and the Media

Although I've never met you, my reader, there are certain things I *think* I know about you. There is one important qualification I must make, however, and that is I must assume that you are a typical American college student taking a course that deals, one way or another, with the subject of this book—media and society. Before I tell you what I might know about you, let me begin by telling a story involving Johnny Q. Public, whom I imagine is someone possibly very much like you.

JOHNNY Q. PUBLIC'S MEDIA USAGE

The hero of this story is Johnny Q. Public who has an apartment in Normal City, USA, about thirty minutes' drive from Central State University, where he is a junior majoring in media studies. At 7:30 AM his clock radio turns on. It is a news show that has information on traffic and a weather report every ten minutes. He takes a shower, brushes his teeth, and has breakfast. Then he jumps in his car to drive to Central State University, in time (or maybe a few minutes late) for his 9:00 AM class. He listens to the radio while he is driving. He's done with classes by 2:00 PM and goes to his part-time job in a gym, where he is a trainer. He works until 5:00 PM. At the gym, popular music is played over the loudspeaker system. He drives back to his apartment, listening to the radio again, and gets home by 5:30 PM. He turns on his television set and cooks dinner. He watches television while he eats. He does an hour of homework while he listens to some music on his iPod. Then he sends a text message to his girlfriend, Emily Greatgal, about going to the movies on Friday night. He sends a few other text messages to friends. Then he turns on his television set and watches for three or four hours.

After watching David Letterman, he checks his e-mail on the Internet. Next he plays a video game for a half an hour. Finally, he washes up, makes sure his clock radio alarm is set for the right time, and goes to bed late at night. He has spent close to the nine hours per day average that Americans spend involved with media of one kind or another. When he wakes up the next morning, he wonders "why am I so tired?"

During the course of a normal day, Johhny has listened to the radio for a couple of hours, watched television for three or four hours, listened to music at work and on his iPod for an hour or so, spent some time on the Internet, played a video game, and sent some text messages using his cell phone. Johnny's media usage is probably typical of people his age.

A GROUP PORTRAIT OF MY READERS

Given the fact that you are reading this book, I can make the following assumptions about you. There is a good possibility that:

1. You are between 17 and 25 years old.
2. You are studying at a college or university.
3. You grew up watching three or four hours of television a day, on average.
4. You have been subjected to hundreds of thousands of print advertisements, television and radio commercials, and online advertisements over the last ten or fifteen years.
5. You believe that while you are aware of these commercials, they do not influence your decision making in important ways.
6. You believe that while you "consume" eight or nine hours of media each day, your media diet doesn't have a significant impact on your life.
7. You also listen to the radio or music an hour or two each day and probably have some kind of gizmo such as an iPod that plays the kind of music you like.
8. You use a computer to do things such as write letters, notes, term papers and other reports, keep journals, and send e-mail to friends. While you work at the computer, you might also be listening to music or to the radio. That is, you often multi-task—you use several different media at the same time.

9. You believe in "individualism," whatever that means, though you may not know where the term comes from, and to some degree in "the American Dream."

Of course, I could be all wrong. You could be a precocious 14-year-old or a 75-year-old retired person and you don't watch television or listen to the radio and you hate popular music. Instead, you spend your days reading poetry and listening to chamber music and opera. You might have gotten this book out of the library, or an older brother or sister had it and you noticed it and picked it up because you're interested in media because you suspect that some media may, in some way, be having some kind of an effect on your life.

It could be that you don't even know who Lady Gaga is.

But I doubt it.

STATISTICS ON MEDIA USE

These assumptions I made are based on data that researchers have accumulated about media usage in the United States. A study released on January 20, 2010, by the Kaiser Family Foundation had some interesting statistics on media usage in the lives of 8- to 18-year-old Americans (www.kff.org). It was based on a survey, a nationally representative sample, of several thousand young people 8 to 18 years of age. It said—and I'm quoting from a news release issued by the Kaiser Family Foundation dealing with recreational (non-school) use of TV, videos, music, video games, movies, computers, and print—the following:

> Five years ago, we reported that young people spent an average of nearly 6½ hours (6:21) a day with media—and managed to pack more than 8½ hours (8:33) worth of media content into that time by multitasking. At that point it seemed that young people's lives were filled to the bursting point with media. Today, however, those levels of use have been shattered. Over the past five years, young people have increased the amount of time they spend consuming media by an hour and seventeen minutes daily, from 6:21 to 7:38—almost the amount of time most adults spend at work each day, except that young people use media seven days a week instead of five. Moreover, given the amount of time they spend using more than one medium at a time, today's youth pack a total of 10 hours and 45 minutes worth of media content into those daily 7½

hours—an increase of almost 2¼ hours of media exposure per day over the past five years.

This means the typical 8- to 18-year-old American is spending more than a full-time work week with media.

These statistics suggest that young people in America consume approximately 3000 hours of media with media each year. More than 1100 of those hours come from watching television, but while they are watching television, they may be doing other things involving media use, such as reading a book or chatting with a friend on the telephone. Contrast that with a typical course in a university that is around 45 hours for a semester and you see how important a place media, of all kinds, has in the lives of most young people.

The Kaiser study found that children and teenagers 8 to 18 have the following in their bedrooms:

	2009	**2004**	**1999**
Radio	75%	84%	86%
TV	71%	68%	65%
CD Player	68%	86%	88%
DVD or VCR Player	57%	54%	36%
Cable/Satellite TV	49%	37%	29%
Computer	36%	31%	21%
Internet Access	33%	20%	10%
Video Game Console	50%	49%	45%
Premium Channels	24%	20%	15%
TiVo/other DVR	13%	10%	n/a

Media in Bedrooms of 8 to 18 Year Olds Over Time

The bedrooms of our children have become media emporia, so to speak.

Data from the National Center for Education Statistics (nces.ed.gov) indicate that there were more than 19.1 million students in two- and four-year colleges and graduate schools in the United States in 2010 and these students have a purchasing power of some $306 billion according to a report on www.MediaPost.com. According to a report by Teenage Research Unlimited mentioned in the January 13, 2003 issue of *The New York Times*, the average 16-year-old spent $104 a week. Given the dire straits the economy has been in recent years, teenagers don't have as much discretionary income now. A recent Census Bureau report states that teens have about $2700 a year from allowances and part time work, or about $50

Some other web sites devoted to children and teenagers, and media are:

http://www.education.com/reference/article/media-influence-children/
http://www.ncbi.nlm.nih.gov/pmc/articles/PMC2594155/
http://pediatrics.aappublications.org/content/117/4/1427.full
http://www.pamf.org/teen/life/bodyimage/media.html
http://www.pbs.org/parents/childrenandmedia/
http://www.commonsensemedia.org/advice-for-parents/side-effects
  -media

---

a week. So teenagers and college students spend a lot of money, and the advertising agencies and marketers are out to do what they can to channel this money into spending for the "right" things—that is, the goods and services that these agencies are selling, such as clothes, fast foods, diet foods, CDs, and going to the movies.

MEDIA EFFECTS AND YOUR LIFE

If I were to ask you, "What effect has the media had on your life?" you might offer the following answer, "I am *aware* of the media, but I'm not really *affected* by it!" I ask this question because several years ago I was interviewed by a reporter from a newspaper in New York. There had been a survey of teenagers who reported that they were "aware" of advertising but not "influenced" by it to any significant decree. The reporter thought that these teenagers were deluding themselves and wanted to know what I thought about the matter.

So the question arises—what influence (or in the language of social science, what effects) has your incredible exposure to the media had on your life—and the lives of all kinds of other people like you who, collectively, form American society, or who are members of any other society. That is the question this book will try to answer, and it will do so by looking at the role media plays in American society and the way American society impacts upon the media. It is a complicated matter, but I will try to get to the heart of the matter in the pages that follow. Let me suggest one way that the media, and television in particular, might affect some people.

TELEVISION VIEWING AND "VICIOUS" CYCLES

In his book *A Psychiatric Study of Myths and Fairy Tales*, psychiatrist Julius E. Heuscher suggests that young children who are exposed to material on television programs that is too adult for them—given their age and developmental levels—become very disturbed. As he explained, (1967:325)

> The child who is being presented with an over-abundance of adult-life conflicts and desires and who thereby is being pushed toward grownup ideas, tends to become afraid of growing up and is therefore stunted in his maturation process. I am talking about stories with nasty arguments between men and women, stories full of violence, stories about broken families, divorces and infidelity and that kind of thing.

This isn't a problem with books, because young children are not able to read material in books that will disturb them. (Heuscher doesn't say but we have to assume quite young.) But children can see the stories on television and follow at least to some extent what happened. As a result of their exposure to this material, some of them become upset and anxious, and this anxiety affects them as they grew older. They fear growing up and becoming adults. They become distrustful of others, especially members of the opposite sex, and avoid intimate relationships with them and with others because they are afraid that they will be rejected or that they will become involved in bad relationships—just like the people in television shows they watched when they were youngsters. This leads to a fear of marriage, to non-relational sexual behavior, and an inability to have intimate relationships of all kinds.

As a result of this kind of behavior, these adults are unhappy, which leads to various kinds of escapism—which often takes the form of compulsive shopping, but especially the viewing of television programs, which they watch to obtain "relief." Thus they become locked in a **vicious cycle**. Because they had difficulty forming relationships with others, they were lonely. To assuage this loneliness they ended up watching a great deal of television, and thus they developed a kind of dependence on television—the same medium that led to their sorry state of affairs. Television provides relief but also, at the same time, reinforces their childhood fears—fears which caused their self-destructive behavior.

This kind of thing can also result from watching movies, but as a rule children don't watch movies as much as they watch television, and movie-watching is often controlled by parents, while television watching often

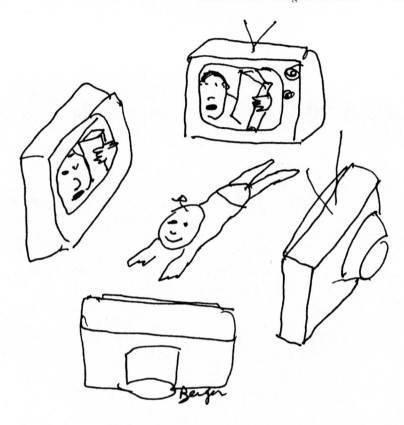

isn't. Is it possible, I ask, that you or someone you know got caught up in a vicious cycle like this? It's an interesting question to consider.

THE MEDIA IN SOCIETY

The media (*media* is the plural form of the term *medium*) are, we must remember, part of society. The media are one of many different institutions that exist within a society—*institutions* being the term used by sociologists to stand for enduring entities and organizations that play an important role in maintaining society. Some of the more important institutions in modern societies are those involving education, the family, religion, politics, and of particular importance to us, the mass media. The media entertain us, socialize us, inform us, educate us, sell things to us (and sell us, as audiences, to advertisers), and indoctrinate us—among other things. The media help shape our identities, our attitudes toward racial and ethnic minorities, and our attitudes about sexuality, and have many other effects.

There are, I should point out, a number of different and conflicting views about how to characterize the media and understand the role they play in society and in our lives. Some scholars see the media as essentially transporting texts while others focus on the way the media use material people have stored in their brains to generate certain responses, what is called the **responsive chord** theory. Some scholars study the broadcast media focusing upon the **genres** they carry (commercials, cop shows, action-adventure shows, game shows, talk shows, and so-called "reality" shows, among other things). Other scholars are concerned with **media aesthetics** and the way light, color, sound, camera angles, kinds of shots, and editing create certain effects. I will be dealing with a number of these matters in various parts of this book.

The **mass communications** media seem to have taken an increasingly dominant role in society in recent years; now the media seem to affect all the other institutions. Our political or governmental institutions have the legal power to help determine how the broadcasting media operate, since the airwaves are public property, but all too often it seems now that the broadcast media, thanks to the power of political advertising, are the tail that is determining where the governmental horse will go.

A CASE STUDY: WHERE DID I GET THAT IDEA?

In the United States, where we believe in the American Dream of the "self-made" man and woman, where we believe in "individualism," many of us have a sense that we alone determine our own destiny, that we have, so to speak, the whole world in our hands. The term *individualism* was first used by Alexis de Tocqueville, a Frenchman who traveled in the United States in 1831 and wrote a fascinating book, *Democracy in America*, about American character and culture based on what he observed. He suggested that Americans were egalitarians and this egalitarianism shaped all our other values and our institutions. Thus, de Tocqueville derives our individualism from our egalitarianism:

> I have shown how it is that, in ages of equality, every man seeks for his opinions within himself: I am now to show how it is that, in the same ages, all his feelings are turned towards himself alone. *Individualism* is a novel expression, to which a novel idea has given birth. Our fathers

were only acquainted with *égoïsme* (selfishness). Selfishness is a passionate and exaggerated love of self, which leads a man to connect everything with himself and to prefer himself to everything in the world. Individualism is a mature and calm feeling, which disposes each member of the community to sever himself from the mass of his fellows, and to draw apart with his family and his friends; so that after he thus formed a little circle of his own, he willingly leaves society at large to itself. Selfishness originates in blind instinct: individualism proceeds from erroneous judgment more than from depraved feelings; it originates as much in deficiencies of mind as in perversity of heart. (1956:193)

Of course de Tocqueville, who didn't think much of our individualism, wrote before we developed our mass media. He argued that individualism eventually becomes transformed into selfishness and becomes as important as egalitarianism. We still are individualists in America, though not in quite the same way that we were in the 1830s, when de Tocqueville visited the country; we are now immersed in media and not all of us (especially when we grow older, get married, and have children) want to leave society to itself.

So the notion of individualism is something that we learn from American society. We are not born knowing about individualism, or the "self-made man and woman" or anything else. We have to be taught about it. Some political figures who believe in a radical or extreme form of individualism argue that there's no such thing as society; it is just an abstraction, a term for a collection of individuals. (That point was made by philosopher Jeremy Bentham, [1748-1832] who wrote "society is a fictitious body, the sum of the several members who compose it," and Margaret Thatcher, who said "There is no such thing as society," when she was Prime Minister in England.)

Thus, ironically, people who learn about individualism from society sometimes find themselves arguing that society doesn't exist. This, in essence, is the point that the sociologist Karl Mannheim made in his book *Ideology and Utopia* when he said "strictly speaking, it is incorrect to say that the single individual thinks."

A French sociologist, Emile Durkheim, offers a solution to this matter of the complicated relationship that exists between individuals and society. He writes, in his classic work *The Elementary Forms of the Religious Life* (first translated into English and published in 1915):

Society is a reality *sui generis;* it has its own peculiar characteristics, which are not found elsewhere and which are not met with again in the same form in all the rest of the universe. The representations which express

it have a wholly different contents from purely individual ones and we may rest assured in advance that the first add something to the second.

. . .Collective representations are the result of an immense co-operation, which stretches out not only into space but into time as well; to make them, a multitude of minds have associated, united and combined their ideas and sentiments; for them, long generations have accumulated their experience and their knowledge. A special intellectual activity is therefore concentrated in them which is infinitely richer and complexer than that of the individual. From that one can understand how the reason has been able to go beyond the limits of empirical knowledge. It does not owe this to any vague, mysterious virtue but simply to the fact that according to the well-known formula, man is double. (1967:29)

These are important ideas. The intellectual activity of society is much richer and more complex than an individual's intellectual activity. And this is because, Durkheim explains, we have history that enriches our thought.

He continues with his analysis of the relation between the individual and society in the following manner, explaining that we all have a complex relationship to society based on the duality of our nature:

There are two beings in him: an individual being which has its foundation in the organism and the circle of whose activities is therefore strictly limited, and a social being which represents the highest reality in the intellectual and moral order that we can know by observation—I mean society. This duality of our nature has as its consequence in the practical

order, the irreducibility of a moral ideal to a utilitarian motive, and in the order of thought, the irreducibility of reason to individual experience. In so far as he belongs to society, the individual transcends himself, both when he thinks and when he acts.

We are all, in a certain sense, then, "double." *On the one hand, we are in society, and on the other hand, society is in us.* We have a physical body and a personality that is our own—that is, we are individuals—but we also are social animals, and much of what we think is based on this fact. We are educated in schools, and we are socialized by our parents, peers, priests, and pop stars (that is the media), so there is a strong social dimension to our lives, even if we believe that somehow we are "self-made."

Marx explained that our consciousness is social. As he put it, in his *Selected Writings in Sociology and Social Philosophy*:

> Morality, religion, metaphysics and other ideologies, and their corresponding forms of consciousness, no longer retain therefore their appearance of an autonomous existence. They have no history, no development; it is men, who in developing their material production and their material intercourse, change, along with this their real existence, their thinking and the products of their thinking. Life is not determined by consciousness, but consciousness by life. (1964:75)

What Marx is arguing here is that life—that is, our social existence—shapes our consciousness, which means that since media play so large a role in our lives, the media help shape our consciousness.

In his book *Marxism and Literature*, the British media and communication theorist Raymond Williams used the term *hegemony* to describe the process by which the ruling classes shaped the consciousness of the masses. He distinguished between rule, which is political and ultimately based on force, and hegemonic ideological domination, which is broader than class-based ideology and which pervades a society, so people are unable to locate what it is that shapes their thoughts and ideas. As he explained:

> Hegemony is then not only the articulate upper level of "ideology," nor are its forms of control only those ordinarily seen as "manipulation" or "indoctrination." It is a whole body of practices and expectations, over the whole of our living: our senses, our assignments of energy, our shaping perceptions of ourselves and our world. It is a lived system of meaning and values—constitutive and constituting—which as they are experienced as practices appear as reciprocally confirming. It thus constitutes a sense of reality for most people in the society, a sense of absolute because experienced reality beyond which it is very difficult for most members of the society to move, in most areas of their lives. (1977:110)

Hegemonial ideological domination can be characterized, then, as that "which goes without saying." We are dominated but cannot recognize that such is the case because it is ubiquitous and seems to be nothing more than common sense. The function of this domination is to help maintain the status quo and solidify the role of the ruling classes in society.

SOCIETY, THE INDIVIDUAL, AND
THE COMMUNICATION PROCESS

In his book *Ferdinand de Saussure*, Jonathan Culler discusses the relationship that exists between individuals and society (Revised Edition, Ithaca, NY: Cornell University Press). He writes (1986:86–87):

> For human beings, society is the primary reality, not just the sum of in-
> dividual activities, nor the contingent manifestations of Mind; and if one
> wishes to study human behavior, one must grant that there is a social
> reality . . . In short, sociology, linguistics, and psychoanalytic psychology
> are possible only when one takes the meanings which are attached to
> and which differentiate objects and actions in society as a primary real-
> ity, as facts to be explained. And since meanings are a social product,
> explanation must be carried out in social terms. It is as if Saussure, Freud,
> and Durkheim had asked, "What makes individual experience possible?
> What enables men and women to operate with meaningful objects and
> actions? What enables them to communicate and act meaningfully?"
> And the answer they postulated was social which, though formed by
> human activities, are the conditions of experience. To understand
> individual experience one must study the social norms which make it
> possible . . . Saussure, Freud, and Durkheim thus reverse the perspec-
> tive which makes society the result of individual behavior and insist that
> behavior is made possible by collective social systems individuals have
> assimilated, consciously or unconsciously.

Culler calls our attention to the ways in which we learn what signs mean. If signs are to be meaningful, there must be a society that, one way or another, teaches people how signs are to be interpreted. The meanings of signs are not natural but determined by society. Individual behavior, Culler argues, is shaped by there being something we call society, and individuals are not the creators of society.

Perhaps extreme individualists like Margaret Thatcher are arguing that society may exist but that it is irrelevant. Many people probably agree with her. They can say this, but if we take into account the nine hours a day most of us spend immersed in the mass media, which require all kinds of social, economic, political, and media institutions to create and disseminate their texts, the argument sounds a bit hollow. It is important that we keep this insight in mind—that we are all, as Durkheim put it, dual creatures and that we are in society and society is in us—as we investigate mass media and its role in society, because the same thing applies to it: the media are in society and society is, in many different and important ways, in the mass media.

Average Number of TVs per U.S. Household: 2.5
Percentage of Americans with 4 or more TVs: 31%
Number of Mobile Phone Users (13+): 228M
Percentage of U.S. Mobile Subscribers with Smartphones: 31%
Number of mobile phone web users: 83.2M

www.onlinemarketing-trends.com/2011

. . . *McLuhan became frustrated trying to teach first year students in required courses how to read English poetry, and began using the technique of analyzing the front page of newspapers, comic strips, ads, and the like as poems* . . . *This new approach to the study of popular culture and popular art form* . . . *eventually resulted in his first book,* The Mechanical Bride, *which some consider to be one of the founding documents of early cultural studies. While the* Bride *was not initially a success, it introduced one aspect of McLuhan's basic method—using poetic methods of analysis in a quasi-poetic style to analyze popular cultural phenomena—in short, assuming such cultural productions to be another type of poem.*

Donald Theall, *The Virtual Marshall McLuhan* (2001:4–5)

2

MEDIA USAGE IN
THE UNITED STATES

The statistics I have offered in this book give us a pretty good idea of media usage in the United States. Surveys reveal that 32 percent of American teenagers never read and that only 50 percent "sometimes" read—a matter that is quite disturbing, since it is reading that is all-important in developing critical thinking skills that are connected both to individual social mobility and to participating intelligently in the political process. Those who don't read become captives of the kinds of media that require relatively little intellectual effort—listening to the radio, watching television, listening to their iPods, watching films, and playing video games.

THE KAISER 2010 MEDIA USAGE STUDY

Let me isolate the figures for time spent with the media to give a better notion of how much time we spend with them in a typical day. The Kaiser media usage study in 2010 provided other data of interest relative to the usage of specific media and reveals that media usage by 8- to 18-year-olds has increased considerably in the years from 2005 to 2009. The study offers a revealing chart on media usage for the years 2009, 2004, and 1999:

MEDIUM	2009	2004	1999
TV Content	4:29	3:50	3:47
Music/Audio	2:31	1:44	1:48
Computer	1:29	1:02	0:27
Video Games	1:13	0:49	0:26
Print	0:38	0:43	0:43
Movies	0:25	0:25	0:18

Total Media Exposure	10:45	8:33	7:29
Multitasking Proportion	29%	26%	18%
TOTAL MEDIA USE	7:35	6:21	6:19

(www.kff.org/entmedia/upload/8010.pdf)

We can see that young people have a total media exposure of almost 11 hours a day, but because they multitask almost 30 percent of the time, the Kaiser figures subtract that time and conclude that the total media use is 7:35 hours a day.

The Kaiser report also had statistics on "Mobile Media Ownership" by 8- to 18-year-olds over the past 5 years:

Item	2009	2004
iPod/MP3 Player	76%	18%
Cell Phone	66%	39%
Laptop	29%	12%

We can see, then, that most 8- to 18-year-olds have some kind of MP3 player and cell phone. As the authors of the report write:

> Not only do more young people own a cell phone, but cells have morphed from a way to hold a conversation with someone into a way to consume more media. Eight- to eighteen-year-olds today spend an average of a half-hour a day (:33) talking on their cell phones, and an average of 49 minutes a day (:49) listening to, playing or watching other media on their phones (:17 with music, :17 playing games, and :15 watching TV)—not to mention the hour and a half a day that 7th- to 12th-graders spend text-messaging (time spent texting is not included in our count of media use, nor is time spent talking on a cell phone).

The Kaiser study also provides information on new media and 8- to 18-year-olds, relative to what devices they have in their bedrooms.

Our 8- to 18-year-olds have the following in their bedrooms:

	2009	2004	1999
Radio	75%	84%	86%
TV	71%	68%	65%
CD Player	68%	86%	88%
DVD or VCR Player	57%	54%	36%
Cable/Satellite TV	49%	37%	29%

Computer	36%	31%	21%
Internet Access	33%	20%	10%
Video Game Console	50%	49%	45%
Premium Channels	24%	20%	15%
TiVo/other DVR	13%	10%	n/a

The bedrooms of our children and teenagers have become media emporia, so to speak. What these statistics suggest is that young people are immersed in media to an extent that can only be described as remarkable. One reason they are exposed to so much media is that more than a quarter of the time they are using two or more media at the same time. We can see that we all spend a lot of time, each day, using consumer media. The question we must ask is—what effect, if any, does this use of consumer media have upon us as individuals and upon our families, friends, and American society?

But young people aren't the only ones living media-dominated lives. Many other people have fallen under the spell of what I call the "Electronic Imperative," and statistics indicate that the average adult in the United States spends 8.5 hours a day looking at screens. In the March 26, 2009, issue of *The New York Times* there was an article with the headline "8 Hours a Day Spent on Screens, Study Finds." The author, Brian Stelter, based this article on data from the Council for Research Excellence. Television dominates our screen watching, but we also watch other kinds of screens such as those found on computer monitors, cell phones, tablets, and GPS devices. Apple sold forty million iPads in 2011, and there were substantial sales of other brands of Android tablets, which means there are many more screens for people to look at. It would seem, then, that the leisure of adults as well as young people is now dominated by various gizmos with screens that we have created and that have an almost hypnotic power over us. And where there is a screen, there usually are advertisements and commercials.

THE KINDS OF MEDIA WE USE

Let me list here the media we use in a typical day. I am using the term *media* in the way it is traditionally used—*as something that carries some kind of communication*. **Communication** involves sending messages from one or more senders to one or more receivers who can decode or understand the message that has been sent. The media not only *carry* "texts" (the term used in scholarly discourse for films, television shows, songs, and works of all kinds); they also *affect* these texts in different ways. The most common media are, then:

> our voices (as in conversations)
> computers
> our bodies (as in body language)
> newspapers
> telephones of all kinds
> magazines
> television
> books
> radio
> billboards
> recordings (compact discs, DVDs, etc.)
> photographs
> films
> videos (including video games)

This list can be broken down in a number of different ways. For example, we could classify media according to whether they are essentially linguistic (using language) or photographic (using such things as images, facial expressions, gestures, and body language).

Communication theorists tell us that in a typical conversation, 70 or 80 percent of the information is generated by our facial expressions, body language, and other forms of **non-verbal communication**. But in some media, such as television programs and films, for example, we find both verbal and non-verbal communication techniques being used to generate messages, so that classification, while interesting, can be improved upon. I will say more about different ways of classifying the media shortly, after a primer on communication.

A PRIMER ON COMMUNICATION

The mass media are, more technically speaking, the mass media of communication. We can distinguish between different levels of communication and see where mass communication and the mass media belong:

Intrapersonal: Internal dialogue (talking to oneself)
Interpersonal: Talking to one person or a few people
Small Group: Communicating with a small group of people
Mass Communication: Using media to communicate with many people

There are many different models and theories of communication. Let me offer two classic and influential ones, which will give you a pretty good idea of how scholars see the communication process working. The first will be that of Roman Jakobson, a linguist, who said there are six elements in any speech act. Let me explain each of these items in more detail.

1. A *Sender* sends (creates)
2. A *Message*: the content of the communication (texts)
3. A *Receiver*: the object of the message (audiences)
4. A *Code*: the way the message is packaged (for example in English)
5. A *Contact*: the medium used (such as conversation or TV)
6. A *Context* which helps us understand the message better (society).

The *sender* can be one person, as in a conversation, or a group of people, some who write scripts and others who perform them (as in a film or television show); the *message* can be words that contain information, or a combination of words and sounds and images; the *receiver* can be one individual or a million, who may be seeing a film or watching a television show; the *code* is the way the message is presented—in a language or by using words, images, and sound, as in films or television programs; the *contact* is the medium used to send the message; and the *context* is the situation in which the message is sent, which helps determine its meaning. For example, the words "pass the hypodermic needle" mean something different if the context is a dark alley or a hospital.

Jakobson's model of communication offers us an insight into the people involved in communication and the way they communicate. It is

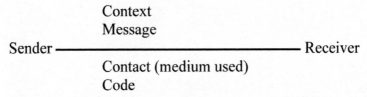

Figure 2.1.   Roman Jakobson's Six Elements of Communication

one of the most famous and most useful models. Let me mention one other model (traditionally a **model** is defined as an abstract representation of what occurs in the real world), another very famous one offered by a political scientist, Harold Lasswell, in 1948. Lasswell asks:

Who?
Says what?
In which channel?
To whom?
With what effect?

Actually, this model by Lasswell is very similar to Jakobson's, as the following chart shows:

Table 2.1.   **Laswell and Jakobson Models Compared**

Lasswell Model	Jakobson Model
Who	Sender
Says	Code
What	Message
In which channel	Contact (Medium)
To whom	Receiver
With what effect	

Jakobson's model doesn't deal with effects, the way Lasswell's model does, but there are, we can see, a number of similarities. Interestingly enough, Lasswell's **theory** has been criticized for bringing in the matter of effects, since *communications* scholars are divided on the matter of whether the mass media have long lasting and important effects.

TRADITIONAL WAYS
OF CLASSIFYING THE MEDIA

Now that we have an understanding of the process of communication, let me discuss the matter of how to classify the media. A commonly used classification breaks the mass media down into electronic, print, and photographic media. This gives us the following:

Table 2.2. Ways of Classifying Media

Electronic Media	Print Media	Photographic Media
telephone	books	photographs
television	magazines	films
radio	newspapers	videos
recordings	billboards	

Some media theorists link electronic media and photographic media into a hybrid they call photo-electronic media. If we use that concept, columns one and three would be merged together. As a rule, we spend a great deal more time with electronic media and photographic media than we do with print media. The average person in the United States watches around four hours of television a day, which means television is the dominant medium in America (and in many other countries as well), followed by radio and listening to music on CD-ROMS and other new technology devices that can store many hours of songs. Americans don't, as the statistics on media use show, spend much time with print media, relatively speaking.

MCLUHAN ON HOT AND COOL MEDIA

The late Canadian media theorist Marshall McLuhan used a different approach and classified media according to whether they were "hot" or "cool." He argued, in a famous aphorism, that "the medium is the message."

That is, the medium is more important than the textual content that the medium carries. While the medium has an important impact on the content it carries, McLuhan's notion that the medium is basic in the communication process—because it alters our sense ratios and modes of perception—is not generally accepted. His theories about hot and cool media, however, are worth considering in some detail.

According to McLuhan, hot media have high definition. By definition, he means that they are full of data, which leads to low participation. Cool media, on the other hand, have low definition, because they have little data, and require high participation.

As McLuhan writes in *Understanding Media* (1956:22, 23):

There is a basic principle that distinguishes a hot medium like radio from a cool one like the telephone, or a hot medium like the movie from a

cool one like TV. A hot medium is one that extends one single sense in "high definition." High definition is the state of being well filled with data. A photograph is visually "high definition." A cartoon is "low definition," simply because very little visual information is provided. Telephone is a cool medium, or one of low definition, because the ear is given a meager amount of information. And speech is a cool medium of low definition, because so little is given and so much has to be filled in by the listener. On the other hand, hot media do not leave so much to be filled in or completed by the audience. Naturally, therefore, a hot medium like the radio has very different effects on the user from a cool medium like the telephone.

This passage offers McLuhan's reasoning behind his classification of media into "hot" and "cool" ones. His discussion of the work that audiences must do to make sense of cool media anticipates some of the thinking of scholars who talk about "reader-response" theory and the role an active audience plays in decoding texts in all media, topics that will be discussed later in this book.

The following chart offers examples of McLuhan's hot and cool media in paired oppositions:

Table 2.3.   McLuhan's Hot and Cool Media

Hot Media	Cool Media
radio	telephone
movie	television show
photograph	cartoon
printed word	speech
book	dialogue
lecture	seminar

We have to be more active in making sense of (or to use a communication theory term, "decoding") the texts carried by cool media. They invite our participation more than hot media do, because hot media supply a great deal of information and there's less for us to do. For example, radio conveys more information than a phone call does, and a photograph has much more information in it than a cartoon does.

McLuhan also speculated on the difference between print media and electronic media. There are, he suggests, certain logical implications that are connected to each kind of media. Print suggests linearity (we read lines of type, typically), logic, rationality, and connectedness. Electronic media, on the other hand, are associated with what might be described as "all-at-once-ness" and emotion. A comparison of McLuhan's notions about these two kinds of media follows:

Table 2.4.   Print and Electronic Media Compared

Print	Electronic Media
the eye	the ear
linearity	all-at-once-ness
interconnectedness	simultaneity
logical thinking	emotional responses
rationality	mythic spheres
books	radio
individualism	community
detachment	involvement
separation	connection
data classification	pattern recognition

I have taken these oppositions from McLuhan's writings—in particular, from his book *Understanding Media*. They reflect the intellectual, social, and political implications that stem from what McLuhan argued are the essential natures of the two different kinds of media.

It is possible to see how McLuhan derives linear thinking and individuality from books. When we read a book, we read letters that form words that form sentences that are printed, generally speaking, in horizontal lines of type. And books are read by individuals, who move through them at their own pace. So we can see how individualism and separation and detachment might be connected to the book. Electronic media are much different—they are often consumed by groups. They can be heard by individuals but also by groups, and thus they tend to bring people together instead of separating them the way books do. The realm of sound involves, McLuhan suggests, pattern recognition rather than data classification, and this brings us much closer together into communities and thus closer to the realm of ritual and the mythic than print does. So a change in the popularity of a medium leads to other important changes in society, changes which ultimately have an impact on individuals, since we are all social beings.

McLuhan's ideas were very popular for a number of years, and he became a media celebrity. Then his theories came under attack by many communications scholars, and he faded from sight. In recent years, long after his death, McLuhan's ideas have been making a comeback, in part because media scholars see a connection between his theories of hot and cold media, for example, and the new digital technologies. His theories might help explain the current passion people have for using cell phones, for example, and why young people prefer texting to talking with their cell phones.

THE MEDIA HELP SHAPE THE TEXTS THEY CARRY

What many communications scholars don't deal with in their theories is the fact that we don't watch television per se. We don't watch television—except when the screens go blank and we stare at the blank screen, like dummies, waiting for the program we were watching to resume. The media always carry texts of one kind or another—news shows, situation comedies, sports programs, commercials, and so on. And because of the power of the media to profoundly influence the sounds we hear and images we watch, by editing and other manipulations, the medium does more than just transport texts. This notion that the media just transport texts is often known as the transportation theory of the media. It suggests that the media are relatively inert, a theory that is not generally accepted today.

Most media theorists believe that the media have an important role in shaping the texts they carry. In television, for example, the shots a director uses—zooming in, quick cutting, fading out, and so on—all of these shape our perception of what is happening in the texts we are watching. Think, for example, of the difference between watching a football game in a stadium and watching the same game on television, where the director can show a given play from three or four different camera angles, where he can zoom in on a player, where there are shots from blimps hovering above the stadium where the game is being played. This matter of the power of a medium to shape the texts it carries will be dealt with in some detail in the following chapter on media aesthetics.

Jacques Aumont . . .suggests there are three functions that graphic images perform and that they are very old . . . He explains these functions as the "symbolic," the "epistemic," and the "aesthetic." In symbolic images the image stands for, or represents, something else. The something else might be a god, an idea or a cultural value . . . Epistemic images (from the ancient Greek word for knowledge) are those which convey information about the world and its contents . . . Aesthetic images are those "intended to please the spectator [or] to produce in the spectator specific sensations . . .and Aumont suggests that this function has become inseparable from the idea of art.

Malcom Bernard, *Graphic Design as Communication* (2005:13)

Everyday media experiences are not usually at the level of a major aesthetic experience, but for many persons the most moving cultural experience will be through popular media rather than classical art. A powerful emotion experience can be triggered by an otherwise trivial song floating out an alley and awakening rich associations. The important quality in the aesthetic experience, whether it is an emotional, earthshaking, life-changing encounter or a quiet, simple, weightless sense of deep appreciation is your subjective response. Seeing a captivating movie, hearing the right popular song as the right time, interacting electronically at maximum capability, getting caught up in a popular novel's sweeping narrative—these are sources of aesthetic experience shorn of artistic pretentiousness. By inspiring such moments, media culture can take on exceptional power, meaning, and importance.

Michael R. Real, *Exploring Media Culture: A Guide* (1996:13)

3

SEMIOTICS AND
MEDIA AESTHETICS

In order to understand why **mass-mediated violence** or any other kind of mass-mediated programming works on its audiences the way it does, we must understand something about **media aesthetics**. Aesthetics is generally defined as a branch of philosophy involved in the study of beauty, but *media aesthetics*, as I will use the term, involves analyzing how creative artists use the technical capacities of the various media to achieve the effects they want. The term *aesthetics* has to do with sense perceptions, and so our concern is with how film, television, and other media shape these perceptions. Media aesthetics deals, then, with how artistic effects are achieved—and these effects, I believe, play an important role in making a text meaningful to audiences. As the quotation from Malcolm Bernard shows, visual images are quite complex and have a number of different functions.

I will be focusing attention mostly on television, but there is an aesthetic dimension to all media. Even in live theater, where performers have only their voices, facial expressions, and body language to use, we find directors using lighting, sound, costuming, action, and settings to create effects.

It is important that we recognize that how a text is edited to clarify and intensify its message often has a social, economic, and political significance. For our purposes here, how a story is told is as revealing as what is told. Thus, for example, the way a political commercial is edited plays an important role in getting the message across. Style in fashion, we recognize, often has social and often political content; we can say the same about the aesthetic aspects of mass-mediated texts. We begin this study of media aesthetics with a brief discussion of semiotics, the science of signs.

35

SAUSSURE ON SIGNS

How do we find meaning in things? How do we know how to interpret a particular facial expression or hair style? These questions are actually quite difficult, but there is a discipline devoted to exploring how we find answers to such questions. It is called **semiotics**, the science of signs. The term *semiotics* comes from the Greek work for sign, *sēmeîon*. A **sign** can be defined as anything that can be used to stand for something else. Thus, for example, a frown generally signifies or stands for the fact that one is displeased. The term *tree* stands for a large, leafy plant.

One of the founding fathers of semiotics, the Swiss linguist Ferdinand de Saussure, said that signs were composed of two components: a *signifier* (a sound or object) and a *signified* (a **concept** or idea). He wrote (1966:67):

> I propose to retain the word sign [*signe*] to designate the whole and to replace concept and sound-image respectively by *signified [signifié]* and *signifier [signifiant]*; the last two terms have the advantage of indicating the opposition that separates them from each other and from the whole of which they are parts.

The relationship between the signifier and signified is arbitrary, based on convention. For example, there is nothing natural or logical in the relation between the word *tree* and the large, leafy plant that we call a tree. It could

easily have been called something else. Words, then, are signs that stand for things, but there are many other kinds of signs.

Saussure wrote, in his book *Course in General Linguistics* (1966):

> Language is a system of signs that express ideas, and is therefore comparable to a system of writing, the alphabet of deaf-mutes, symbolic rites, polite formulas, military signals, etc. But it is the most important of these systems.
>
> *A science that studies the life of signs within society* is conceivable; it would be a part of social psychology and consequently of general psychology. I shall call it *semiology* (from Greek *semeion* "sign"). Semiology would show what constitutes signs, what laws govern them.

This may be considered one of the charter statements of semiotics. Saussure called his science *semiology*, but that term has been replaced in recent years by the term *semiotics*, used by another founding father of the science, C. S. Peirce.

Saussure made another point that is very important. Concepts have meaning because of the web of relationships in which they are found; they don't have meaning by themselves. He wrote [my italics], "*concepts are purely differential* and defined not by their positive content but negatively by their relations with the other terms of the system" (1966:117). He added that "*the most precise characteristics*" of these concepts "*is in being what the others are not.*" What that means is that it isn't content, per se, that determines

meaning but *relationships* among the elements in a system. We make sense of concepts, then, by seeing them as the opposite of something else. Rich is the opposite of poor and weak is the opposite of strong.

For Saussure, nothing has meaning by itself, and the meaning of everything has to be learned. What this means is that we all have to learn media aesthetics, informally and on our own, as we watch films and television programs and play video games, if we are to understand everything that is going on in them.

PEIRCE ON ICONS, INDEXES, AND SYMBOLS

The other founding father of semiotics was the American philosopher Charles Sanders Peirce (pronounced "purse"). He had a different theory than Saussure's, though both were interested in signs. Peirce said there were three kinds of signs: *icons*, which communicate by resemblance; *indexes*, which communicate by cause and effect; and *symbols*, which have to be learned. The chart below shows these three kinds of signs:

Table 3.1. Peirce s Three Kinds of Signs

Kind of Sign	Icon	Index	Symbol
Signify by	resemblance	cause/effect	convention
Example	photographs	fire/smoke	flags
Process	can see	can figure out	must be taught

We can see that there is a difference between Saussure's ideas about signs and Peirce's. For Peirce, only symbols are conventional and have to be learned. He once said "the universe is perfused with signs, it is not composed exclusively of signs," which suggests that for Peirce semiotics is the key to finding meaning in anything and everything.

We can combine Saussure and Peirce, and suggest that we find meaning in the world by seeing everything as either a signifier of something else (a signified—that is, a concept or idea) or as generating meaning by being iconic, indexical, or symbolic. We swim, like fish, in a sea of signs; everything is a sign, then, of something else. An **image**, for our purposes, can be defined as a visual sign system or a collection of visual signs. In many cases, of course, we have signs within signs. For example, the White perfume advertisement shown in figure 3.1 has two figures in it, two bottles of perfume, and words—so there are many smaller signs within the larger collection of signs that we can describe as an image. The expressions on the faces of the models, the clothes they are wearing, their ages, their body language, the jewels in the woman's bellybutton, the design of the ad, its lighting, and its color also function as signs.

LYING WITH SIGNS

One problem with signs is that they can be used to lie. As Umberto Eco, the distinguished semiotician and novelist, wrote in his book *A Theory of Semiotics* (1976:7):

> Semiotics is concerned with everything that can be taken as a sign. A sign is everything which can be taken as significantly substituting for something else. This something else does not necessarily have to exist or to actually be somewhere at the moment in which a sign stands for it. Thus semiotics is in principle the discipline studying everything which can be used in order to lie. If something cannot be used to tell a lie, conversely it cannot be used to tell the truth; it cannot be used "to tell" at all.

Bald men who wear wigs, brunettes who dye their hair blonde, malingerers who pretend to be ill—there are any number of examples of people lying, in varying degrees of seriousness, with signs. Eco's point is that if a sign can be used to tell the truth, it must also be able to be used to lie.

So, as I write this book, I pause for a moment and look out the window of my study. I see very tall plants (trees) and large objects (houses)

Figure 3.1.   This perfume advertisement is filled with signs, from the expressions of the models to the design of the ad.

with rectangular shapes in them (windows). When we are born, we know almost nothing. What we do, as we grow up, is learn a language or perhaps a number of languages. And what are languages—they are, simply put, composed of words (a kind of sign) that tell us what things are and rules that tell us how to use these words (grammar). We also unconsciously learn various **codes**, which can be defined as systems of signs and symbols that have meaning—one that is often not apparent. In espionage, codes are secret rules for unlocking the meaning in coded messages, but we can also think of codes in a cultural sense as being very similar to the codes spies use.

From a semiotic perspective, actors and actresses, if you think about it, lie with signs. They pretend to be certain characters who have certain emotions, which they express by such things as what they say, by the way they speak their lines, by their facial expressions, by their body language, and by the clothes they wear. We don't consider this kind of "lying" to be serious; in fact, we seek it out. We know what it going on with plays, films, and television shows but are caught up in a temporary "willing suspension of disbelief," and so we become emotionally involved with what these performers are doing. When you move from the theater, from live performances, to mediated texts such as those found in videos, video games, television shows, and films, things become much more complicated. In the case of video games, for example, we are not merely spectators but actually become involved, interactively, in the story, and our actions can affect a game's outcome.

EDITING TECHNIQUES AND SEMIOTICS

When we consider texts in visual media such as film and television, we are dealing with works in which editing, different kinds of camera shots, lighting, music, and sound effects play an important role—perhaps, in some cases, a more important one than the dialogue spoken by the performers. It is useful to apply Saussure's distinction between *signifiers* (sound-image) and *signifieds* (concept, meaning) to different kinds of camera shots, camera movements, and editing techniques. Different camera shots and editing techniques function as signs, or cues to viewers—cues that tell them what to think and feel. These cues are based on aesthetic codes people learn while watching television and films. Editing, for our purposes, will be considered to be the sequencing of different kinds of camera shots to create a sense of continuity in a text and generate certain desired effects. These camera shots and editing techniques are used with other matters such as sound, music, color, and lighting.

Camera Shot (signifier)	Definition of Shot	Meaning (signified)
establishing shot	large overview	location
close-up	head and shoulders	intimacy
extreme close-up	part of face	inspection
medium shot	head and torso	personal relations
full shot	complete body of person	social ambiance
long shot	setting and people	context, scope
extreme long shot	person in wider context	orientation
z-axis	vertical action from screen	involvement

As we grow up and become used to watching television, we learn the meanings of the various camera shots. We may not be able to articulate these meanings, but we get a sense of what the shot means. If we move to camera work, we find other meanings of interest.

Camera Movement	Definition	Meaning for Viewer
pans down	camera looks down on	power and authority
pans up	camera looks up to	weakness, smallness
dollies in	camera moves in	interest, observation
dollies out	camera moves out	scope, context
zoom in	lens moves in on	detail, focus
zoom out	lens moves out from	scope, context
arc	semi-circular movement	investigation
truck left/right	horizontal movement	different perspective

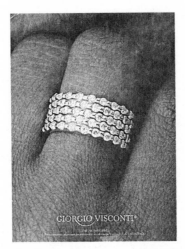

Figure 3.2. This print advertisement uses an extreme close up photograph to at tract attention.

Now I will deal with some of the more important transitional editing techniques that are conventionally used. These techniques enable editors to move from one image to another. The cut is the most commonly used editing techniques, but there are others that are available:

Signifier	Definition	Signified
fade in	black to image	beginning
fade out	image to black	ending
cut	switch from one image	simultaneity
wipe	screen image replaced by other	imposed ending
dissolve	image dissolves into next	weak ending

We can see, then, that there are many possibilities that directors and editors can use in shooting a text, and I haven't covered all of the different things that can be done in post-production to a text. In some commercials, there is an incredible amount of quick cutting—some of them can have as many as sixty different images in a 30 second commercial. So editing is an important element of the mass-mediated arts.

We should think of the use of different kinds of shots and editing techniques as "instructions" to viewers to think certain things or have certain emotions. The order of images conveys meaning to viewers in the same way that the order of words does, and these meanings often have a social as well as a psychological dimension to them.

Editing involves the way media makers use different kinds of shots and different kinds of camera work to create the effects they want. As viewers watch a television program, for example, their ideas and emotions are affected by the words the characters utter and their actions, but also by the different shots and combinations of shots and by the lighting, the sound, the music, and the colors used, among other things. I will now list and briefly discuss some of the techniques, mentioned above, that directors and production artists can use to intensify the meanings of texts.

Color

Colors have culturally important meanings to people, which differ from country to country. We know, for example, that black means a certain thing in the United States and something different in other countries. Villains in American cowboy films were conventionally dressed in black and heroes were dressed in white. Hospitals now paint their walls peach and similar colors because they've found that these colors relax people.

Lighting

Lighting is an important cue for us about what is happening in a dramatic text. If the lighting is dark, we are in the realm of mystery and, in some cases, horror. Bright lighting, on the other hand, means something quite different and is associated with less dramatic entertainment genres, such as situation comedies.

Music

Music is used to help viewers of films and television programs connect, emotionally, to what is being shown on the screen. Music offers cues to audiences that help them understand better what they are seeing and anticipate what might be coming. It establishes the emotional mood that the filmmakers want to generate and also connects to the pace or rhythm of the images being shown.

Sound Effects

Sound also plays a role in giving audiences a better idea of what is going on in a text and helps intensify their experiences. We live in a world

of sound and it is only natural that films, television programs, video games, and all audio-visual texts use the sounds that we are used to so as to make their texts seem more realistic. As we grow up, we learn what certain sounds mean, so using sounds is a way of conveying information to audiences about how they should feel or what they might expect when they are watching a text.

THE NATURE OF NARRATIVES: VLADIMIR PROPP

A large percentage of the texts people watch on television and see at the movies are **narratives**—that is, stories. Stories have two axes: a linear or *syntagmatic* one, which involves one action following another sequentially (like words in a sentence or links in a chain) in time, and a horizontal or *paradigmatic* one, in which actions and characters take their meaning the way concepts do—by differentiation—that is, by being the opposite of something else. Vladimir Propp is the theorist connected with syntagmatic analysis and Claude Lévi-Strauss is the theorist connected with paradigmatic analysis. I discuss their theories below.

Linear Axis	**Horizontal Axis**
syntagmatic	paradigmatic
sequence of events	relations among events

meaning from place in story	meaning from sets of oppositions
Vladimir Propp	Claude Lévi-Strauss

There have been many different attempts to understand how texts generate meaning as their plots develop sequentially. One of the most influential theories was developed by a Russian folklorist, Vladimir Propp. He said the most important thing to deal with in narratives are the actions of the characters, which he called "functions." He listed thirty-one functions that he found in Russian fairy tales, but which we can find (with minor modifications and updating necessary) in contemporary narratives—from fairy tales to James Bond films.

His thirty-one functions are listed in the chart below. (Note: the initial situation is not considered to be a function.) These functions frequently are paired, and there is a logical nature, based on how the mind works, to the way they are used in narrative texts. Propp believed that the sequence of events in narrative was invariable, but we don't need to accept his idea about the invariability of sequences of events to benefit from his analysis of narrative texts.

Initial Situation	*Members of family introduced, Hero introduced*
1. Absentation	One of the members of the family absents self.
2. Interdiction	Interdiction addressed to hero. (Can be reversed)
3. Violation	Interdiction is violated.
4. Reconnaissance	The villain makes attempt to get information.
5. Delivery	The villain gets information about his victim.
6. Trickery	The villain tries to deceive his victim.
7. Complicity	Victim is deceived.
8. Villainy	Villain causes harm to a member of a family.
8a. Lack	Member of family lacks something, desires something.
9. Mediation	Misfortune made known. Hero dispatched.
10. Counteraction	Hero (Seeker) agrees to counteraction.
11. Departure	Hero leaves home.
12. 1st Donor Function	Hero tested, receives magical agent or helper.

13.	Hero's Reaction	Hero reacts to agent or donor.
14.	Receipt of Agent	Hero acquires use of magical agent.
15.	Spatial Change	Hero led to object of search.
16.	Struggle	Hero and villain join in direct combat.
17.	Branding	Hero is branded.
18.	Victory	Villain is defeated.
19.	Liquidation	Initial misfortune or lack is liquidated.
20.	Return	Hero returns.
21.	Pursuit, Chase	Hero is pursued.
22.	Rescue	Hero rescued from pursuit.
23.	Unrecognized Arrival	Hero, unrecognized, arrives home or elsewhere.
24.	Unfounded Claims	False hero presents unfounded claims.
25.	Difficult Task	Difficult task is proposed to hero.
26.	Solution	The task is resolved.
27.	Recognition	The hero is recognized.
28.	Exposure	The false hero or villain is exposed.
29.	Transfiguration	The hero is given a new appearance.
30.	Punishment	The villain is punished.
31.	Wedding	The hero is married, ascends the throne.

A PROPPIAN ANALYSIS OF
JAMES BOND NOVELS AND FILMS

Propp also believed that there are only two kinds of heroes: *victim* heroes (who suffer from some action) and *seeker* heroes (who are sent on missions to accomplish something). In stories with victim heroes (and heroines), the focus is on how they are victimized and how they end their victimization. In stories with seeker heroes and heroines, the focus is on the way they help others who have suffered from some kind of villainy or are in danger. (To avoid the awkward nature of writing *heroes and heroines* all the time, I will use the term *heroes* to stand for male and females henceforth.) Seeker heroes often have helpers who aid them in various ways—they often have special powers or they give heroes some kind of magic agent that enables them to prevail over villains.

In *Dr. No*, Bond is sent by the spy master M to Jamaica to find out what is going on; before he leaves he is given certain weapons by Q. While in Jamaica he undertakes a hazardous mission to explore a small island controlled by Doctor No. He is captured by the villain, Doctor No (an example here of personal victimization), and must undergo an ordeal of escaping from his confinement, during which time his life is continually threatened, so he can kill Doctor No (who had a mad plan to conquer the world) and end up in bed with Honeychile Rider, a beautiful woman he has befriended (the moral equivalent of marrying the princess). She is introduced in a chapter titled "The Elegant Venus."

Some Proppian functions found in *Dr. No* follow:

Initial Situation	*Members of family are introduced*
8. Villainy	Villain causes harm to members of a family.
9. Mediation	Misfortune made known, hero is dispatched.
14. Receipt of agent	Hero acquires use of magical agent (from Q).
15. Spatial Change	Hero is led to object of search.
16. Struggle	Hero and villain join in direct combat.
17. Branding	Hero is branded (captured, imprisoned).
30. Punishment	The villain is punished (Dr. No is killed).
31. Wedding	Hero is married (goes to bed with Honeychile).

The Bond novels and films, then, can be seen as updated versions of fairy tales, and we can find many Proppian functions in them, though in modernized versions and not in the rigid order Propp thought all narratives had to obey. (We can do the same for many television shows and films, and it might be an interesting thing to use Propp's list of functions to analyze some contemporary film or television show.)

This particular Bond novel had negative portrayals of people of color, in particular black people and Asians, leading to many critics describing the book as racist. In recent years, we have become increasingly aware of the role the media play in giving people of color, women, ethnic minorities, gays, and other groups negative stereotypes that have destructive effects upon them. This use of negative stereotyping continues to be a problem with the media. Writers use stereotypes because doing so enables them to "explain," quickly and easily, why characters act the way they do.

Propps's theory of looking at the order of actions or events in a narrative is known as syntagmatic analysis. A syntagm is a chain, so Propp's analysis looks at the chain of functions he believed all stories must have. Syntagmatic analysis tells us what happens in a text, but to understand the deeper or hidden meaning of the events in a text we must apply a different theory, based on the work of the French anthropologist Claude Lévi-Strauss.

THE NATURE OF NARRATIVES:
CLAUDE LÉVI-STRAUSS

Lévi-Strauss's theory is known as paradigmatic analysis and is based on Saussure's notion that concepts don't mean anything in themselves. I quoted Saussure earlier to the effect that "concepts are purely differential." We can extend this notion of concepts to include heroes and villains and their actions in narrative texts.

Lévi-Strauss is known as a structuralist; that is, he was interested in how the elements in something—a myth or a story—related to one another. The literary critic Jonathan Culler has explained (1976:15) structuralists take "the binary opposition as a fundamental operation of the human mind basic to the production of meaning." We make sense of things in general, then, by fitting them into sets of polar oppositions that our mind supplies to us. And we make sense of texts by seeing every action and every character in terms of the binary oppositions that exists in all texts—oppositions whose meaning we all know. Our minds decode texts like computers, then, providing us with oppositions that enable us to make sense of what is going on in a text at all times.

It is possible to see some of Propp's functions in terms of oppositions between heroes and villains, the two main characters in narratives. What follows are very general oppositions that aren't always the case in every text, of course.

You can see from this list that there are many important oppositions that can be found in narratives, and this list is only suggestive. We are continually setting up oppositions in our mind's eye as we read a book or

Table 3.2. Oppositions in Propp's Functions

Heroes	Villains
young (sons)	old (fathers)
handsome	ugly (often grotesque and monstrous)
love	lust
heroines (rescued by heroes)	enchantresses (bewitch heroes)
seeming villainesses	false heroines
imagination, invention	technology, manpower
seeks something	hinders hero
suffers from acts of villain	punishes hero
is dispatched	engages in reconnaissance
gets helpers (magic powers)	has henchmen
undergoes ordeals	creates ordeals
defeats villains	loses to hero

see a movie or television program between the characters, events, objects, and so on that we see and their imagined or real opposites—that is how we find meaning in texts, and by extension, everyday life. It's quite easy, for example, to apply these oppositions to the various *Star Wars* films, James Bond films, and most films, as a matter of fact.

While many of these villains are evil individuals, criminals, and monsters of one sort or another, they have a social significance beyond the role they play in a particular text. The triumph of the hero over these characters confirms our sense that there is justice in the world and that good must inevitably triumph over evil, thereby reinforcing our belief in goodness and the value of democratic institutions. Thus, when James Bond defeats the monstrous Doctor No, Bond's victory is both personal and political. There are, of course, many texts that are overtly political, such as the television shows about the White House (*The West Wing*) and the Supreme Court and, when elections come around, the numerous political commercials that are broadcast on radio and television.

THE IMPORTANCE OF NARRATIVES

Narratives are important in more ways than we might imagine. As Laurel Richardson writes ("Narrative and Sociology," *Journal of Contemporary Ethnology,* 19, 118):

> Narrative is the primary way through which humans organize their experiences into temporally meaningful episodes . . . Narrative is both a

mode of reasoning *and* a mode of representation. People can "apprehend" the world narratively and people can "tell" about the world narratively. According to Jerome Bruner . . .narrative reasoning is one of the two basic and universal human cognition modes. The other mode is the logico-scientific . . . the logico-scientific mode looks for universal truth conditions, whereas the narrative mode looks for particular connections between events. Explanation in the narrative mode is contextually embedded, whereas the logico-scientific explanation is extracted from spatial and temporal events. Both modes are "rational" ways of making meaning.

So narratives are more than entertainments. They are a means by which we seek to make sense of the world, both to ourselves and to others. This means that the conversations you have, the stories you read, the television shows you watch, the films you see, the songs you listen to, the comics you read, the video games you play, the jokes you tell and that people tell you, and every other narrative that you experience—they all play an important role in your consciousness and the development of your identity. Your "story" (by which I mean your identity) is, in a sense, a story you build out of all the other stories you know and to which you have been exposed.

One thing that this investigation of narratives reveals is that members of audiences are much more active than we might imagine. They have to interpret the meaning of every shot and sequence of shots they see; they have to interpret the meaning of the camera work; they have to make sense of the lighting, the music, and the sound. They also have to find meaning in what the characters in a text look like, what they say, what they do, and so on. In short, there's a great deal that we must do every time we read a passage in a book or see a film or television program or video. Of course we have a lot of practice and experience doing this kind of work.

POSTMODERNISM AND MEDIA AESTHETICS

There is a great deal of controversy about what postmodernism is and isn't, and its influence on society and culture in the United States and elsewhere. Scholars suggest that the movement known as **modernism** lasted from approximately 1900 to around 1960 and was replaced by **postmodernism**— a philosophical system which argues that the old philosophical beliefs, what the French scholar Lyotard calls metanarratives, that used to guide people—such as a faith in progress and reason—no longer were accepted as valid. Some theorists have argued that postmodernism is really another name for the advanced form of capitalism found in the United States and elsewhere. In the chart that follows, I offer some contrasts between post-modernism and modernism that will help you see the difference between the two more clearly:

Modernism 1900–1960	**Postmodernism** 1960–present
Master narratives accepted	Incredulity toward master narratives
Belief in progress	Skepticism about progress
Can know reality	Can't know reality
Acceptance of hierarchy: elitism	Rejection of hierarchy: egalitarian
Separation of reality and simulations	Simulations and mediated experiences basic
Unified style	Eclecticism, many styles at same time
Serious	Playful
Elite arts versus popular arts	Elite arts and popular arts unified
Unified, coherent self	Fragmented, shattered, and decentered self
Pablo Picasso	Andy Warhol
Print culture	Electronic culture
New York architecture	Las Vegas architecture
Unitary works of art	Pastiche (pieces patched together)

You can see, from this chart, that modernism and postmodernism are quite different, and that postmodernism best describes our aesthetic sensibilities in the United States and many other advanced societies.

Sociologist Norman Denzin describes the postmodern sensibility, as reflected in the cinema and television, in his book *Images of Postmodern Society: Social Theory and Contemporary Cinema*, as follows:

> The ingredients of the postmodern self are given in three key cultural identities, those derived from the performances that define gender, social class, race and ethnicity . . . These cultural identities are filtered through the personal troubles and the emotional experiences that flow from the individual's interactions with everyday life. These existential troubles look back to the dominant cultural themes of the postmodern era, including the cult of Eros, and its idealized conceptions of love and intimacy. The raw economic, racial, and sexual edges of contemporary life produce anxiety, alienation, a radical isolation from others, madness, violence, and insanity. Large cultural groupings (young women,

the elderly, racial and ethnic minorities, gays and lesbians) are unable either to live out their ideological versions of the American dream or to experience personal happiness. They are victims of anhedonia, they are unable to experience pleasure . . . They bear witness to an economy, a political ideology, and a popular culture which can never deliver the promised goods to their households. (1991:viii)

Among the films Denzin deals with in his study of postmodern film are *Blue Velvet, Wall Street, Crimes and Misdemeanors,* and *Sex, Lies, and Videotape.* Other writers have included such films as *Blade Runner* and *The Terminator,* among others, to this list.

These postmodern films, videos, and television programs reflect with great power many of the problems that different groups of people—ethnic minorities, women, gays and lesbians—face in society, and the alienation they feel. These works also play a role in giving young people identities and belief systems. From the postmodern perspective, identities are flexible: you change your identity when you feel like it. The notion that identity involves something constant and non-changing is a modernist one; nowadays, you try on and cast off identities as often as you wish.

BLADE RUNNER, RASHOMON, AND *SURVIVOR:* THREE POSTMODERN TEXTS

Blade Runner raises the problem of what it means to be human. In the film, there are replicants who look exactly like humans, but they are really androids. One of them, it seems, has been programmed to think that she is a human. The hero of the film falls in love with her. The film raises the question of what it means to be a human being. The ambiance of the film, in a seamy Los Angeles, is also very postmodern.

Another postmodern film is the Japanese masterpiece by Akira Kurosawa, *Rashomon.* In *Rashomon* a bandit overcomes a samurai in a grove and ties him up. Then he fetches the samurai's wife, who has been waiting near the grove, brings her back to the grove, and rapes her in front of her husband. The events are also seen by a woodcutter, who stumbles onto the little drama taking place in a grove and observes them from a distance. The samurai is found dead. At a trial scene, each person involved gives a different interpretation of what went on. The bandit says he killed the samurai after a tremendous battle; the wife says that in a trance, caused by her husband's hateful stare, she killed him; the husband, speaking through a medium, says that, broken-hearted, he committed suicide; and the woodcutter said the battle between the bandit and the samurai was pathetic, as each was scared to death of the other. The problem the film raises involves the matter of whether we can know reality. Can we ever know what happened in that grove?

Reality television shows such as *Survivor* can also be seen as postmodern in nature. One of the dominant motifs of postmodernism is the pastiche, the blending of different styles and, in this case, genres. Consider the different genres found in *Survivor*:

- A sex-driven, beach-bunny show, with women in bikinis and various stages of undress running around
- A soap opera, with various intrigues by participants trying to win a million dollars
- An action-adventure show, with various tasks required of the team members
- A game/contest show, with numerous contests that teams have to win and activities they are involved in.

These shows are highly edited, so although they are not scripted, the editing process functions as a kind of script to generate drama and excitement.

The postmodern sensibility can also be seen in television commercials that don't seem to mean anything and don't seem to convey a message (this applies to any number of perfume commercials) and in novels that don't come to a logical ending, such as Thomas Pynchon's *The Crying of Lot 49*. As a result of exposure to postmodern works, it has been suggested that contemporary youth now have a postmodern sensibility, which puts them at odds with older generations, which have a modernist perspective on things. What is called "generational conflict" is based not only on age but on the difference between a modernist and postmodernist sensibility—one that is reflected in many of the films and television programs of the last forty years. (I will discuss other aspects of postmodernism, as it involves the relationship between elite and popular culture, in a later chapter.)

What media aesthetics attempts to do is determine, with some precision, how texts work and bring to consciousness the way individuals "decode" or make sense of these texts, hour after hour, day after day, without a second thought. It also is concerned with how aesthetic factors help shape text and consciousness. This is important if we wish to understand the social and cultural significance of images and of characters and their activities in narratives and other mass-mediated texts of all kinds.

Advertising texts are rarely the work of lone creatives; rather, they are scripted by committee, vetted, and redrafted. Advertising is the embodiment of compromise. Survey research and studies on how audiences are imagined also inform message design. From the perspective of decoding, or how messages are received by audiences, the text is complicated again: While advertising texts fix symbols or images, they do not fix meaning, which requires reader's active interpretation.

William Leiss, Stephen Kline, Sut Jhally, and
Jacqueline Botterill, *Social Communication in Advertising:
Consumption in the Mediated Marketplace* (2005:162)

. . . Ad agencies are so very useful. They express for the collective that which dreams and uncensored behavior do in individuals. They give spatial form to hidden impulse and, when analyzed, make possible bringing into reasonable order a great deal that could not otherwise be observed or discussed. Gouging away at the surface of public sales resistance, the ad men are constantly breaking through into the Alice in Wonderland territory behind the looking glass which is the world of subrational impulse and appetites . . . The ad agencies and Hollywood, in their different ways, are always trying to get inside the public mind in order to impose their collective dreams on that inner stage . . . The ad agencies flood the daytime world of conscious purpose and control with erotic imagery from the night world in order to drown, by suggestion, all sales resistance.

Marshall McLuhan, *The Mechanical Bride* (1951:97)

4

MEDIA AND TEXTUAL ANALYSIS

Texts—the works carried (and to some degree shaped) by the media—are often neglected in analyses of social aspects of the media made by communication researchers. This is because, in part, media analysts and researchers are interested in making generalized statements about the media or doing statistical analyses of matters such as violence in the media, and texts (that is specific works) do not fit comfortably into these kinds of studies.

And yet, as I have suggested earlier, people do not watch television, per se, but watch certain programs; they don't just listen to the radio but listen to specific stations that carry the kind of music they like or some other kind of programming to which they are attracted. The same applies to the other media—people choose to watch certain television shows, listen to certain radio stations, play certain video games, or go to particular films of interest to them. (In some cases, when people watching television channel surf, and switch from one program to another rapidly—looking for something to amuse themselves—the composite of all the shows they have glanced at, a pastiche, can be considered a postmodern text.)

YURI LOTMAN ON TEXTS

Yuri Lotman, a famous Russian semiotician, points out that texts are incredibly complex and function as very rich storehouses of information for those who know how to access this material. This explains why we can read certain novels over again, with pleasure—because we get different things out of each reading. The same applies to certain films and television programs. The more you know, the more you can find in a given text.

Texts may seem simple, but in reality, Lotman argues, they are incredibly complex. As he writes:

> Since it can concentrate a tremendous amount of information into the "area" of a very small text (cf. The length of a short story by Checkov and a psychology textbook) an artistic text manifests yet another feature: it transmits different information to different readers in proportion to each one's comprehension; it provides the reader with a language in which each successive portion of information may be assimilated with repeated reading. It behaves as a kind of living organism which has a feedback channel to the reader and thereby instructs him. (1977:23)

Lotman has also suggested that every aspect of a text is important. As he writes (1977:17), "The tendency to interpret *everything* in an artistic text as meaningful is so great that we rightfully consider nothing accidental in a work of art." This means that texts are remarkably complicated, since everything in them is important, and analyzing them and interpreting them is a difficult matter. It is understandable, then, why certain great texts have fascinated readers/viewers and critics, who keep finding new things in them over the years, decades—and in some cases, such as *Hamlet* and other classic works, over the centuries.

When we deal with mass-mediated texts, such as films and television programs, we have to consider every aspect of these texts as important—not only the dialogue and narrative elements, but also the editing and other aspects of media aesthetics. It's worth considering what texts do—or, in a more general sense, what art is and what it does.

THEORIES OF ART: WHAT TEXTS DO

M. H. Abrams, a literature professor, wrote an influential book, *The Mirror and the Lamp: Romantic Theory and the Critical Tradition*, in which he suggests that there are four important critical orientations to the arts. I use the acronym POEM to deal with these approaches:

1. *Pragmatic*. Art is functional and does things.
2. *Objective*. Art projects its own reality.
3. *Expressive*. Art expresses the reality of the artist.
4. *Mimetic*. Art imitates life.

In my work on focal points (see diagram on page 2), I added Media to the mix and changed "Universe" to "Society." Abrams was writing about literary works, so the medium—print—was not an important consideration for him. In my analysis, however, there are many different media, and they play varying roles in the creation and dissemination of texts.

Debates about what art is and how it functions have been with us since Aristotle's time. Aristotle argued that art is an "imitation" of life, a key statement of the **mimetic theory of art**. (I will discuss this matter in

more detail shortly.) The **objective theory of art** is the opposite of this, suggesting the artists create and project their own reality. Another pair of opposites involves the **pragmatic theory of art**, which argues that art has certain functions, and the **expressive theory of art**, which focuses on the emotional impact of works of art.

Alan Gowans, a professor of the history of art, argues for the pragmatic theory. In his book *The Unchanging Arts: New Forms for the Traditional Functions of Art in Society*, he discusses the functions of art, which, from our point of view, involves works of art or texts carried by the media. He argues that we shouldn't waste our time debating what art is, and, in terms of our interest in the media, whether texts carried by the mass media are "art," but focus instead on what the functions of the art (and the media) are. As he explains (1971:12–13):

> Instead of asking "What is Art?" we need to ask "What kinds of things have been done by that activity traditionally called Art?" And then we will find that activity historically performed four functions: substitute imagery; illustration; conviction and persuasion; and beautification. (1) In cases where the appearance of something needed to be preserved for one reason or another, art made pictures that could be substituted for the actual thing. (2) Art made images or shapes (including pictographs) that could be used in whole or part to tell stories or record events vividly ("illustrate," "illuminate," "elucidate," all come from the same root "lux" = "light"). (3) Art made images which by association of shapes with ideas set forth the fundamental convictions or realized ideals of societies (usually in what we call architectural or sculptural form); or conversely art made images intended to persuade people to new or different beliefs (usually in more ephemeral media). (4) Art beautified the world by pleasing the eye or gratifying the mind; what particular combinations of forms, arrangements, colors, proportions or ornament accomplished this end in any given society depended, of course, on what kinds of illustration or conviction or persuasion a given society required its arts to provide.

So, for Gowans, the arts have certain functions: first, they preserve the appearance of things; second, they make images that can be used to tell stories; third, they are used to persuade; and fourth, they help beautify the world. What Abrams and Gowans write about the various theories of the arts, in general, can be applied to the media and raise interesting questions for us to think about. I should add that debates about what art is and how it functions have been with us since Aristotle's time.

THE TEXTS THE MEDIA CARRY HAVE POWER

In thinking about the media, we must keep in mind the texts they carry and help shape. These texts have the **power**, as I suggested in my discussion of vicious cycles in Chapter 1, to help shape our consciousness and give us notions about how to live, what is right and wrong, and so on. Some people get some of their social identity from television programs. For example, there are people known as "Trekkies," who attend numerous *Star Trek* conventions dressed up in *Star Trek* uniforms and buy various artifacts connected with the show. There are fan groups (and websites) for scores of movie franchises and TV shows, from *Star Wars* and *The X-Files* to *Buffy the Vampire Slayer* (and now, many vampire novels and television shows), *Alias*, *Lost*, and *24*. There are many different *kinds* of texts or shows carried by television. Some of the more important of these genres are:

Table. 4.1.   Genres: Kinds of Texts on Television

commercials	action-adventure shows	media events
news shows	science fiction	sports shows
talk shows	religious shows	horror shows
soap operas	cooking shows	cop shows
situation comedies	music videos	plays
crime shows	documentaries	award shows

Each of these genres or kinds of programs has certain conventions that make it what it is and differentiate it from other genres. The conventions involve the kinds of characters we find, the actions they are involved in, the way they speak, and that kind of thing. As we grow up and watch different kinds of programs, we learn these conventions and become able to distinguish one genre from another. This is a kind of **incidental learning** that takes place; after watching a number of episodes of a certain genre, we learn what to expect in soap operas or cop shows or any of the other popular genres. That is, most genres are formulaic and rely, to a considerable extent, on knowledge audiences bring to the shows and desires audiences have for certain kinds of entertainment.

CONVENTION AND INVENTION IN TEXTS

There is a continuum line that can be drawn between texts that are primarily based on convention and those that are essentially based on invention. In the mass media, because radio and television stations want to attract as large an audience as possible, you tend to get texts closer to the convention side of the continuum—texts that audiences can easily understand and which don't challenge them very much. At the opposite end you have works that are very challenging. For example, think of the difference between a television show like *CSI: Crime Scene Investigation* and a novel like James Joyce's *Ulysses*.

Convention _____ *Invention*

CSI: Crime Scene Investigation   **Ulysses**

1   2   3   4   5   6   7   8   9   10

Figure 4.1.   Convention⊓Invention Continuum

We can use this diagram to think about where certain films and television shows might be placed on the above continuum. If *Crime Scene Investigation* = 1 and *Ulysses* = 10, it's an interesting problem to consider where any of the following texts might fall: *Star Wars, The Matrix, Tomb Raider: The Angel of Darkness* (film and video game), *War of the Worlds, Gran Turismo 3, 60 Minutes, The Sims, Chicago, Titanic, The X-Files, Terminator I, Alias, Annie Hall, Mission Impossible: Ghost Protocol, Avatar,* and *The Girl with the Dragon Tattoo.*

This continuum line between convention and invention was dealt with in John Cawelti's classic study of westerns, *The Six-Gun Mystique*:

> All cultural products contain a mixture of two elements: conventions and inventions. Conventions are elements which are known to both the creator and his audience beforehand—they consists of things like favorite plots, stereotyped characters, accepted ideas, commonly known metaphors and other linguistic devices, etc. Inventions, on the other hand, are elements which are uniquely imagined by the creator such as new kinds of characters, ideas, or linguistic forms. (1971:27)

Most mass-mediated texts are conventional, but that doesn't mean they have to be, and one finds a good deal of experimentation and even so-called avant garde textual practices in certain genres, such as science fiction, music videos, and in commercials.

THE POWER OF COMMERCIALS

In the United States, the most important television genre by far—from an economic standpoint, that is—is the commercial. It may be somewhat simplistic and reductionistic to put it this way, but as I've pointed out earlier, many critics argue that from an economic perspective, the essential thing that television does is to deliver audiences to advertisers for their commercials. The nature of these audiences is very important since different genres and different shows within a genre attract different kinds of audiences, with different levels of education, different degrees of sophistication, and different income levels (that is, different demographics).

We've all heard about how money is spent by advertisers on commercials during the Super Bowl (a 30 second commercial in the 2012 Super Bowl cost $3.5 million), but consider this: The annual NCAA basketball tournament known as March Madness brings in more advertising money that either the Super Bowl or the World Series. A report on NCAA advertising in 2010 by KantarMedia reveals the following:

> The NCAA men's basketball tournament has grown into the second most lucrative post-season sports franchise as measured by national TV ad revenue. It consistently brings in more money than the post-season playoffs for Major League Baseball, the National Basketball Association or college football. Only the National Football League playoffs, which include the Super Bowl, bring in more ad spending. (http:// kantarmediana.com/intelligence/press/march-madness-advertising -trends-report)

In the final analysis, the system we have in the United States for financing television is all about attracting audiences for commercials and making money for the companies that advertise on television and the stations and networks that broadcast their commercials. The price we pay in the United States for our so-called "free" television is advertising; commercials now take up as much as 20 minutes on an hour-long show in some cases. The average situation comedy is written to take up 22 minutes; the remainder of the half hour is for commercials and promos.

It has been estimated that Americans spend approximately nine years of their lives watching television and one year of their lives just watching television commercials. Typically American teenagers are exposed to approximately 360,000 television commercials by the time they graduate from high school (some have estimated the number at closer to 500,000). So the television commercial is what makes television, as we know it here in the United States, possible. There are other countries where people pay fees to the government to watch television and aren't exposed to the number of commercials that we are in the United States. So our system of providing

"free" television, which we pay for by allowing for commercials on our programs, isn't the only one around. Now that we can time shift with devices like TiVo and are able to watch television shows on our computers, cell phones, and tablets (and will soon have smart television sets), the role of advertising on television is changing.

It is important to remember, also, that we eventually pay for our "free" television programs by generally being charged more by the makers of the products and services we purchase that advertise; they pass their costs on to consumers. We pay many hundreds of dollars for advertising every time we purchase a new car. We also pay psychologically by having our attention interrupted by commercials so often.

Commercials not only affect our minds (that is, our decision making about products and services) but also have the power to affect our bodies. As a result of the growth of the fast-food industry—which makes great use of commercials—an increasingly large percentage of our children and adolescents, as well as adults, in the United States are now obese. Many of them suffer from clogged arteries, heart problems, and diabetes from eating all those french fries and hamburgers and all the other fat-laden and calorie-laden junk food that they saw advertised on television. This obesity problem is now found in many other countries, as well.

Prescription drug advertisements fill our magazines and airwaves. The people who are exposed to these advertisements then put pressure on their physicians to prescribe these drugs. This has resulted in the incredible growth in the popularity of, and also a significant rise in the price of, certain prescription drugs. There is a good deal of support now for doing something to restrain the amount of advertising these drugs companies do, as it is felt that the impact of this advertising is having negative consequences on the medical industry and the health of Americans.

Television commercials, then, often have a social and cultural significance—in the broadest sense of the term—that goes far beyond the products they are advertising. There is a biological, psychological, and social dimension to commercials; these narratives—or perhaps micro-narratives is more correct—have important consequences.

ANALYZING COMMERCIALS

Here are some topics to consider when analyzing commercials. You should record commercials you analyze.

1. What is the *plot* of the commercial? That is, what happens in the commercial?
2. What is the *theme* of the commercial? Is it success, happiness, reward or some other subject?
3. What *linguistic devices* are used to persuade viewers to purchase the product or service? Analyze whatever is said by actors or printed on the screen.
4. What role does the *product* play in American society?
5. *What do the actors do* to sell the product? Analyze their clothes, body type, body language, facial expression, tone of voice, etc.
6. *What are the actors like?* Are they beautiful women, handsome men, ordinary citizens? Why were they chosen to sell the product?
7. Analyze the use of *color, lighting, music, sound effects,* and all other technical aspects of the commercial.
8. What is the *target audience* of the commercial? Do you think the commercial will be successful in motivating those who view it to purchase the product? Explain your answer.

Note: You can make the same kind of analysis with print advertisements, except that you have to consider things like the typefaces used, the graphic design of the text, and the quality of the artwork or photography. Print advertisements and television commercials are very important art forms that demand serious attention.

NARRATIVES IN THE MEDIA

Our lives are saturated with media, and the media are saturated with narratives. This point is made by the French scholar Michel de Certeau, who explains in his book *The Practice of Everyday Life*:

> From morning to night, narrations constantly haunt streets and buildings. They articulate our existences by teaching us what they must be. They "cover the event," that is to say, they *make* our legends (*legenda*, what is to be read and said) out of it. Captured by the radio (the voice is the law) as soon as he awakens, the listener walks all day long through the forest of narrativities from journalism, advertising, and television narrativities that still find time, as he is getting ready for bed, to slip a few final messages under the portals of sleep. Even more than the God told about by the theologians of earlier days, these stories have a providential and predestining function: they organize in advance our work, our celebrations, and even our dreams. Social life multiplies the gestures and modes of behavior *(im)printed* by narrative models; it ceaselessly reproduces and accumulates "copies" of stories. Our society has become a recited society, in three senses: it is defined by *stories* (*recits*, the fables constituted by our advertising and informational media), by *citations* of stories, and by the interminable *recitation* of stories. (1984:186)

What Certeau points out is that these narratives are not simply entertainments; he calls our attention to the fact that they have a powerful social and cultural significance to them. We learn certain physical gestures from them, and we learn how to behave in many cases by imitating those we see in these narratives, who become "models" for us. These narratives, Certeau argues, even organize our lives and permeate our dreams.

In the last thirty years the amount of television viewing people do on a daily basis has increased, and it is reasonable to suggest that we see more televised narratives now than in earlier times. It is the nature of these narratives, which tend to be full of violence and exploitative sexuality, and the power narratives have to affect our emotions and our ideas about ourselves and "life," that is of importance here. The term *mimesis* means "imitation," and it is to that subject, as explained by Aristotle, that we now turn.

ARISTOTLE ON NARRATIVES

We all know what narratives are—stories. But the matter is a bit more complicated. The earliest and one of the most important philosophers to

write about narratives was Aristotle. In his *Poetics*, written around 330 B.C., he suggests that literary works—and now we include works such as films, television shows, novels, and plays—are always imitations of reality; that is, they can be thought of as being like mirrors. The term for imitation in Greek is *mimesis*.

There are three topics that relate to imitation for Aristotle:

1. *The medium of imitation* (language)
2. *The mode of imitation* (comedy or tragedy)
3. *The objects imitated* (men in action)

He points out that some works just use language while others use many different media. The mode of imitation involves whether a work is comic or tragic or some combination of both. Then Aristotle moves on to the object of imitation, which is "men in action." This matter of dealing with "men in action" he later describes as plot—namely the structure of the interactions or arrangement of incidents in a story. So a narrative, for our purposes, is a story of men (and women) in action.

Aristotle offered rules that were observed for centuries about plots having a beginning, middle, and end (in which the action is resolved) and about the nature of comedy and tragedy, among other things. Aristotle's rules are no longer slavishly observed, but he did offer a description of the basic elements of narratives that is useful for our purposes: a narrative tells a story by having characters interact with one another and can use many

different techniques and media, involving matters such as lighting, music, sound, scenery and costuming, to do so.

TEXTS AND OTHER TEXTS: INTERTEXTUALITY

One of the reasons that narrative texts such as films and television programs have such an emotional impact and affect us so powerfully is that they often draw upon (consciously or unconsciously) other texts with which we are familiar—a concept known as *intertextuality*. There is a considerable amount of controversy about what intertextuality means, but for our purposes we will consider it to involve making allusion to, imitating, adapting, and modifying previously created texts, styles of expression, or genres. Often this intertextual borrowing is not done consciously by the creators of texts; I should point out, though, that sometimes—especially in the case of parodies—it is. Think, for example, of the *Saturday Night Live* spoofs of news programs.

In *Understanding Media Semiotics*, Marcel Danesi offers us an excellent example of intertextuality with his discussion of *Blade Runner* (2002:63):

> The main text of the movie *Blade Runner* . . .unfolds as a science fiction detective story, but its subtext is, arguably, a religious one—the search for a Creator. This interpretation is bolstered by the many intertextual allusions to Biblical themes and symbols in the movie.
>
> The search for replicants in the film also ties it into postmodern thought, which is concerned with simulations of all kinds and their relation to reality.

Some films pay homage, stylistically, to the works of great filmmakers such as Orson Welles and Sergei Eisenstein; other films "remake" other films (such as *Contraband*); some films adapt novels; and there are many other examples of intertextuality that can be found in all media.

Texts exist, then, in a kind of limbo—suspended between the past, that is earlier texts, and the future, or forthcoming texts. All texts, it could be said, are intertextual in that they borrow from, are based on, or are affected, to varying degrees, by texts that have preceded them. These earlier texts have impacted on the psyches and sense of possibility of the creators of later texts in different ways. Bakhtin's stress on the importance of dialogue (technically known as Dialogism) offers us new insights into the creative process; it also shows how important the social and cultural context is for creators of all kinds. That is because the creators of artistic texts are profoundly affected by the social and cultural milieu in which they find themselves—whether they recognize this to be the case or not. And by extension, all texts and other creative works that already exist cast a long shadow, so to speak, or provide a compelling frame of reference on all texts being created at a given moment.

In many cases artists and creative people in all media are unaware of the extent to which their work has been influenced by previously created texts; in other cases, in parody for example, artists are aware of earlier works and imitate them in a ridiculous manner. M. M. Bakhtin deals with the difficulties of separating one person's speech—by which we can read "text"—from another (1981:69):

> The relationship to another's word was equally complex and ambivalent in the Middle Ages. The role of the others' word was enormous at that time: there were quotations that were openly and reverently emphasized as such, or that were half-hidden, completely hidden, half-conscious, unconscious, correct, intentionally distorted, deliberately reinterpreted and so forth. The boundary lines between someone else's speech and one's own speech were flexible, ambiguous, often deliberately distorted and confused. Certain types of texts were constructed like mosaics out of the texts of others . . . One of the best authorities on medieval parody, Paul Lehmann, states outright that the history of medieval literature and its Latin literature in particular "is the history of the appropriation, re-working and imitation of someone else's property."

So intertexuality is nothing new; the concept helps us understand why it is that some "new" texts can seem so familiar and why texts often have remarkable emotional power; in part it is because these texts often connect—stylistically or in terms of content—to other texts with which we are familiar.

An interesting example of intertextuality is discussed in *Pulp Politics: How Political Advertising Tells the Stories of American Politics* by Glenn W. Richardson. He discusses the 1988 presidential campaign of George H. Bush (2003:4–5):

> The appeal of invoking associations drawn from popular culture was not lost on George H. Bush's advisors in 1988 when they considered what turned out to be one of the most important phrases the vice president

would ever utter. In August, Bush's speechwriting team was sharply divided over whether to include in his acceptance speech at the Republican National Convention the now infamous line, "Read my lips: no new taxes." "Read my lips" was a catch-phrase of the hyper-macho action-film hero "Dirty Harry" Callahan, played by actor Clint Eastwood . . . By merely aping the language of a familiar Hollywood icon, the vice president was able to activate a deep web of preexisting associations in his audience. Campaign ads can do this even more effectively, by using audio, visual, and narrative elements to tap viewers' cognitive maps, literally evoking neural networks in our brains to communicate campaign themes with emotional force.

We see here how an intertextual reference to a well-known popular culture text can have enormous consequences, and much political advertising makes use of such references in print advertisements and television commercials.

THE QUESTION OF THE "UR TEXT"

If all texts are related to one another—stylistically, in terms of their adoption of certain technical or genre conventions, or content-wise (that is, in terms of imitating or alluding to a particular text)—the question arises as to whether all texts are related to one, primal, "Ur" text. This text would be a kind of template for all other texts, a "mother of all texts."

Let me suggest that the fairy tale is the foundational model or Ur form of the narrative. Fairy tales, which psychoanalytic critics such as Bruno Bettelheim say are the first important narratives to which we are exposed, are Ur texts. Collectively, fairy tales contain all the elements found in the more important contemporary narrative genres, and a given tale may contain all of them:

> *science fiction*: characters ride on magic carpets, have magic weapons
> *horror*: various monsters and dragons need to be dealt with
> *action adventure*: heroes have tasks to do or battles to fight
> *detective*: characters must solve puzzles and crimes
> *romance*: the hero marries the princess

In modern narratives we generally find updating of these primal elements, but the origin of our more important genres can be traced back to the fairy tale and to the psychological gratifications and instructions about how one is to function in society that these fairy tales provided.

NEWS ON TELEVISION

The coverage of the 9/11 attack and the events that followed showed that television can perform a valuable service. In times of crisis, it is invaluable. At other times, however, the news falls victim to the same forces that operate on television—the need to maximize profits. At one time news was considered a service that networks provided to audiences, even if news shows lost money. Now, news—especially national news broadcasts—have been "lightened up," and broadcast news, in general, suffers from being turned into entertainment and from increased tabloidization. Local television news can, generally speaking, only be described as a disaster.

The tyranny of audience demographics, the role of the Internet (and sites like Facebook), and the quest of advertisers for younger audiences now dominate the advertising industry. A friend of mine in the advertising industry told me recently that the hottest demographic is now 12 to 32; advertisers are after 12-year-olds, hoping to "brand" them and recruit them to life-long purchasing of their products and services. Young children have also been taught to be brand conscious. I can only wonder what the impact of all this branding will be on American culture and society.

I would suggest that news and commercials are, in terms of their social, economic, and political impact, the most important genres carried by television; selected texts from these genres, I have suggested, can have a significant impact upon our psyches, our bodies, and our society. Curiously, however, it may be that it is the commercials we watch that have the most profound and long-lasting impact on us as individuals—especially commercials for food products that affect and in some cases shape our food preferences and political commercials that play an important role in electing politicians and thus helping determine social policy.

Now, in the age of the Internet, we must add photographs and videos on the Internet as being very powerful. The video of a few American marines urinating on dead Afghans went viral in January 2012 and created enormous problems for the American State Department, the American military services, and the American government. In the age of the Internet, every photograph and video has global reach and can be politically explosive.

9/11 AND THE SOCIAL AND POLITICAL
IMPACT OF MEDIA IMAGES

When it comes to the matter of the social impact of the mass media, the 9/11 tragedy is of signal importance. For people in the United States, and elsewhere as well, there are probably no television images in recent history as horrifying as those of the two planes, controlled by terrorists, crashing into the World Trade Center. These images were followed shortly by horrific images of people jumping to their death from the buildings, and then of the giant buildings collapsing into a gigantic pile of rubble, with smoke from the fires filling the sky. Some people who were asked about viewing these events on television said it looked like a film or television program to them.

Those images, and the news programs that were on the airwaves for the next few days, changed America in many profound ways. There was an immediate sea change in our foreign policy, which went from being quasi-isolationist to internationalist, as we suddenly recognized that what was going on in a poor country like Afghanistan, thousands of miles away from our shores, could affect the United States in profound ways.

A new villainous figure emerged—the international terrorist—and with his emergence, all kinds of things that we used to take for granted, such as having superficial examinations of our baggage at airports, ended. Suddenly, we became conscious of the danger terrorists represented and made major changes in our law enforcement practices. The American Muslim community, which had never received much press, became the subject of intense interest, and a number of atrocities and hate crimes were committed against Muslims and people who were thought to be Muslims.

At the same time, new heroes suddenly presented themselves—the firefighters and police who risked their lives trying valiantly to save people in the World Trade Center; many of these brave men and women in the New York City fire department and police department lost their lives doing so. The attacks on our country led to a new sense of nationalism in the American public; all of a sudden, people started displaying the American flag on their homes, on their automobiles, and wherever else they could.

There were reports also about large numbers of people who watched the newscasts suffering from increased anxiety and post-traumatic shock. (Many young children were traumatized by the events of 9/11 and required therapy.) Some psychiatrists even suggested it would be best if people didn't watch so much television in the immediate aftermath of 9/11, but people's curiosity about the event, who was responsible for it, and its consequences was so strong that many people watched an enormous amount of the news coverage. Even a decade after the attack, 9/11 still lingers in our collective consciousness as a terrible wound.

We see, then, how powerful a text can be. In this case, I am dealing with the most serious attack on the American mainland in our history—an attack that cost nearly 3,000 lives. The news shows about the 9/11 attack show how a particular event—and images of that event—can have an enormous impact on individuals and on entire societies. The same applies to the impact of the television coverage of hurricanes Katrina and Rita in 2005, the tsunami in Japan in 2011, and countless other natural events whose full impact on our economy and collective psyche has yet to be determined.

BY WORDS ALONE

This chapter has dealt with the power of narratives (including commercials) and of images in a text—especially with respect to the horrific 9/11 tragedy. In narrative texts such as films, television shows, and video games, we find that some acts of violence may be much more important than other acts of violence, so merely counting the number of violent incidents in a text or a given time period, while important, doesn't tell the whole story. We may talk about television in general terms, but it is really the texts carried by television, often in combination with one another during an evening's viewing (what is sometimes called "flow"), that affect our beliefs and emotions and, as we have seen, these beliefs and emotions have considerable economic, social, and cultural significance.

A question now suggests itself. If we did not have television coverage of this event, if we didn't *see* all those terrifying images, if we only heard about the attack on the radio or only read about it in newspapers, would the 9/11 attack have had the impact it did? Eventually, I would imagine, we would have made the same decisions we made about foreign policy and all the other aspects of our lives affected by the attack, but I don't think that reading about the attack, or even listening to a radio report of it, would have had the impact that seeing the events on television had.

Still, words alone can have serious impact. A different mass-mediated text, a 2005 report in *Newsweek* magazine that American troops at the Guantanamo Bay detention site had flushed a copy of the Koran down the toilet, led to riots and several deaths and many injuries in Afghanistan. *Newsweek* later repudiated the article, but the damage had been done. There is considerable debate as to what degree *Newsweek* was responsible (if at all) for the riots and deaths, but the event shows that what seems like a minor detail in a news story can have enormous repercussions.

Janet Thumim has demonstrated, in her feminist analysis of the development of television culture in the 1950s and 1960s, that it is possible to assess the profound impact that television has made on society and culture. For Thumim, a generation of young women who watched the multiple, competing, and contradictory representations of women on television in this period went on to become feminist scholars in the 1970s . . . Crucial to Thumim's analysis is John Ellis' theory of "witness." For Ellis, the twentieth century was the century of "witness" where, through the media of photography, film and television, mass audiences could see new places, people, objects and events from afar. These audiences, by becoming witnesses to events then became complicit in them.

Rob Turnock, *Television and Consumer Culture* (2007:5)

. . . The critic may have access to a demographic profile of the audience, which includes the sociocultural categories that the audience members belong to: sexual identity, sexual orientation, religion, ethnicity, race, profession, educational level, income level, age, and political affiliation, to mention a few. The demographic profile will suggest a psychographic profile . . . There are always individual differences and variations from the norm, but most public messages are designed to make sense to the largest possible audience, and they do. Even though Americans, for instance, may identify with very different cultural groups, they are exposed to many of the same messages via school, parents, and media, and therefore develop many of the same codes for making sense of messages.

Jodi R. Cohen, *Communication Criticism:*
Developing Your Critical Powers (1998:20)

5

AUDIENCES I: CATEGORIES

In this chapter I deal with different categories of audiences. Individuals may not be aware of it, but media and marketing organizations have developed elaborate ways of classifying people into different categories—of interest to advertising agencies, who are trying to reach people to sell them goods and services. We may think of ourselves as unique individuals, but for marketers our distinctive identities are of no concern—we're all, as far as they are concerned, members of some group or category based on **demographics** (our age, gender, race, religion, ethnicity), **psychographics** (values and beliefs), or something else.

AUDIENCES ARE SPECIALIZED

Audiences for many mass media texts are now global—think, for example, of audiences for American **popular** music, films, or the broadcasts of the Olympics and the Super Bowl. In this chapter, I will focus on audiences in the United States, though what I write has applications to global audiences. We must remember that audiences are part of a larger entity, namely the society (or societies with access to global media) in which they are found.

In the United States, for example, we have a number of different and specialized audiences for the various genres (that is, kinds) of radio shows: news, talk shows, sports broadcasts, and music shows, such as country western, classical, hard rock, light rock, rap, jazz, blues, and easy listening—I could go on and on. There are probably a dozen or more niche audiences for specific kinds of music on radio. That is why radio can be considered to be a **narrowcasting** medium—appealing, as a rule, to limited and very specific audiences, as contrasted with **broadcasting**, which aims for much larger audiences.

In many cases, people in what we can describe as micro-audiences are members of various **subcultures** that exist within the broader category of American **culture**. There are, for example, many different genres of video games; gamers can be broken down not only by their preferred game genre, but also by which kind of console they use or whether they play video games on personal computers. Audiences are much more active than we might imagine, both in terms of the texts they select and the way they interpret these texts.

PROBLEMS ADVERTISERS FACE

Since radio and television commercials are sold on the basis of the size and characteristics of the audiences of specific shows, radio stations, television stations, and radio and television networks are interested in knowing how many people are listening to and watching their shows and what these audiences are like. If you're selling a luxury car, it doesn't pay to advertise on a television program mainly watched by viewers who cannot afford these cars. So advertisers have to pay careful attention to the programs on which they advertise.

The development of new digital video recording technologies, such as TiVo, which enable people to record television programs and delete commercials, is causing all kinds of problems for advertisers. Some of them are dealing with this problem by increasing the use of **product placements** in shows—paying to have their products used in films and television programs, which is a kind of "stealth" approach to advertising. But product placement cannot solve the problem new technologies pose to the advertising industry and the companies for which the advertising agencies work. Just showing a bottle of soda pop isn't the same thing as having a commercial about it.

There is also the problem of **clutter**, in which viewers of television programs are assaulted by so many commercials that they forget what they have seen and get the commercials all mixed up in their head. As advertisers become more and more desperate to attract the attention of audiences by finding new and more fantastic images, they become involved in an ultimately self-defeating war for viewers. In addition, people quickly learn that the promises advertisers make are often spurious and so audiences have become increasingly skeptical and more difficult to reach.

SHARES AND RATINGS

Media researchers distinguish between **ratings** and **shares** when dealing with audiences. The difference between the two is explained in Barry L. Sherman's *Telecommunications Management: Broadcasting/Cable and the New Technologies*. Sherman writes (1995:389):

> *Rating* refers to the percentage of people or households in an area tuned to a specific station, program, or network. For example, if, in a Nielsen sample of 1000 homes, 250 households were tuned to the ABC network, the rating for ABC during that time period would be (250 div 1000), or 25%. For ease of reporting, the percentage sign is dropped in the ratings book. *Share* refers to the number of people or households tuned to a particular station, program or network correlated with sets in use. Continuing the above example, if only 750 of the sampled households were actually watching television in the time period covered, ABC's share would be (250 div 750) = 33%. Since there are always more sets in a market than there are sets in use, the share figure is always higher than the rating.

These figures are important because radio and television networks are "selling" their audiences to advertisers, so a show with very high ratings and a high share (and the right kind of listeners and viewers) can charge much more for commercials than one with low ratings and a low share or with the "wrong" kind of listeners and viewers. For example, the 2012 Super Bowl charged $3.5 million for each 30 second commercial because it knew it would have a huge audience. Advertising works on a cost-per-thousand (CPM) basis, so a television show that is seen by hundreds of millions of people may actually cost less on a CPM basis than a show that doesn't charge very much, relatively speaking, but has a very small audience.

There is also the question of how reliable the various ratings systems are. Nielsen, for example, asks people to keep a "Peoplemeter" for its national ratings. Sherman describes how Nielsen gets its data (*Telecommunications Management*, 1995:383):

> The national Nielsens are produced through the use of the Nielsen Peoplemeter, a device resembling a cable box with a remote control. Over 4000 homes in the United States comprise a sample which, theoretically at least, represents TV viewing in America's more than 94 million TV homes. The peoplemeter is attached to each set in the participating household. Viewers push buttons assigned to them to track their viewing

activity. The data are transmitted to the Nielsen Company and processed overnight so that ratings information can be used by programmers and advertisers by the beginning of business the following day.

A sample size of 4000 people can get fairly accurate information about a television viewing population of 300 million people—if the sample is truly *representative* and if the people using the Peoplemeter are diligent.

There are some questions about how representative the Nielsen sample is and how accurately the people using the Peoplemeters report their television viewing. The only way to be absolutely certain about television usage in America would be for all station changes to be recorded automatically in each household and for a camera to record how many people are in front of a given television set when it is on. Obviously, this is quite impossible. So we have to make do with statistical sampling, which, while not perfect, yields quite accurate information if done correctly.

We cannot separate media organizations that rely on the Nielsen ratings, such as radio, television, and cable networks, and the marketing organizations that are so intimately connected with them. Advertising agencies have to choose certain programs on which to broadcast the commercials they produce, for example. So the broadcast media and marketing organizations are joined at the hip. Media broadcasting organizations and marketing organizations are, it is fair to say, different sides of the same coin.

NEW DEVELOPMENTS IN OBTAINING RATINGS

An article in the April 20, 2003, *New York Magazine* by Jon Gertner, "Our Ratings, Ourselves," deals with new developments in obtaining more accurate ratings. The Nielsen corporation has teamed up with Arbitron to test out a device called the Portable People Meter (PPM) that records which television and radio programs individuals wearing these devices are exposed to during the day. The PPM works by encoding an inaudible digital code in the audio tracks of most of the radio and television stations broadcasting wherever it is used. It has stirred up a great deal of controversy in recent years by groups that claim that they are under-represented. An article on October 16, 2008, by Hoag Levins in *Advertising Age* describes the controversy in New York and New Jersey:

> Arbitron's commercialization of its Portable People Meter system in
> New York and New Jersey radio markets this week triggered a flurry

of conflict. The attorneys general of both states filed suit to block implementation of the system, which, they charge, undercounts African American and Hispanic audiences. Arbitron then counter sued. Meanwhile, the Hispanic Radio Association and the National Association of Black-Owned Broadcasters joined with regional minority radio stations on the steps of New York's City Hall to blast the Arbitron system as inaccurate. Arbitron defends the accuracy of its data gathering.

These devices are "passive" in that people don't have to record what they've listened to on the radio or watched on television, the way they do in "active" research testing—the way Nielsen currently obtains information on ratings. It's been evident for some time that although Nielsen obtains information from a representative sampling of Americans, asking people to record what they've seen or listened to is not terribly accurate. This is not a problem with digital cable. As Gertner points out, the digital cable companies can obtain detailed information about what people who use their services are watching whenever they are watching cable television. In 2006, around 58 percent of American households subscribed to basic cable services, but cable services have been losing customers recently due to economic conditions and Internet video. Since so many Americans subscribe to cable services, the digital cable companies have an enormous amount of information about viewer preferences. Federal laws, and problems caused by people using analog set-top boxes because of our switch to digital television, have prevented the digital cable companies from utilizing this information. But now, Gertner says, third-party companies are trying to figure out how to protect viewer privacy yet use the information they obtain.

All of this effort to secure more accurate ratings is being made so television networks and stations and radio stations can provide advertisers with detailed information about how many people, and what kind of people, are watching broadcast or television cable programs or listening to radio stations. Ultimately, the ratings companies hope to be able to provide advertising agencies with information about how specific campaigns are working. Advertising executives commonly say that they know that advertising works, but they don't know how it works. It is hoped, Gertner writes, that the new, detailed information about preferences in media will help companies and advertising agencies learn how certain advertisements and commercials work their magic.

The development of digital video recorders has led to a great deal of time shifting in the way Americans watch television. As Pat McDonough, a senior vice president at Nielsen, explained on a 2000 Nielsenwire blog, "DVRs are changing the way Americans watch TV. Despite the competition for viewers' attention from the Internet, video games, and other media, TV viewership continues to rise. As with other vehicles, convenience is key—allowing people to consume content when they want. DVRs are a relatively inexpensive and useful tool for viewers to do that."

DEMOGRAPHICS AND AUDIENCES

I will now consider some of the different ways of breaking down the American market as being equivalent to segments of audiences in America. I will also use other typologies (classification systems) to distinguish between different ways of classifying audiences in America. We will start with demographics, which can be defined, broadly speaking, as the study of the social, economic, and other characteristics of human populations.

Marketers classify audiences into demographic categories, based on distinguishing characteristics such as age, education, income, race, gender, ethnicity, marital status, and residence. Let me list some of the titles of books on marketing to different demographic groups that are found in a catalogue of marketing books I was sent a number of years ago (*Marketing Power: The Marketer's Reference Library*):

> *Wise Up to Teens*
> *Everybody Eats: Supermarket Consumers in the 1990s*
> *Kids as Customers*
> *Marketing To and Through Kids*
> *Mature Americans: Myths and Markets*
> *Hispanic Market Handbook*
> *Mindstyle of the Affluent*
> *Marketing to Women*
> *Target the U.S. Asian Market*

These groups are all "target audiences" that marketers try to reach, since members of these audiences presumably have special characteristics and purchasing patterns.

I will offer the blurbs for two of the books listed above. The first is *Wise Up to Teens: Insights into Marketing and Advertising to Teenagers* by Peter Zollo:

Here at last is the expert analysis that will help you capture your share of the nearly $100 billion that teenagers spend. This book explains where teenagers get their money, how and why they spend it, and what they think about themselves and the world around them. It presents five rules that will make your advertising more appealing to teens. Learn about brands teens think are cool, words to use in advertising to teens, which media and promotions teens prefer, and how much influence teens have over what their parents buy. This is a fascinating look into the world of teens—a market whose income is almost all discretionary.

Zollo's book deals with an important demographic group for broadcasters and film studios—teenagers. It is probably somewhat of an exaggeration, but a large percentage of the movies that are made now have this segment of the American public (and teens in other countries, as well) in mind.

For my second example, let's consider the book *Target the U.S. Asian Market* by Angi Ma Wong, which is described in the following blurb:

This book explains how to effectively reach the most affluent, well-educated, and fastest-growing consumer group in the nation—one that numbers 7.3 million, with an impressive $225 billion in purchasing power. These consumers are a fascinating blend of centuries-old traditions and contemporary American culture. This marketing guide shows you where to get information: the impact of education and culture on the decision-making process; how to avoid potentially offensive intercultural mistakes; how number, colors, names, and *feng shui* affect your business; basic etiquette and much more.

We see that, for marketers, the United States is a collection of different demographic groups, each of which can be seen as an audience, each of which has particular characteristics, and each of which can be reached by advertisers, so their decision making about purchasing products and services will be the way advertisers want this decision making to be—for the products and services they are selling.

As I suggested earlier, we all think about ourselves as discrete and unique individuals, and, in terms of our personal identity—our genetic make-up, our personalities, the way we look and think—we are. But for marketers we don't exist as individuals. They see us as targets who can be classified as members of various market segments and groups that theoretically can be "reached" by those who know how to "press the buttons" that motivate members of these groups, including each of us. In this respect, you might think about your behavior as a consumer: why it is that you buy certain brands of clothes, watch certain television shows, go to certain films, use certain shampoos, eat certain foods, and the extent to which, as advertisers would put it, you have been "branded."

In addition to matters like age, race, and religion, some marketers look at audiences in other ways, such as in terms of the magazines they read. According to a survey conducted by the research company Yankelovich and Partners, the magazines people read are a more valuable indication of consumer behavior than demographic factors. The authors of this study argue that people choose magazines primarily based on their editorial content, and this editorial content is generally a reflection of their values, beliefs, and interests. The Yankelovich survey claims that people's behavior as consumers is coherent and logical and their choice of magazines is an index, so to speak, of other choices they make as consumers.

It is useful for us to remember that the radio stations we choose to listen to and the television programs we choose to watch are also a form of consumption, though we may not think of it as such. And as the Yankelovich survey suggests, there is a connection between the media we consume and our other kinds of consumption—namely goods and services advertised in the media.

Marketers also look at groups in terms of their zip codes (that is, specific locations in cities) and the **lifestyles** that researchers have associated with these zip codes. For example, families that live in the 10021 zip code, in the Upper East Side of New York City, have an average income of $200,000 (2010 figures); are liberal and moderate in their politics; have a "high use" of aperitifs, specialty wines, and champagne; and read publications such as *New York* and the *New York Times*.

What this means is that advertisers for companies that make and sell aperitifs, specialty wines, and champagne will look for the kinds of radio shows and television programs that people who live in the 10021 code most likely will listen to and watch. Our media, we must remember, are businesses. They must sell advertisements and commercials to audiences they attract in order to survive.

One marketing research company, Claritas Nielsen, has divided American society into more than sixty different groups, based primarily on their zip codes. Claritas Nielsen argues that "birds of a feather flock together," and suggests that people who live in a certain zip codes have many similarities in terms of their tastes in products and, I would suggest, tastes in media as well.

I suggest that this list of sixty-six consumer clusters applies to media tastes as well as general consumer preferences. A number of different clus-

Table 5.1.   One Market Research Company's Lifestyles Groupings

1. Upper Crust	34. White Picket Fences
2. Blue Blood Estates	35. Boomtown Singles
3. Movers and Shakers	36. Blue-Chip Blues
4. Young Digerati	37. Mayberry-ville
5. Country Squires	38. Simple Pleasures
6. Winner's Circle	39. Domestic Duos
7. Money and Brains	40. Close-in Couples
8. Executive Suites	41. Sunset City Blues
9. Big Fish, Small Pond	42. Red, White, and Blues
10. Second City Elite	43. Heartlanders
11. God's Country	44. New Beginnings
12. Brite Lites Li'l City	45. Blue Highways
13. Upward Bound	46. Old Glories
14. New Empty Nests	47. City Startups
15. Pools and Patios	48. Young and Rustic
16. Bohemian Mix	49. American Classics
17. Beltway Boomers	50. Kid Country USA
18. Kids and Cul-de-Sacs	51. Shotguns and Pickups
19. Home Sweet Home	52. Suburban Pioneers
20. Fast-Track Families	53. Mobility Blues
21. Gray Power	54. Multi-Culti Mosaic
22. Young Influentials	55. Golden Ponds
23. Greenbelt Sports	56. Crossroads Villagers
24. Up-and-Comers	57. Old Miltowns
25. Country Casuals	58. Back Country Folks
26. The Cosmopolitans	59. Urban Elders
27. Middleburg Managers	60. Park Bench Seniors
28. Traditional Times	61. City Roots
29. American Dreams	62. Hometown Retired
30. Suburban Sprawl	63. Family Thrifts
31. Urban Achievers	64. Bedrock America
32. New Homesteaders	65. Big-City Blues
33. Big Sky Families	66. Low-Rise Living

ters may be found in a given zip code, I should add, so not everyone in a given zip code is like everyone else in that zip code.

PSYCHOGRAPHICS AND AUDIENCES

Marketers and media researchers also break audiences down in terms of psychographics—the psychological characteristics of audiences. Research organizations have come up with a number of interesting classification systems, that is typologies, for various audience sub-groupings based on whether members are "inner-directed" (think for themselves) or "outer-directed" (follow others) and categories like that. The psychographic marketing theorists suggest that values and beliefs are more important than demographics. Consumer motivations, psychographic marketers tell us, are not always identical to **socio-economic** status and other demographic factors.

This means that people watch television programs, for example, because these shows reflect and reinforce their values and beliefs (which they may never have articulated or brought to consciousness) and are congruent with their lifestyles. People who watch *American Idol* and *Survivor* have different values and beliefs than people who watch *The PBS News Hour*. Thus, the psychographic theorists argue, the psychological profile of an audience can be more important than its age and income level. Let me offer, as an example, a well-known psychographic typology called VALS—for Values and Life Styles.

THE VALS TYPOLOGY

This **typology** or classification system was developed a number of years ago by SRI International, a think tank in Menlo Park, California, and focuses on people's lifestyles rather than demographic statistics about them. The VALS 1 typology is based on theories of psychological development and divides audiences into nine different and distinctive kinds of people. There have been changes to the VALS typology over the years, but I will focus on the original system here. Breaking the market down into nine categories of consumers is important, SRI suggests, because advertisers can target their appeals to the specific values of each kind of consumer, or, for our purposes, members of each kind of audience.

In the preface to *The Nine American Lifestyles: Who We Are & Where We are Going*, Arnold Mitchell, director of the Stanford Research Institute's Values and Lifestyles Program, writes (1983:vii):

> By the term "values" we mean the entire constellation of a person's attitudes, beliefs, opinions, hopes, fears, prejudices, needs, desires and aspirations that, taken together, govern how one behaves. One's interior set of values—numerous, complex, overlapping, and contradictory though they are—finds holistic expression in a lifestyle . . . We now have powerful evidence that the classification of an individual on the ba-

sis of a few dozen attitudes and demographics tells us a good deal about what to expect of that person in hundreds of other domains.

So, if Mitchell is correct, knowing people's values enables marketers and broadcasters to know a great deal about them and their tastes and preferences in many different areas.

The description of the VALS 1 typology that follows uses material from articles by Niles Howard (*Dun's Review*, August 1981) and Laurie Itow (*San Francisco Sunday Examiner and Chronicle*, June 27, 1982). In her article, Itow explains the VALS system as follows:

> The system . . . draws on behavioral science to categorize consumers, not only by demographics such as age, sex, and the products they use, but according to their state of mind. Marie Spengler, VALS director at SRI, says the program is based on an analysis of cultural trends that can be used to develop products and target markets as well as match employees with jobs and make long-range business decisions such as where to build plants . . .

CATEGORIES OF CONSUMERS

VALS, Spengler says, captures "a deep, underlying sense of what motivates the consumer," using data from a thirty-question survey. Consumers are questioned about demographics, such as age and sex. But more importantly, they're also asked about their **attitudes** and **values**. This provides SRI with the data needed to create the various categories of consumers found in VALS. For our purposes, in this discussion of audiences, we can think of each of these categories of consumers as a segment of the more general American audience. The nine categories of consumers in the VALS typology are as follows:

Need-Driven. These consumers are "money restricted" and have a hard time just affording their basic needs. They are divided into two subcategories:

1. *Survivors:* old, poor, and out of the cultural mainstream.
2. *Sustainers:* young, crafty, and on the edge of poverty but want to get ahead in the world.

Outer-Directed. These consumers, who often live in Middle America, want others to feel positive about them. There are three subcategories of outer-directed consumers:

3. *Belongers:* conservative and conventional in their tastes, nostalgic, sentimental, and not experimental.
4. *Emulators:* upwardly mobile, status conscious, competitive, and distrustful of the establishment. They want to "make it big."
5. *Achievers:* the leaders of society, who have been successful in the professions, in business, and in the government. They have status, comfort, fame, and materialistic values.

Inner-Directed. These consumers tend to purchase products to meet their inner needs rather than thinking about the opinions of other people. There are three subcategories of inner-directed consumers:

6. *I-Am-Me's:* young, narcissistic, exhibitionist, inventive, impulsive, and strongly individualistic.
7. *Experientals:* in essence an older version of the I Am-Me's and concerned with inner growth and naturalism.
8. *Societally Conscious Individuals:* believe in simple living and smallness of scale, and supporter of causes like environmentalism, consumerism (not the same thing as consumption), and conservation.

Integrateds

9. *Integrateds:* the last subcategory, one that is characterized by psychological maturity, tolerance, assuredness, and a self-actualizing philosophy. They tend to ignore advertising, and relatively few advertisements are made to appeal to them. Integrateds make up only around 2 percent of the adult American population, but they are very influential and are disproportionately found among corporate and national leaders. While integrateds may not be as susceptible to advertising as other groups, their taste in lifestyle products may be highly influential and they may function as what might be described as "taste opinion leaders."

This typology, which focuses on kinds of consumers, can also be thought of as listing what we might call micro-audiences, segments of the larger audi-

ence that are different from one another based on their values and beliefs and the way these values and beliefs are expressed in consuming products and services—but also, I would suggest, in consuming media. We can think of the programs the media carry as products to be consumed by segments of the American public, or other publics and audiences in other countries in certain cases. As you read the above list of VALS categories, you might want to consider which one of them applies to you, to your friends, to your parents, and other people you know.

POLITICAL CULTURES AND
LIFESTYLES AS AUDIENCES

The late Aaron Wildavsky, an extremely influential political scientist who taught at the University of California for many years, developed a way of breaking down democratic societies into four discrete political cultures.

In an unpublished paper, "Conditions for a Pluralist Democracy or Cultural Pluralism Means More Than One Political Culture in a Country," he explained how he derived his four political cultures (1982:7):

> What matters to people is how they should live with other people. The great questions of social life are "Who am I?" (To what kind of a group do I belong) and "What should I do?" (Are there many or few prescriptions I am expected to obey?). Groups are strong or weak according to whether they have boundaries separating them from others. Decisions are taken either for the group as a whole (strong boundaries) or for individuals or families (weak boundaries). Prescriptions are few or many indicating the individual internalizes a large or a small number of behavioral norms to which he or she is bound. By combining boundaries with prescriptions . . . the most general answers to the questions of social life can be combined to form four different political cultures.

There are, then, two basic questions: *who am I?* (does the group I belong to have strong or weak boundaries) and *what should I do?* (does the group I belong to have few or many prescriptions or rules). These two questions lead to four political cultures based on whether the boundaries are strong or weak and there are few or many rules. The four political cultures are, Wildavsky suggested:

Political Culture	Rules	Group Boundaries
Fatalists	numerous	weak
Individualists	few	weak
Elitists	numerous	strong
Egalitarians	few	strong

Fatalists think they are victims of bad luck and are apolitical; individualists believe in free competition and stress the importance of limited government, which should do little more than protect private property; elitists believe that stratification in society is necessary but also have a sense of obligation towards those below them, unlike the individualists; egalitarians emphasize that everyone has certain needs that must be taken care of (especially the downtrodden fatalists) and tend to oppose mainstream political thought in America.

According to Wildavsky, you need all four groups for democracy to flourish in a country, and the four groups need one another. He saw the individualists and elitists as being the dominant or core groups in America (the establishment) and the egalitarians as the loyal opposition. People in

America may not recognize that they belong to one of these political cultures or be able to articulate the beliefs of a given political culture. But their membership in one of these political cultures (and there can be no more than four) influences their decision making. The matter is further complicated by the fact that people sometimes move from one group to another, except for the fatalists, who are stuck down at the bottom of the totem pole and seldom have the chance to rise.

If you think about it, each of these four political cultures also represents a kind of audience for books, radio shows, television programs, films, and other media. I used to play a learning game with my students when I taught courses on media and **popular culture** in which we looked at these groups as audiences. One premise we use is that people seek **reinforcement** in the media for their basic beliefs and values and wish to avoid **cognitive dissonance**. Thus they will watch television programs that affirm and support the values they believe (that provide reinforcement) and avoid ones that attack their values and beliefs (and generate cognitive dissonance). The table below, adapted from one of our game-playing sessions a number of years ago, offers an example of the four political cultures as audiences:

Table 5.2.   Political Cultures and Representative Popular Texts

Kind of Text	Elitist	Individualist	Egalitarian	Fatalist
Books	The Prince	Looking Out for Number One	I'm Okay, You're Okay	1984
Films	Top Gun	Color of Money	Woodstock	Rambo
TV Shows	News Hour (PBS)	Survivor	American Idol	Smack Down Wrestling
Songs	God Save the Queen	I Did It My Way	We Are the World	Anarchy in the UK
Sports	Polo	Tennis	Frisbee	Roller Derby
Games	Chess	Monopoly	New Games	Russian Roulette

From this table, you can see how it might be that members of different political cultures, with different core values and beliefs, might choose to read certain books, watch certain films, as well as decide on which candidates to vote for in elections. These four audiences may not always articulate their beliefs to themselves or others and may not be conscious of what motivates them, but it can be seen that there is a logic, in many cases, to the choices members of audiences make as far as consuming media is concerned. It seems rather obvious that people who watch *American Idol* or *CSI* are probably quite different from those who watch *Nova* or *Nature*.

What complicates matters is that in some cases an individual who is a member of one political culture (for example, individualists) may be thinking of moving to another one (for example, elitists) which means the media choice could be based on the change the person is thinking of making in political cultures rather than reinforcing the political culture to which he or she belongs.

Wildavsky made use of the work of a British social anthropologist named Mary Douglas, with whom he collaborated on a number of projects. Douglas developed what is known as grid/group theory. She wrote an influential article, "In Defence of Shopping," in which she asserted that what Wildavsky described as political cultures were what she called "lifestyles," and these four (and only four exist in any society) lifestyles shape our preferences. "We have to make a radical shift away from thinking about consumption as a manifestation of individual choice," she wrote, explaining that our choice of a lifestyle shaped all our other consumption choices (1997:17). This means that, as she explained, "cultural alignment is the strongest predictor of preferences in a wide variety of fields" (1997:23), including, I would suggest, media preferences.

ACTIVE AUDIENCES:
DECODING MASS-MEDIATED TEXTS

In recent years, we have begun to recognize that members of audiences are more active than we thought they were. When the **hypodermic needle theory** of the media was popular, and we believed that everyone got exactly the same message from a mass-mediated text, the role of members of an audience (from one individual watching a television show to the huge numbers of people who are watching that show) was not considered important.

Now, however, the hypodermic theory has been abandoned and been replaced by what might be described as **reader-response theory** or sometimes as **reception theory**, which is the opposite of the hypodermic theory. Wolfgang Iser, one of the leading advocates of reader-response theory, explains his thinking as follows (1988:212):

> The text as such offers different "schematized views" through which the subject matter of the work can come to light, but the actual bringing of light is an action of *Konkretisation*. If this is so, then the literary

work has two poles, which we might call the artistic and the aesthetic: the artistic refers to the text created by the author, and the aesthetic to the realization accomplished by the reader. From this polarity it follows that the literary work cannot be completely identical with the text, or with the realization of the text, but in fact must lie halfway between the two. The work is more than the text, for the text only takes life when it is realized and furthermore the realization is by no means independent of the individual disposition of the reader—though this in turn is acted upon by the different patterns of the text.

Iser is talking about literary works, but we can extend the notion of a literary work to cover any text carried by the mass media. Everyone who watches a mass-mediated text interprets it on the basis of his or her temperament, education, background, and knowledge base.

For example, when we watch a show on television, we bring to the process of watching that show our culturally shaped knowledge base that enables us to make sense of what we are watching. This involves applying the aesthetic "codes" that we've picked up as we grew up watching television, our knowledge of rules of behavior, our understanding of spoken language and body language, and any number of other things. That is, we are always decoding the texts we see on television.

In the case of a novel, for example, according to Iser, that novel without a reader is inert; it takes a reader to bring a novel to life, and readers play an important part in interpreting novels and other kinds of mass-mediated texts. At the very least, in the case of films and television shows, audiences have to interpret visual phenomena, sound effects, and dialogue.

Iser's approach may seem a bit extreme, but it serves to point out the role audiences play in the scheme of things. They are not, at the very least, passive receivers of texts. We have to learn how to "read" television programs and films and all kinds of other texts in ways analogous to the way we read books. And where we are in the social structure, as the British media scholar Graeme Burton points out, also affects the way we read texts. All of these complications involved in interpreting texts suggest that the question we must ask when dealing with a film or television program or any other text is not whether our interpretation is right or wrong but whether it is interesting and comprehensive—whether it reveals important matters found in the text and explains the power the text has over audiences.

In other words, our reading of texts is based on our experiences in our societies and on the "grid" that growing up in a given culture and time period imposes on our minds. This helps explain why works of art are

so useful in understanding the society and culture in which they are produced—for that grid or schema is also, to varying degrees, in the mind of
the creator of a given text. We can say that it doesn't make sense to argue
whether the interpretation or a text is correct or incorrect. And taste is not
important, for tastes vary and one might say that in a postmodern world
taste is irrelevant. You may or may not have liked *The Matrix* or *Avatar*,
but that's not important. What is important is the degree to which your
interpretation of those movies adequately explains them in interesting ways
and can relate them to social, psychological, and cultural concerns, thus
providing a stimulating analysis.

ACTIVE AUDIENCES: USES AND GRATIFICATIONS

This notion, that there is often a logic to the choices people make in se-
lecting one or another television program, for example, leads to my next
topic—the uses people make of the television shows and the films they
watch and the gratifications which these television shows and films (and by
extension all kinds of other texts in other media) provide. The **uses and
gratifications** approach to audiences contrasts with the most commonly
used approach, which focuses on the media's "effects" on individuals,
groups of people, and society. There are some who argue that uses and
effects is dated, but it seems to me that it is important that we think about
how people use mass-mediated texts and, conversely, how these texts use
people.

Let me offer here a list of some of the more important uses and gratifications. This list was compiled from various sources and studies. I will separate uses and gratifications and will assume that *uses* involves the relation of
individuals to society and that *gratifications* refers primarily to psychological
matters, though my separation of uses from gratifications is, admittedly,
somewhat arbitrary.

Uses

1. To share experiences with others in some group or community.
2. To find models to imitate.
3. To help gain an identity and a personal style.
4. To obtain information about the world.
5. To affirm and support basic values.
6. To see order imposed upon the world.

Gratifications

1. To see authority figures deflated or exalted.
2. To experience beautiful things.
3. To identify with the divine.
4. To find diversions and distractions.
5. To empathize with others.
6. To experience extreme emotions in a guilt-free and controlled situation.
7. To reinforce a belief in the ultimate triumph of justice.
8. To reinforce a belief in romantic love.
9. To reinforce a belief in the magical, the marvelous, and the miraculous.
10. To see others make mistakes (and feel satisfaction in not having made those mistakes oneself).
11. To participate in history and events of historical significance in a vicarious manner.
12. To be purged of unpleasant feelings and emotions (a catharsis).
13. To obtain outlets for sexual drives in a guilt-free manner.
14. To explore taboo subjects with impunity and with no risk.
15. To experience the ugly and the grotesque.
16. To affirm moral, spiritual, and cultural values.
17. To see villains in action.

We must recognize that a given text might provide a number of different uses and gratifications, and different people will obtain different gratifications and make different uses of events in a given text. For example, viewers of talk shows might get information about how to deal with problems they face, gain information about topics of interest, and see models they wish to imitate (in terms of the guests on a show and their clothes, the way they talk, their "style," and so on).

Our knowledge of these uses and gratifications comes, in large measure, from surveys in which social scientists asked people (who, for our purposes, can be seen as members of audiences) questions about why they watched soap operas or what they got from listening to certain kinds of music. One problem with uses and gratifications is that it is difficult for researchers to determine, in an objective manner, which uses and gratifications are generated by specific events in a given text, and it is also difficult to quantify the results of this kind of research. Nevertheless, it seems pretty obvious that audiences are attracted to various specific mass-mediated texts because there is some payoff for them, and these payoffs are the uses these texts can be put to and the gratifications they provide. That explains why huge numbers of people watched the final episodes of *Frasier* and *Everybody Loves Raymond* and a long documentary about Michael Jackson that aired in February 2003, and why the media were so obsessed about his trial in 2005 and his funeral in 2011.

USES AND GRATIFICATIONS AND GENRES

As I explained earlier, the texts we watch can be classified according to their genres, such as a sitcom, police procedural, talk show, and so on. I suggest that genres provide for certain gratifications and are made use of in various ways by media consumers. A chart with these gratifications by genres follows.

Table 5.3.   Media Uses and Gratifications by Genre

Uses and Gratifications	Genres
To satisfy curiosity and be informed	Documentaries, news shows, talk shows, quiz shows
To be amused	Situation comedies, comedy shows
To identify with the deity and divine	Religious shows
To reinforce belief in justice	Police shows, law shows
To reinforce belief in romantic love	Romance novels, soap operas
To participate vicariously in history	Media events, sports shows
To see villains in action	Police shows, action-adventure shows
To obtain outlets for sexual drives in a guilt-free context	Pornography, fashion shows, soft-core commercials, soap operas
To experience the ugly	Horror shows
To find models to imitate	Talk shows, action shows, award shows, sports shows, commercials
To experience the beautiful	Travel shows, art shows, culture shows (symphony concerts, operas, ballet)

Texts and the genres we use to classify them also have many different effects on people, a matter of great interest to media researchers and the subject of the next chapter. And people use these texts in a number of different ways, as well.

In her book *Reading the Romance*, which is based upon research she conducted with readers of romance novels, Janice Radway offers some insights about the way individuals and groups of readers can resist the power of those who control the media. As Radway explains (1991:222):

If we can learn, then, to look at the ways in which various groups appropriate and use the mass-produced art of our culture, I suspect we may well begin to understand that although the ideological power of contemporary cultural forms is enormous, indeed sometimes even frightening, that power is not yet all-pervasive, totally vigilant, or complete. Interstices still exist with the social fabric where opposition is carried on by people who are not satisfied by their place within it or by the restricted material and emotional rewards that accompany it.

We can conclude then that people use the media and the media use—or attempt to use, influence, or manipulate—people, and the relationship between users or consumers of media and producers of media remains a complex one.

In his often-emotional lectures, Marshall McLuhan (1911–80) would be wont to warn his students at the University of Toronto in the 1960s and 1970s that the media to which they were exposed on a daily basis constituted a blessing and a curse at the same time. While they do indeed make information more available and accessible to larger and larger groups of people, he argued, the media also engender a general feeling of alienation and "disembodiment" in people. Since then, it has become obvious to virtually everyone that McLuhan's caveat was well founded. Our modern mediated world is indeed a two-edged sword. The "disembodiment" and "de-personalization" that McLuhan warned about just a few decades ago has, seemingly, become widespread, at the same time that more and more people gain access to information that was once the privilege of the few.

Marcel Danesi, *Understanding Media Semiotics* (2002:1)

The entire study of mass communication is based on the premise that the media have significant effects, yet there is little agreement on the nature and extent of these assumed effects. This uncertainty is the more surprising since everyday experience provides countless, if minor, examples of influence. We dress for the weather as forecast, buy something because of an advertisement, go to a film mentioned in a newspaper, react in countless ways to media news, to films, to music on the radio, and so on. There are many reported cases of negative media publicity concerning, for instance, food contamination or adulteration, leading to significant changes in food consumption behaviour. Our minds are full of media-derived information and impressions. We live in a world saturated by media sounds and images, where politics, government and business operate on the assumption that we know what is going on in the wider world. Few of us cannot think of some personal instance of gaining significant information or of forming an opinion because of the media.

Denis McQuail, *Mass Communication Theory:
An Introduction* (1994:327)

6

AUDIENCES II: EFFECTS

The media affect us on many levels: they give us ideas, they help shape our opinions and attitudes, they affect our emotions, they affect us physiologically, and they affect our behavior, among other things. But are these effects significant, and are they long lasting? Are the media doing things to us that may be harmful? Are the media doing anything socially constructive? Let me begin this chapter on media effects with a question that is at the heart of many of the criticisms of the mass media and mass culture.

IS MASS CULTURE MAKING US ALL MORONS?

Some media theorists argue that the mass media and popular culture—sometimes combined into "mass-mediated culture"—*must* destroy the elite arts (by which I mean things like serious novels, poetry, classical music, and plays) since Gresham's law suggests that junk art always drives out good art. But this doesn't appear to have come true. Let me cite some statistics about the book publishing industry for the year 2009 taken from www.bowker. com. I've not offered data for certain categories of books, such as those on medicine, home economics, and music.

Category	2009
Arts	9860
Biography	13,795
Business	9351
Education	9578

Fiction	48,738
History	15,480
Juveniles	32,638
Literature	11,456
Philosophy	13,949
Poetry, Drama	13,474
Religion	20,527
Science	15,608
Sociology, Economics	25,904
Technology	8068
Travel	4800

http://www.bowker.com/en-US/aboutus/press_room/2011/pr_05182011.shtml

Traditional book publishers put out 302,000 books in the United States in 2009, and the projected figure for 2010 is more than 315,000 book titles. This means that traditional publishers came out with more than 850 new titles every day. There were more than 760,000 self-published book titles in 2009, and it was estimated that there would be more than a million titles in 2010. In 2008, the book publishing industry was a $43 billion industry, larger than the film industry and the video-game industry combined. We must also consider the rising importance of electronic books (e-books). A report on e-publishing on Gracebooks (www.gracebooks .org/e-books/ebook-publishing-statistics-) states that e-books will be a $3 billion-a-year industry by the 2015. Amazon.com now sells twice as many e-books as what it describes as DTB books (dead tree books).

A large number of books are, no doubt, of poor quality—formulaic romances, trashy novels, and so on—but we must remember that a large percentage of books published in the so-called elite art forms—"serious" novels, poems, plays, and so on—are also second-rate or third-rate works. In the final analysis it is the skills and abilities of the writers and artists, not the art forms they use, that counts. A great writer like Dashiell Hammett can take a low-brow genre like the tough-guy detective novel and turn it into a masterpiece like *The Maltese Falcon*.

It is reasonable to argue that popular taste is not, as a rule, elevated—and that has been the case for centuries. But we still produce a considerable amount of great art for a relatively small percentage of the population, generally speaking—and is it unlikely that popular culture is driving out good art and rapidly moronizing us all, or even most of us.

JOHNNY AND EMILY MAKE DINNER

In this vignette, we find Johnny and Emily multi-tasking like so many media users around the world.

> Johnny and Emily are making dinner at her apartment before watching *CSI: Crime Scene Investigation*. They are in the kitchen, but the television set, located in the living room, is turned on. Emily is washing lettuce and making a salad of lettuce, tomatoes, cucumbers, and avocados. Johnny is grilling hamburgers on a George Foreman electric grilling machine. They are both "listening" to the television program that is on and occasionally walking into the living room to glance at it. For dinner they have the salad Emily made, grilled hamburgers on buns, and frozen french-fried potatoes that Johnny zapped in the microwave. For dessert they have ice cream and coffee. After dinner they go into the living room to watch *CSI*.

Johnny and Emily are like millions of other people who do other things while they are "watching" television. The fact is that, generally speaking, most people do not sit, hour after hour, with their eyes glued to the television set, but do a number of different things while their sets are on. Life goes on in front of the television set—people pet their dogs, go to the bathroom, chat with one another, go to the kitchen for snacks, read newspapers and magazines, and so on. So we have to make a distinction between watching television and simply having a television set on; not everyone watches television with undivided attention.

We must keep this in mind when we read about the number of hours people watch television and the effect that television has on people. Television is part of our lives, and relatively small numbers of us give it all our attention. The "boob tube" is blaring away, but Johnny and Emily are doing a number of things at the same time. Like many people, they are just using television programs as a kind of background to their activities.

The preceding chapter dealt with different ways of classifying audiences, with some of the ways that members of audiences use the media, and with the gratifications they obtain from them. Now, let's take a different approach and consider the effects that the media *may* be having on members of audiences. Denis McQuail, in the quote at the beginning of this chapter, makes an important point: We all believe that the media have effects—or, more precisely, from my point of view, the texts carried by the

media (and, in part shaped by them) have effects. But we have a very hard time proving, to the satisfaction of scholarly researchers, that these mass-mediated texts have long-term and important effects.

THE CONCEPT OF MEDIA EFFECTS
NEEDS QUALIFICATION

I think it is somewhat of a simplification to talk about "media effects" when dealing with television since we don't watch television per se but watch specific texts: programs carried by television (and other means such as cable and satellites). And the same, of course, applies to all media. The reason we talk about media effects the way we do is because we're looking for ways of dealing with large aggregates of people and texts, and so we simplify things and talk, for example, about the amount of violence on television (generally, on an hourly basis) or the way television portrays women (in commercials or in narratives or other genres).

This is perfectly understandable, but we should always remember that texts play an important role in providing a context for and characterizing events that take place in them—as the example "Pass the hypodermic needle" in a dark alley or hospital demonstrates. I will focus my attention on television here, since it is the medium with which we spend the most time and is the most powerful of our daily media experiences. But what I say about television can be applied to movies, music videos, video games, and other media.

Many of the texts we see on television are narratives of one sort or another—that is, they tell a story and have some kind of a beginning, some kind of conflict to be worked out or problem to be solved, and some kind of a resolution. This is important because narratives have the power to move us and to affect us in profound ways, emotionally and intellectually. I alluded to this in my discussion of the vicious cycles in television (see Chapter 1). We should also keep in mind the fact that genres commonly not seen as narratives, such as commercials (which are often micro-dramas), sports programs, talk shows, and game shows, often have powerful narrative and dramatic components to them. Even news shows can be seen as being composed of little narratives that form a larger narrative.

With all these qualifications and caveats in mind, let me offer some of the most commonly held criticisms of the mass media and the popular culture texts they carry.

CRITICISMS OF THE MASS MEDIA AND THE TEXTS THEY CARRY

Here are a number of commonly made criticisms of our mass-mediated texts, sometimes offered as attacks on the mass media in general and at other times as attacks on television, the medium everyone loves to hate. Throughout history, members of various social, intellectual, and aesthetic elites have attacked the taste of the common people and made arguments like these.

You may find some of the attacks quite convincing, and others you might consider rather extreme. The important thing is to be aware of what many critics consider to be the numerous negative effects that come from spending the amount of time we do with the media, in general, and television, in particular.

Viewers' Critical Faculties Overwhelmed

This argument is that television "overwhelms" us. Due to the amount of television to which we are exposed and the power of this medium, we eventually and inevitably abandon our critical faculties and our capacity for clear thinking and rational decision making. If we don't completely abandon it, our capacity to think clearly is certainly greatly diminished. The constant bombardment of our sensorium by rapidly moving images, music, and sound effects eventually make it very difficult for us to make rational decisions about anything. In this respect, the subtitle of Todd Gitlin's book on media is most interesting—*Media Unlimited: How the Torrent of Images and Sound Overwhelms Our Lives.* The metaphor that informs this title is that media is a wildly charging river that carries everyone along with it.

Viewers Desensitized to Violence

As a result of all the violence to which we as viewers of television are exposed, we become desensitized to violence's real nature, leading to a lack of concern about violence and, perhaps, a tendency by some viewers to rely on violence in their own lives to solve problems. This desensitization to violence may also have an impact on our attitudes toward sexuality, since it can be argued that there is often a psychosexual dimension to violence.

Picture of Reality Distorted

Television doesn't show the world the way it really is, but offers a highly distorted picture of it. The world shown on television is full of violence and sexual innuendo; we watch countless killings and murders on television while most people never see anyone killed or murdered in real life. The new, so-called reality programs such as *Survivor* and *The Real World* are, in a sense, frauds—they are highly edited and the people in them are not a cross section of the kind of people we see in our everyday lives.

Many of the people we see on television are unusual. For example, the female models in commercials tend to be tall and exceedingly slim, and the men often are very handsome. Ethnic minorities, those with disabilities, people of color, children, the elderly, and women are all underrepresented. We don't get a representative sampling of American society on television by any means. The reality we find on television, we must remember, is always a mediated, highly edited, distorted image of reality.

As Todd Gitlin points out in his book *Media Unlimited*, even the news is a distorted picture of life. He writes (2001:2):

> The news is not in any simple way a "mirror" on the world; it is a conduit for ideas and symbols, an industrial product that promotes packages of ideas and ideologies, and serves, consequently, as social ballast, though at times also a harbinger of social change. The news is a cognitive warp. The world is this way; the media make it appear that way.

Gitlin's point is that the media don't mirror the world but, instead, project a world as interpreted by editors and others who control the images we are allowed to see and the words we are allowed to hear on news shows.

Serious Creative Artists Diverted

Because television pays such incredible salaries, it seduces many serious writers, directors, and performers into working for it, diverting them from the theater and other elite art forms and depriving the audiences for this kind of art of their contributions. (This is particularly true of the film industry, which once used to hire stables of great writers to crank out film scripts.) The attractions of the media are so great that it is difficult for serious artists to resist them, which means that fewer serious dramatic and literary works are created.

Escapism

Television provides essentially escapist fare—silly situation comedies, violence-ridden action-adventure shows, and similar kinds of material with little redeeming social and aesthetic value. Because these shows don't deal with serious issues and are so superficial, people can consume enormous quantities of this material. Even news shows have become dominated by the need to entertain. Local news shows can only be described as a disaster area as far as news is concerned. It has been pointed out by media critics that nowadays there are relatively few television documentaries dealing with serious issues compared to twenty or thirty years ago.

False Consciousness Created

The stories shown on television tend to suggest that the so-called American Dream is alive and well and that anyone with enough determination and willpower will, inevitably, succeed. Most of the characters on television narratives tend to be middle-class or affluent people. This implies we live in a society that is classless in that it is, for all practical purposes, all middle class. Minorities, ethnic groups, and racial and other groups tend to be ignored, and the terrible difficulties people in the working classes face are seldom dealt with. Some critics of television argue that it should be seen as a subtle kind of brainwashing, meant to convince people to accept the status quo and to assume that nothing can be changed.

The notion that we are a classless, all-middle-class society has come under attack in recent years by the Occupy Wall Street movement and reports about the incredible amounts of money earned by corporate executives and the difference in incomes of various classes in America.

Formulaic Nature

In order to enable audiences to understand quickly what is going on in narratives, television script writers tend to use very conventional, stereotyped characters and story lines. That is, television is very formulaic and avoids material that might be challenging because it is original and inventive and requires a certain amount of effort on the part of viewers. Because watching television and films requires so little intellectual effort, many children and adolescents find it difficult to put in the effort required to read a book.

Fragmentation

The way a typical hour of television broadcasting is broken up, with numerous commercials and station promos, leads to a sense of life in general as fragmented and disorderly. In addition, the fact that we often see a large number of commercials for different products, one after another, often exacerbates the problem. Finally, in the course of an evening's viewing, we can see any number of different kinds or genres of programs: news, sitcoms, horror shows, and action adventure, which also reinforces the sense of life as fragmentary, cluttered, and lacking coherence. Postmodern theorists argue that the *pastiche* or hodgepodge (that is, a mixture of different styles and genres) is the dominant metaphor for understanding contemporary American culture, so it might be that our mass media both reflect and reinforce a postmodern sensibility.

Todd Gitlin deals with this matter of fragmentation in his book *Media Unlimited*. Discussing the research of Professor Berndt Ostendorf of the

University of Munich, Gitlin writes about how the formulaic storytelling and stereotypical characters in television shows fit together (2001:109–110):

> To make spaces for commercial breaks, and keep viewers' attention, production companies divided programs into short units—*acts,* producers still call them, hanging on to the theatrical precedent, even if they are but a few minutes long. Viewers, disposed to be fidgety, came to expect these breaks. Now, Ostendorf writes, the plot, with its traditional unities of time, place, and action, "is chopped up into short sequential bursts, each with their own simulacrum of a microplot . . . The goal is to create an unending series of reversals, moments of ecstasy and anticipation, which then may be usurped by the commercial." Interruption was thus built into the program. Not surprisingly, in the era of television, the term *attention span* began to be heard—and worried about.

So television's very nature more or less requires that television shows be designed to have many interruptions—for commercials—and the impact of this process has been a decrease in the attention spans of many individuals.

Homogenization

The other side of the psychological fragmentation argument is that television, film, and American popular culture in general are spreading American culture all over the world (especially in Third World countries). This media imperialism **hypothesis** leads, it is held, to a destruction of these "weaker" native cultures and the dominance of American and First World culture and, ultimately, a kind of global homogenization—in which all cultures are more or less alike: watching American films, eating McDonald's hamburgers, drinking Starbucks espressos, and abandoning their native traditions and culture. In addition, some critics argue that our popular culture also spreads our capitalist ideology, which is hidden in the texts and not obvious to those who consume them. (Some scholars, I should point out, do not accept this media imperialism hypothesis.)

Hyperactivity

As a result of the rapid bombardment of images and the kind of instant gratification that television provides, there is reason to suspect that television viewing contributes to hyperactive behavior in many children. Children who watch television are used to being endlessly amused and entertained and do not develop the ability to be quiet in classrooms and to concentrate on their studies. The incredible rise in the number of children (and now adults) diagnosed with Attention Deficit Disorder (ADD) or Attention Deficit Hyperactivity Disorder (ADHD) may be connected to high levels of television viewing and media exposure.

Irresponsibility

The argument that the people who decide what to show on television are irresponsible and more interested in profit than the well-being of their audiences raises an ethical concern. The airwaves are owned by the public and, in principle, television and radio should further the public's well-being. Instead, in a mad quest for ratings, television producers broadcast a great deal of junk that has wide appeal but is harmful. For example, many of the commercials for beer are directed towards adolescent sensibilities and shown on programs that adolescents tend to watch. This, critics assert, has led to a serious drinking problem in many young people—large percentages of whom are binge drinkers.

Isolation

Although television creates a huge audience of viewers, almost all of the people viewing television programs are isolated into little family groups. Statistic reveal that a large percentage of school-age children have their own television sets in their rooms, which means that even the family group is no longer a television-viewing audience because now children watch television shows in their own rooms. This argument ultimately suggests that television leads to increased alienation in people, who cut themselves off from others—even, sometimes, those in their own families. Marshall McLuhan dealt with this matter of alienation in the quotation at the beginning of this chapter.

Lowest Common Denominator

One of the most commonly made attacks on television (and the mass media in general) is that it is aimed at the lowest common denominator. This means that TV waters things down, oversimplifies things, and avoids important issues, in an effort to please as many people as it can. In theory, the "lower" you go, the more people you'll attract, which implies that ultimately there are forces at work to generate works that are best described as

Experts Rip ▢Sesame▢ TV Aimed at Tiniest Tots

How young is too young to park a baby in front of the TV set? The American Academy of Pediatrics's rule has been steadfast: No television under age 2. Now the venerable educational organization that pioneered "Sesame Street" is lowering that age limit with a new DVD series, "Sesame Beginnings," which targets babies and toddlers from 6 months to 2 years. Due in stores April 4, the videos feature baby versions of "Sesame Street's" most beloved characters—Elmo, Big Bird, Cookie Monster and Prairie Dawn—dancing and singing with their Muppet parents and other relatives.

"This could be the beginning of some beautiful friendships!" baby Elmo's dad says enthusiastically in one scene. But the product's launch has frayed some friendships and professional alliances among experts who monitor the impact of media on young minds.

"Essentially it is a betrayal of babies and families," says Harvard Medical School psychologist Susan Linn, founder of the Campaign for a Commercial-Free Childhood. "There is no evidence that media is beneficial for babies, and they are starting to find evidence that it may be harmful. Until we know for sure, we shouldn't risk putting them in front of the television."

Sesame Workshop, which for 37 years has pioneered children's educational television, teamed up with Zero to Three, a respected Washington, D.C.–based, nonprofit child-development and advocacy organization, to produce the DVDs. It's the first time the workshop has trained its marketing savvy on children under age 2 and their parents.

Don Oldenburg, *The Washington Post,* March 21, 2006

moronic—such as the infamous celebrity boxing match with Tonya Harding and Paula Jones in March 2002. This show received very high ratings, supporting the Gresham's Law theory some critics have which suggests that bad programming drives out good programming.

Manipulation

Television, it is asserted, manipulates its viewers by using humor, sexuality, and anything else it can to attract audiences and to get people to purchase the products and services it advertises. In addition, because television only shows certain perspectives on news events, it manipulates public opinion. People say "seeing is believing" without thinking that when they watch television, someone always determines what they see and that what they see may be taken out of context, or in scholarly jargon, *decontextualized*.

Narcotic

There is reason to suggest that television functions like a narcotic with a number of people who become psychologically dependent on it and sometimes even describe themselves as "hooked" on it. That is, they become television addicts. Like many addicts, they lack an awareness of their addiction, seeing themselves as people who "like" television but can live without it. Some viewers develop **para-social relationships** with certain characters they watch on television, and feel that they actually "know" these characters and the performers who play them. These viewers have a need to be with these characters on their favorite shows, which can be seen as a pathetic substitute for real relationships with other people.

Obsession with Narrow Range of Topics

Television is obsessed with a relatively narrow range of topics—violence, sexuality, consumption, youth, celebrity and a few others—if we judge from the vast number of topics relative to the human condition that it could deal with. Television executives argue "we only give people what they want," neglecting the fact that audiences can only "select" from what is available on television, satellite, or cable that night. This narrowness of focus in television leads, ultimately, to a diminished sense of possibility in viewers and a constricted notion of what it means to be a human being. Television, it could be said, doesn't give us what we want but teaches us to want what we can get.

Passivity Induced

Watching television is, generally speaking, a passive experience—we sit and watch. The only physical activity might be pressing a button and zapping a program. This television viewing experience is typically punctuated by trips to the bathroom and refrigerator. As a result of all the television viewing that young people do, they are now are growing obese in alarming numbers. Obesity is now an epidemic in America. Thus, television watching has certain biological, as well as psychological, effects on members of audiences. And these biological changes have social implications, because obese people tend to suffer from many medical problems such as heart trouble and diabetes, which leads to higher medical costs for everyone. In some cases we find an interesting contrast—passivity, while watching television, and hyperactivity, when not watching television.

Privatism

The argument that television leads to privatism means that viewers of television learn to focus on their own lives and personal concerns and neglect social matters and the public realm in general. We become distracted from serious matters—involving politics, decisions about social issues, and that kind of thing—and focus, instead, on our own concerns, and in particular our desires for consumer products and services. Thus television viewing leads to materialism. Researchers have found, for example, many young people know very little about our history or anything else, in many cases, but know everything about pop culture celebrities and have incredible "product knowledge" (which they've learned from advertising). This privatism on the part of the general public means that small groups that are politically motivated and organized exercise inordinate power over our social and political agenda. Large numbers of people do not vote in elections because they are all wrapped up in themselves, so the argument goes,

---

What We Know

According to a recent survey of America's most elite universities, nearly all college seniors could identify *Beavis and Butthead,* but 40 percent could not place the Civil War in the right half-century. A national history test of high-school seniors found a majority of them identifying Germany, Italy, or Japan as a U.S. ally in World War II. Still another survey of Americans at large found a third attributing the line "from each according to his ability, to each according to his needs" to the Constitution rather than Karl Marx.

The Wall Street Journal, February 4, 2003:W15.

and can't be bothered with anything else, even though decisions made by elected officials affect their lives in profound ways.

Sentimentalism

Television dramas are often criticized for being excessively sentimental, for generally having "happy endings," for calling up more emotion than is necessary in the various kinds of narratives they broadcast. Television, it is argued, tends to neglect the tragic dimensions of human life, washing everything over with a veneer of optimism and seeing everything through rose-colored glasses.

Sexploitation

The roles women are given in television dramas and the way they are portrayed in television commercials and other texts exploit their sexuality and use them to create sexual excitement and sell products. Even though feminists have spent many years attacking the roles women are given in narratives and the way television exploits female sexuality, there has been little improvement. Generally speaking, women are not portrayed in realistic ways; the focus is on their bodies and their sexuality and not on their minds, character, or personalities.

It might be that there is so much vicarious sexuality available on television (and on videos) that the interest of viewers in real sexual activity becomes diminished or that the erotic fantasies generated by television dominates their thinking, leading to negative feelings towards real-world partners.

Trendmaking

Interestingly enough, large numbers of Americans pride themselves on their individuality and uniqueness, on "doing their own thing," yet television has incredible power to create trends, fads, and crazes—usually involving matters like clothing styles, hair styles, and the use of new slang terms. It has been argued then, perhaps carrying things to extremes, that we are a nation of sheep. Each of us has the illusion that we are different from others—even though we may look like everyone else and talk like everyone else—in our culture in general or in some subculture to which we belong. We are caught in a contradiction—we want to be ourselves but we also aspire to be "trendy" or "hip."

Violence as a Solution

It has been suggested that many mass-mediated narratives use violence as an easy solution to dramatic problems. Much of what we know about the world is based on what is called "incidental learning," learning that we pick up outside of the classroom, and it may be that what many people learn from these dramas, without being conscious of what they are learning, is that violence is the best way to deal with certain difficulties. This may help explain why, all of a sudden or so it seems, we read about all kinds of newly identified "rages," such as road rage and air rage.

There is now evidence to suggest that media organizations are cutting down somewhat on the amount of violence and sexploitation in the texts they carry. A survey taken in 2002 shows a decrease in the amount of violence and sexuality in television—perhaps in response to all the negative publicity media organizations have received about violence and sexual exploitation in the media. But this decrease does not mean that there is not still excessive use of violence and sexploitation on television, in films, and in many music videos.

These are the criticisms that commonly are made about the mass media and especially television. I offer next a discussion of some extreme attacks on the media that have been made in earlier years—examples of what I call anti-media rage.

ANTI-MEDIA RAGE

It is interesting to consider the vehemence with which the mass media have been attacked by some scholars. Is this, perhaps, in an era of road rage and other such rages, an example of what might be called anti-media rage? As an example, let me cite from the introduction by Bernard Rosenberg to a book he co-edited with David Manning White, *Mass Culture: The Popular Arts in America*—an important anthology on the media published in 1957. It is generally considered one of the first books to seriously examine the mass media and popular culture—or mass-mediated culture. I have eliminated a number of phrases and similar material in the interest of economy, but offer Rosenberg's indictment in all its fury:

> People in mass cultures become *dehumanized, deadened, anxiety-ridden, exploited, entrapped, lonely, debased,* and their lives are *standardized, vulgarized* and *manipulated* by mass culture, which is a threat to our autonomy,

and this situation is exacerbated by things such as *sleazy fiction, trashy films, bathetic soap operas,* creating, in the general public, *unrest, lives emptied of meaning and trivialized,* as well as *alienation* (from the past, work, community and possibly one's self) leading to that horrendous entity, mass man. Mass culture is *cultural pap* and *gruel* that *cretinizes* our taste, *brutalizes* our senses (paving the way for totalitarianism), and destroys our taste so that all we like is kitsch. (my italics)

Rosenberg, quite obviously, thinks that popular culture, the mass media, and **mass culture** are highly destructive of our well-being as individuals and collectively, as a society. He hypothesizes that it is mass culture, made possible by modern technology, that lies at the root of our problems—not our national character or our economic system. In essence, he is suggesting that mass culture is the logical and necessary result of the development of modern technology.

DEFENDERS OF THE MASS MEDIA AND POPULAR CULTURE

Not everyone is as negative as Rosenberg, of course. His co-editor, David Manning White, offers a different and more positive assessment of television. He writes:

> Take, for example, the offerings of the television networks on Sunday, March 18, 1956, a Sunday which I chose at random. The televiewer would have been able to see on this day a discussion of the times and work of Toulouse-Lautrec by three prominent art critics; an inspiring interview with Dr. Paul Tillich, the noted theologian; a sensitive adaptation of Walter von Tilburg Clark's "Hook," a story of a hawk's life; a powerful documentary on mental illness with Orson Welles and Dr. William Menninger; an interview with the Secretary of Health, Welfare and Education; an interview with the Governor of Minnesota on the eve of the primary elections in his state; an hour and a half performance of *Taming of the Shrew* in color with Maurice Evans and Lilli Palmer.

White points out that there is a lot of excellent programming on television, and adds that critics of mass culture "will invariably choose the mediocre and meretricious" to focus their attention on when they deal with the media and popular culture. In other words, their attention is highly selective; they neglect anything that is good and focus their attention and fury on anything that is mediocre or bad.

Let's look at an updated version of David Manning White's 1956 review. Television offerings for March 18, 2006, were affected by the fact that it was a Saturday and the annual NCAA college basketball tournament (March Madness) was in full swing. Here are some programs that aired March 18, 2006, in San Francisco as listed by the *San Francisco Chronicle*.

Channel 9: Public Television
American Soundtrack: This Land Is Your Land
Benise Night of Fire
Roy Orbison and Friends: A Black and White Night

Channel 5: CBS
College basketball
The King of Queens
Everybody Loves Raymond
CBS News Special

Channel 7: ABC
Jeopardy
Wheel of Fortune
The Sixth Sense (film)

Channel 11: NBC
Access Hollywood
Saturday Night's Main Event

Based on this listing of programs, was broadcast television offering anything of cultural significance? I would say that it was not and that these offerings were, instead, trying to reach an audience representing the mythical "lowest common denominator." On cable, few programs were of radically different cultural importance. This lineup would have given David Manning White little reason to argue that television and cable were bringing culture to the millions.

There are, it is fair to say, many scholars who defend television and the mass media, on a number of different fronts. I will deal with some of these defenses below.

OTHER DEFENSES OF THE MASS MEDIA
AND THE TEXTS THEY CARRY

Defenders of the mass media, mass-mediated culture, and popular culture (or, for our purposes, the texts carried by the mass media) have a number of points to offer concerning the attacks made by critics of the media and some arguments to make on their own behalf. I once wrote an article with the title "Why Is Popular Culture So Unpopular?" My point in the article was that popular culture was very popular with the masses of people for whom it was created; it is unpopular with academics, scholars, and various elites, who argue most popular culture is junk (which is generally true) and its effects have generally been very harmful (which is debatable).

William McGuire, a psychologist at Yale University, has offered the following assessment of what might be called the debate over television and the mass media. His essay "Who's Afraid of the Big Bad Media?" discusses research on a variety of subjects related to media effects. He writes:

> Evidence in support of the claim that the media have sizable direct impact on the public is weak as regards each of the dozen most often-mentioned intended or unintended effects of the media. The most commonly mentioned intended effects include: (1) the influence of commercial advertising on buying behavior; (2) the impact of mass media political campaigns on voting; (3) public service announcements' efficacy in promoting beneficial behavior; (4) the role of prolonged multimedia campaigns in changing lifestyles; (5) monolithic indoctrination effects on ideology; and (6) the effects of mass-mediated ritual displays on maintaining social control. The most often cited unintended effects of the mass media include: (1) the impact of program violence on viewers' antisocial aggression; (2) representation on the media as a determinant of social visibility; (3) biased presentation of media as a influencing the public's stereotyping of groups; (4) effects of erotic materials on objectionable sexual behavior; (5) modes of media presentation as affecting cognitive styles; and (6) the impact of introducing new media on public thought processes. (quoted in Berger, 1991:274)

McGuire argues that there is little evidence that the media have the effects they are held to have by critics. Thus, many of the criticisms found in the section above on effects can be attacked as speculative, theoretical, and perhaps ideological—that is, not based on empirical evidence—or as involving short-lived and relatively limited phenomena.

Defenders of television and the mass media also suggest, like David Manning White, that it has brought millions of people ballet, opera, serious drama, and other works of so-called elite culture—works that they never would have seen otherwise. Thus, it is argued, the mass media have, on balance, positive effects for their audiences. This assertion that television has brought culture to the masses is correct, but I would counter that the amount of "culture" is minimal contrasted with the amount of third-rate material that is available.

I would suggest that now the dominant view among researchers is that most of the evidence available leads to the notion that media effects are not weak and limited, but are strong and powerful. For example, as a colleague of mine, Chaim Eyal, has written:

> The limited effects notions are conceptualizations of the past. Very few, if any, theoreticians cling to those ideas. In the first place, the notion of null, or limited, effects originated from a very narrow line of research— the impact of political campaigns, studies in the late 1940s and early 1950s. Not much later it was recognized effects are not only in the realm of behavior but also in the area of cognition: awareness, knowledge, opinions, etc. With this recognition, which paralleled the development of the concept of attitudes by social psychologists, came the recognition that the mass media do have an impact—indeed different types of impact—in specific areas of people's thoughts, information processing and life in general. (Personal communication, 1999)

There is reason to believe that the effects of television and the mass media are not as limited and minor as defenders of the mass media argue.

THE POSTMODERN SOLUTION

Earlier I discussed postmodernism with a focus on the way it is reflected in films (see Chapter 3). I pointed out that postmodern society is characterized by a lack of adherence to overarching philosophical systems and beliefs. The phrase that Jean-François Lyotard, a French scholar, used to characterize postmodernism in *The Postmodern Condition: A Report on Knowledge* is "incredulity toward metanarratives." In postmodern societies, people no long accept the old philosophical systems that were used to justify beliefs and actions. I should point out that he is dealing with the

Figure 6.1.   The pastiche, which combines fragments from many images, is consid ered a quintessential postmodern art form.

condition of knowledge in the most highly developed societies. He writes (xxiii, xxiv):

> I have decided to use the word *postmodern* to describe the condition. The word is in current use on the American continent among sociolo- gists and critics; it designates the state of our culture following the trans-

formations which since the end of the nineteenth century have altered the game rules for science, literature, and the arts.

He then suggests that the transformations should be understood as involving a crisis of narratives and offers his definition of postmodernism.

Eclecticism and the pastiche have become the dominant metaphors for postmodern societies. People can have multiple identities, which means they can, at different times, be members of many different audiences. As Lyotard explains,

> Eclecticism is the degree zero of contemporary general culture: one listens to reggae, watches a western, eats McDonald's food for lunch and local cuisine for dinner, wears Paris perfume in Tokyo and "retro" clothes in Hong Kong; knowledge is a matter for TV games. (1984:76)

That is, an individual can have multiple identities and consume many different kinds of culture in the course of a day or week.

One significant thing about postmodern thought is that it breaks down the barrier between elite culture and popular culture. In essence, postmodernists argue, elite culture and popular culture aren't that different,

and in many cases it is hard to tell the difference between them. Take, for example, an Andy Warhol painting of a comic strip hero, Dick Tracy. Is that elite culture or popular culture? So, for postmodernists, there is just culture and different kinds of culture appeal to different groups, subcultures, media audiences, or interpretive communities within society. As Douglas Kellner writes in "Postmodernism as Social Theory: Some Challenges and Problems" (*Theory, Culture & Society*, 5, Nos. 2–3, 239):

> As opposed to the seriousness of "high modernism," postmodernism exhibited a new insouciance, a new playfulness, and a new eclecticism embodied above all in Andy Warhol's "pop art" but also manifested in celebrations of Las Vegas architecture, found objects, happenings, Nam June Paik's video-installations, underground film, and the novels of Thomas Pynchon. In opposition to the well-wrought, formally sophisticated, and aesthetically demanding modernist art, postmodernist art was fragmentary and eclectic, mixing forms from "high culture" and "popular culture," subverting aesthetic boundaries and expanding the domain of art to encompass the images of advertising, the kaleidoscopic mosaics of television, the experiences of the post holocaust nuclear age, and an always proliferating consumer capitalism. The moral seriousness of high modernism was replaced by irony, pastiche, cynicism, commercialism, and in some cases downright nihilism.

Thus, it can be argued that postmodernist thought cuts the Gordian knot created by the tangled and complicated debate over elite and popular culture by slicing through the barrier that critics had used to separate them. If popular culture and elite culture are more or less the same, as the postmodernists argue, then the debate over the effects of popular culture and the mass media becomes irrelevant.

Contemporary Western citizens are surrounded by media, immersed in media, dependent on media . . . we have become, quite literally, a media culture. We spend our everyday lives reading newspapers, perusing magazines, watching television, playing video games, surfing the internet, and listening to music, without thinking about what we are doing—or what the media are doing. Media have become "like the air we breathe, ever present yet rarely considered."

Media, with their images of utopian lifestyles and bodily perfection, are a key site for the construction of identity in contemporary Western society.

Kelley Massoni, *Fashioning Teenagers:*
A Cultural History of Seventeen *Magazine* (2010:17)

There is no "mass" communication because there is no "mass" audience. Instead, there are many audiences, some with structures and leadership and others without these characteristics. Some audiences last only a few hours (Super-bowl viewers) while others last for a whole season (diehard football fans). Some audiences are based on a need for immediate information (viewers of CNN), some on in-depth information (readers of news magazines), some on a need for a religious experience (viewers of the PTL Club), some on a need for political stimulation, musical entertainment, romantic fantasy, and on and on . . . Each of us is a member of multiple audiences. You are a member of a local community that the local newspaper and cable TV franchise targets. You are a member of virtual communities when you are on the Internet—communities that quickly form and may last for only one evening. You are a member of certain hobby groups that are targeted by certain magazines . . .

W. James Potter, *Media Literacy* (1998:246–247).

7

THE MASS CULTURE/
MASS SOCIETY HYPOTHESIS

In this chapter I deal with an argument that was very popular a number of years ago—that the mass media were turning America in what was known as a "mass society." I will call this the Mass Culture/Mass Society hypothesis. The hypothesis is that mass culture inevitably would lead to a mass society, in which individualism is destroyed and a slave-like "mass man" (and now we would add "mass woman") is created. Although this debate about mass culture stems from the 1950s, it is still relevant today—and perhaps, due to the increased power of the media, it is even more important now than it was when it was originally propounded.

THE MASS CULTURE HYPOTHESIS:
MYTH OR REALITY?

In America there is, I would suggest, a kind of diffuse obsequiousness regarding European philosophers, culture critics, and theorists of one sort or another. Culturally speaking, we still see ourselves, I would argue, as spiritual orphans, as "sons and daughters" who have abandoned our intellectual motherlands and fatherlands in Europe and elsewhere, in a desperate but futile attempt to escape from history or, more precisely, historical consciousness (though, of course, we probably have half the historians in the world in America).

Our intellectuals and deep thinkers on cultural matters, especially those found in literature departments and communications departments, now bend their knees to French cultural theorists more than those from other countries. (In the fifties it was German thinkers, many of whom were escaping from the Nazis, who dominated our theorizing, as I shall

explain shortly.) Today we derive many of our concepts and ideas, as far as cultural criticism is concerned, from the likes of Roland Barthes, Claude Lévi-Strauss, Jean Baudrillard, Jacques Derrida, Jean-François Lyotard, and one could go on and on here—with a few Russians, Bulgarians, Italians, Germans, and others bringing up the rear, so to speak.

ROUND UP THE USUAL INDICTMENTS; OR, THE LANGUAGE OF CRITICISM IN THE FIFTIES

In recent years the critics of American media and culture don't seem to be as certain about things as they were in earlier times. Perhaps the demise of communism and the questions many now raise about Marxism have contributed to this feeling. In the fifties, however, many American intellectuals and others interested in media, culture, and society learned and became indoctrinated, one might say, with the jargon of a number of social theorists and culture critics who had fled from Germany and other countries in Europe. They were members of what was known as the Frankfurt School of media theorizing. Let me cite two examples.

In an important collection of essays edited by Bernard Rosenberg and David Manning White, *Mass Culture: The Popular Arts in America*, published in 1957, Gunther Anders explained to us, in his essay "The Phantom World of TV," that "modern mass consumption is a sum of solo performances: each consumer, an unpaid homeworker employed in the production of the mass man" (358). This leads, he adds, to the creation of mass-produced hermits who don't want to renounce the world but, instead, want "to be sure they won't miss the slightest crumb of the world as image on a screen" (359). Eventually, he predicted—tongue-in-cheek, perhaps—we would lose our ability to talk. "Because the receiving sets speak in our place, they gradually deprive us of the power of speech, thus transforming us into passive dependents" (361).

T. W. Adorno is represented in the book with an essay, "Television and the Patterns of Mass Culture," that suggests that "popular culture is no longer confined to certain forms such as novels or dance music, but has seized all media of artistic expression" (475). The media, for Adorno, seem all-powerful. He describes modern mass culture as repetitive, boring, and ubiquitous and suggests that these aspects of modern mass culture "tend to make for automated reactions and weaken the force of individual resistance" (475). Eventually, he adds, people not only lose their ability to see reality as it is, but also their capacity for life experience may be dulled.

WHERE ARE THE MASS MEN AND MASS WOMEN THE CRITICS OF THE FIFTIES WARNED US ABOUT?

The theorists we have been discussing believed that popular culture and the mass media would automatically generate mass culture and it, in turn, would lead to the development of mass man and mass woman—the cretinized, dehumanized, moronized, kitsch-loving, de-individuated inhabitants of mass societies that, as an additional and ominous feature, lent themselves to becoming totalitarian. This would happen because—and this is implicit in the arguments of the early elitists—the media would affect everyone more or less the same way. According to these theorists, individuals living in mass societies are essentially isolated or atomized and thus are highly susceptible to messages from the media.

This theory, that the media not so much affect or shape but actually determine the consciousness of individuals, is very close to what used to be called the hypodermic theory or magic bullet theory of the media, a theory that is now generally discredited and considered simplistic. According to this theory, as we discussed in Chapter 6, messages in the media are interpreted essentially the same way by everyone and these messages generate responses that are direct and more or less automatic and immediate.

Media scholars now recognize that things are not as simple as the hypodermic theorists thought they were and that such matters as race, religion, age, ethnicity, gender, education, values, personality, and a host of other variables affect our decisions about the media we will watch or listen to and the way we respond to the texts carried by this media. This does not mean that the media don't have effects on large numbers of people, but there is good reason to argue that the effects are not universal and not everyone is affected the same way.

There is some question in my mind as to whether mass culture actually exists or can exist. Of course there are countries, such as America, where an enormous amount of media are available to people, but is that the same thing as mass culture? The Eastern European societies, under the thumb of Russia and their national communist parties, were subjected to forty years of totalitarian rule, continual propaganda, and a rigidly controlled mass media, but the people in these countries ditched the communists with hardly a second thought when they discovered that the Red Army wouldn't be invading them.

DOES POPULAR CULTURE DESTROY OUR ABILITY TO ENJOY ELITE CULTURE?

According to Adorno and a number of other theorists of mass culture, popular culture drives out elite culture, and as people become more and more exposed to popular culture, they lose their interest in the elite arts and the ability to enjoy them. This may sound plausible in theory, but in practice it doesn't seem to work out very well.

Let me offer a hypothetical situation here that most people have had some experience with, and put the theory to the test. Take fast foods and, in particular, McDonald's hamburgers: one of the most important symbols of American culture. As the theory goes, because McDonald's is fast and relatively cheap, this chain of restaurants (or others like it) will drive out other kinds of restaurants that are less technologically advanced and involve individual choices (delicatessens, coffee shops, regular restaurants, and ethnic restaurants, for example), and eventually, following the logic of the elite theorists, we will only have McDonald's and other fast-food restaurants in America, and then all over the world because we have lost our taste for good food.

(Those interested in the impact of McDonald's on society might consult two books by sociologist George Ritzer: *The McDonaldization of Society* [1993], which he wrote, and *McDonaldization: The Reader* [2002], which he edited.)

I think we can see, from our own experience, that fast-food restaurants have not driven other restaurants out of business. These fast-food restaurants do have a social cost, however, which I alluded to earlier. As a result of the popularity of these restaurants, childhood and adult obesity is growing at an alarming rate, and with it many diseases tied to obesity such as diabetes and heart disease. Research on the growth of obesity in America suggests it is slowing down, but it still is widespread. Fast-food restaurants are now trying to cope with the anxiety many people have about eating fast food by experimenting with salads and less fatty food.

People use fast-food restaurants for their own purposes and do not necessarily lose their capacity to enjoy other kinds of foods. Just the opposite happens frequently. In the San Francisco area where I live, for example, there has been an explosion of Thai and Vietnamese restaurants, and as other ethnic groups settle in America, other ethnic foods become increasingly popular. The same applies to more upscale French and Italian restaurants.

I wrote an essay in 1963, "The Evangelical Hamburger," in which (somewhat tongue-in-cheek) I suggested that the dynamics of McDonald's restaurants were similar to those of evangelical Protestantism and that McDonald's would spread all over the world. Many people thought these ideas were simply ridiculous. I also suggested, playing with the Marxist concept of *embourgeoisment* (which argues that capitalism generates bourgeois, middle-class mentalities) that McDonald's involves "hambourgeoisment" and functions so as to convince people that they are middle class because they have ready access to ground meat. We now see a similar evangelical thrust in the incredible growth of Starbucks coffee shops. The argument that popular culture will destroy the so-called elite arts—and in this case, French, Italian, and other ethnic restaurants—doesn't appear to have come true.

ARE WE BECOMING HOMOGENIZED?
ARE THE MASS MEDIA UNIFORM?

One assumption of mass culture theorists is that the mass media are, in some way, uniform and thus can perform their task of destroying our sense of individuality and making Americans, and people in other countries, mass men and women. But a look at the media shows that there is a great deal of competition in a given medium, such as television or the magazine industry, and among the media an equally vigorous competition for the attention of people. The growth of video games, for example, has been explosive. (There has, of course, been a great deal of consolidation of control of the media—a subject I deal with in Chapter 10, on media and politics.) The networks are continually battling one another for viewers, since they must deliver audiences to advertisers to make money.

Most of what the networks carry is highly formulaic junk, of course, but even formulaic texts can be done well from time to time. And there are many excellent dramas and comedies on television and cable and in film. It is not the media themselves that are the problem but the beliefs of many of the people running the media about what kind of material will be popular. This is what is responsible, to a great degree, for the low level of entertainment in most of the media. I might note that the arts are always risky, and it is fair to say that many of our serious novels and plays today, though thought to be elite works of art, are, in fact, second rate.

In the world of magazines, we find incredible diversity. There are magazines for every interest conceivable, and some that are not conceivable. In addition to regularly published magazines, there are also huge numbers of "zines," small specialty publications on everything from ecology to Zen that are put out by individuals or groups. Now that computers and laser printers are inexpensive, it is easy and cheap for people to publish their own zines or makes their views known on their own web sites.

Many individuals now have become publishers with their creations on a web site on the Internet. Blogging has become a very important part of the Internet now also. Bloggers have had an impact on the political scene as bloggers from the left and right now make their ideas known, and now Google and other search engines are making it possible for people to search out blogs that deal with matters of interest to them.

Now, of course, we have Twitter, which allows people to offer 140-word "tweets" (or micro-blogs) on anything of interest to them, and Facebook. Twitter has actually played a role in numerous political uprisings in recent years, such as the Arab Spring awakening and in the Occupy Wall Street movement in 2012.

So there is good reason to question the assumption that the media are **culturally homogenizing** us and can perform the needed "mobilization" of people required to create a mass society. Rather than finding a mass society in America (and the same would apply to many other countries), we find just the opposite—what might be described as cultural and pop cultural pluralism, with large numbers of subcultures and groups putting out their own publications, making their own films, and broadcasting their own radio and television shows. This does not mean, however, that these groups all see themselves as estranged from American culture and society.

MASS CULTURE AND THE MELTING POT

With this discussion of popular culture, the mass media, and the theory of mass society as a background, we can now gain some insights into the question of whether there have been fundamental changes in American society and culture in the last few decades, and if so, what role the media might have played in this matter.

If the mass media were as powerful as elitists believed they were, how do we explain the fact that American society has so many subcultures and groups based on everything from race, religion, and ethnicity to political persuasion and geographic location? We are not diminished by having these various social entities, but enriched.

A knowledge of urban geography is helpful in gaining an understanding of what America was like fifty or seventy-five years ago. When we look at cities then (and today, as well) we find that they are often divided up into enclaves, in which the population is predominantly Italian, Jewish, black, Irish, Vietnamese, Iranian, Chinese, or some other group. At the time, these groups often had publications written in their native languages and directed toward their particular interests. Today, many of these groups have television stations that broadcast in their native languages. It would seem that the fabled "melting pot" was more a theory of what some analysts think happened or would like to have happened than a description of what America was like when your grandparents were born—or even today, in many cases.

Many different ethnic groups were thrown, so to speak, into the melting pot (American society), but they didn't melt into one smooth,

homogenous mass but maintained their identities, even while they went about finding their place in America and realizing or trying to realize the American Dream.

Proponents of the mass society thesis would have to argue that though America may not be monolithic now, it once was because of the exposure of immigrants and others to America's ubiquitous and all-powerful mass media. If the media are as powerful as they are supposed to be, how did the earlier Americans resist becoming unified into a mass society, a resistance evident in the ethnic enclaves of American cities fifty or seventy-five years ago? And why haven't we remained a mass society?

It could be argued, perhaps, that the mass media no longer are as effective as they once were in unifying Americans and providing them with a common frame of reference, with some kind of a consensus and national consciousness. But Americans are exposed to more media than they were earlier. We watch enormous amounts of television, the most powerful medium, and have digital video recorders (DVRs) to capture other shows, so we can do **time shifting** (watching a program at a time other than when it was broadcast). The growth of cable and satellite television means there are huge numbers of channels available to viewers, and new technologies are being developed that, it is estimated, will open as many as 500 channels to viewers. (What all the channels of communication carry is another matter—essentially the same old genres found in the movies and on television, with an occasional mixture of genres, such as MTV or single-genre stations, such as all-sports and all-news stations.)

The existence of a society full of subcultures and characterized by what I've described as popular cultural pluralism (some might say near anarchy) suggests the media are not as all-powerful as we, or more precisely some communications theorists, once thought they were and also suggests that our notion that America was a huge melting pot was more an illusion (of consensus historians and social scientists) than a reality. Though various groups in the melting pot didn't melt, they were still in the same pot. Some have suggested that "beef stew" would be a better metaphor than a melting pot where everything blends together into an amorphous mass.

Societies are always evolving, so it would be incorrect to argue that there have not been changes in America. The question is whether these changes mark radical new directions in which our society is moving or whether they are more evolutionary. America, it has often been said, is a country continually undergoing revolution, and thus change is constant. This notion that we are continually undergoing change is different from a conservative perspective that argues, as I see it, that there have been no fundamental changes in American culture and society or that any changes have been minimal.

My argument would be that in America everything is always in the process of change and evolution. The question is—what is the nature of the changes, and how do these changes relate to continuities in American society and culture?

MASS CULTURE AND AMERICAN SOCIETY: THE MYTH OF THE MONOLITH

In an essay in *Public Perspective*, "The Polarization of America: The Decline of Mass Culture" (Sept/Oct. 1992), Paul Jerome Croce argues that mass culture has lost its ability to shape consensus and suggests that this decline is a fundamental cause of what he sees as an increasingly polarized America. He writes, "Through their popularity, the mass culture's productions shaped taste, established goals and values, and defined the kind of people most people thought they should be." This consensus has now broken down, he adds, and we now find ourselves in a post–mass culture society in which mass culture has "metastacized, with individuals still pursuing different styles, but doing so in clusters broken off from a single massive standard."

I don't believe we ever had the "single massive standard" Croce thinks we had, or that the mass media ever had the power he suggests it had to shape a society. And I don't think we ever were as "unified" as Croce thinks. Mass media tend to reinforce values we already have—such as individualism, equality, freedom, and achievement. The media tend to reflect the societies in which they are found, although, of course, they also affect them. There's always been a great deal of conflict in American society, between classes, among races, between geographic sections of the country, and to some degree among religious groups.

People who burn with "passionate intensity" and belong to subcultures, groups that attack this or that aspect of our society, are nothing new:

we have a long history of utopian communities and morally defined groups such as the Abolitionists. (We still have people living in communes.)

What the mass media do, I would suggest, is reflect the changes going on in society at a given point in time. They may add impetus to them and speed things up, they may help set agendas, they may increase our awareness and show us things many of us don't like, but I find it hard to believe that they ever had the ability to homogenize us the way they allegedly did. We never were unified to the extent Croce believes, except, perhaps, in terms of our basic values, so the media are being attacked for not continuing to do what they did not and could not do. There are plenty of other reasons to find fault with our mass media, but we can dismiss as false this charge against them that they no longer unify our society. If anything has ever unified Americans it is the public school system, not the media.

America, if the postmodern theorists are correct, is a society in which elite art and popular culture no longer are seen as distinct and in which eclecticism and fragmentation are the norms. Earlier we noted Jean-François Lyotard's example of someone who "listens to reggae, watches a western, eats McDonald's for lunch and local cuisine for dinner," and so on. This doesn't sound like the homogenized culture that mass culture theorists predicted. And this has been the case since around 1960 when, it has been suggested, the postmodern mind-set took over. What all this suggests is that American society is one in which diversity is celebrated, in which differences are accepted as part of the scheme of things. Rather than splitting apart, everything in American society is getting mixed up, yet different groups still are able to maintain their identities. That, in fact, is the story of America—a country of immigrants, where people from many different nations come in search of the American Dream. Different groups may have different versions of this dream and take different paths to realize this dream, and may be different in many ways—but there still is a commonality behind these differences.

As evidence of this, let me mention a recent poll that was taken of Hispanics in America. The poll discovered that Hispanics want to assimilate into America, that they believe there's too much immigration in America, that they think residents of America should learn to speak English, and that Hispanics are, in fact, not as unified as we used to believe they were. In *Latino Voices* we read "A large majority of Hispanics born in the United States speaks English better than Spanish," as a matter of fact, and there's a high degree of English literacy among foreign-born immigrants who prefer to speak Spanish. The Latino National Political Survey, in *Latino Voices*, concludes that "the [survey's] results should dispel any notions that their political attitudes separate them from the majority of the American population or define them as a monolithic interest group."

G. William Domhoff writes in "Who Rules America":

In the United States, wealth is highly concentrated in a relatively few hands. As of 2007, the top 1% of households (the upper class) owned 34.6% of all privately held wealth, and the next 19% (the managerial, professional, and small business stratum) had 50.5%, which means that just 20% of the people owned a remarkable 85%, leaving only 15% of the wealth for the bottom 80% (wage and salary workers).

http://sociology.ucsc.edu/whorulesamerica/power/wealth.html

What this survey suggests is that the United States is truly a multi-cultural society in which various subcultures exist, but multi-culturalism doesn't mean separateness and alienation but, rather, a different kind of co-existence. Our mass media and popular culture have neither turned us into a mass society (on the road to totalitarianism) nor into one in which "the center cannot hold." But political decisions in recent years have caused great difficulties for many Americans, and our faith in the American Dream is now weakened.

The tensions and anxieties found in America have been generated and exacerbated in large measure by the unfair and grossly distorted distribution of income that has occurred here, especially since 1980, with the poorest segments of our society actually losing ground and large numbers of people in the middle classes not gaining any ground. Since 2000, the inequities in the distribution of wealth in America have become worse, with many members of the middle class now finding it difficult to maintain that status and with many poor people sinking deeper into poverty.

An editorial in the *New York Times* with the subtitle "New Hope for the Fabulously Wealthy" (June 7, 2005) points out that since 2000, the income of the top 0.1 percent of American society, the super-rich, has more than doubled while the share earned by the top 10 percent rose a great deal less and the bottom 90 percent's share actually declined. The middle class, the upper-middle class, and even the wealthy, it seems, are being left behind "into the dust," by the super wealthy as a result of tax policies. Hurricane Katrina revealed to many Americans just how desperate the situation was for many poor people living in New Orleans and elsewhere in America.

It is politics, not popular culture, that is most responsible for our social disorganization and our many problems, and it will be political decisions, not our popular culture or the mass media, that will lead to the amelioration of the situation in which we find ourselves.

As communication instruments become part of our daily routine, they free us from many of the spatial and temporal constraints that govern our lives. Significantly, overcoming such restraints has ramifications beyond the ability to effectively manage the multiple, simultaneous tasks that characterize contemporary life. This purely practical function conceals deeper cultural and societal issues, because these technologies prompt us to rethink and recreate the ways we live together.

Andre H. Caron and Letizia Caronia, *Moving Cultures: Mobile Communications in Everyday Life* (2007:5)

If I may be allowed a historical analogy: the technically advanced societies are at a point in their history similar to that of the emergence of an urban, merchant culture in the midst of feudal society in the Middle Ages. At that point practices of the exchange of commodities required individuals to act and speak in new ways, ways drastically different from the aristocratic code of honor with its face-to-face encounters based on trust for one's word and its hierarchical bonds of interdependency: Interacting with total strangers, sometimes at great distances, the merchants required written documents guaranteeing spoken promises and an "arm's length distance" attitude even when face-to-face with the other, so as to afford a "space" for calculations of self interest. A new identity was constructed, gradually and in a most circuitous path to be sure, among the merchants, in which a coherent, stable sense of individuality was grounded in independent, cognitive abilities. In this way the cultural bias for the modern world was begun, one that eventually would rely upon print media to encourage and disseminate these urban forms of identity.

In the 20th century, electronic media are supporting an equally profound transformation of cultural identity. Telephone, radio, film, television, the computer and now their integration as "multimedia" reconfigure words, sound and images so as to cultivate new configurations of individuality.

Mark Poster, "Postmodern Virtualities," in Arthur Asa Berger (ed.) (1998:255, 256)

8

THE SOCIAL IMPACT OF
NEW MEDIA TECHNOLOGIES

We tend to think of the new media technologies that are developing so rapidly now in terms of their primary functions, which involve entertainment or communication. The impact of these new technologies on these areas has been incredible. But these new media technologies also are having important social, economic, cultural, and political consequences as the quotations on the previous page suggest. Most people are aware that American culture and society are changing (and the rest of the world, as well) as the new technologies start making their impact felt, but we don't, as a rule, appreciate the incredible impact these new technologies are having on American culture and society.

We can see how many Americans use new media technologies from the following statistics from various Pew Research reports in recent years:

85 percent own cell phones
59 percent own desktop computers
57 percent own laptop computers
52 percent own DVRs
44 percent own MP3 players
42 percent own video-game consoles
12 percent own electronic book readers
8 percent own tablet computers

These figures show that Americans love the new media technologies, especially cell phones. Some countries have a higher penetration of cell phones, so the 85 percent figure is not remarkable now.

THE IMPACT OF CELL PHONES

Large numbers of people now have cell phones because they are very con-
venient and useful in many different circumstances. But some cell phone
users, who make terrible nuisances of themselves, conduct the most intimate conversations, often in a loud voice, anywhere they happen to be—in
restaurants, in airport lounges, and even in toilets. Cell phones now ring
in the middle of plays, at symphony concerts, in school lecture halls, and
while religious services are being conducted. Often this happens because
people forget to turn their phones off, but not always. Some people consider it vitally important to be accessible at all times and don't care whether
or not they disturb other people. Interestingly enough, many people now
consider it chic *not* to be reachable by cell phone—that is, they wish to
guard their privacy and limit their accessibility to others. Cell phones used
to be signifiers of importance, but they are now so common that they have
lost their cachet.

Howard Rheingold argues that cell phones have had a profound
impact on the cultures and societies where they are used and have led to
the creation of what he calls "smart mobs." As he explains (*Smart Mobs*,
2004:xi–xii)

> On a Spring afternoon in the year 2000 . . . I began to notice people
> on the streets of Tokyo staring at their mobile phones instead of talking
> to them. The sight of this behavior, now commonplace in much of the
> world, triggered a sensation I had experienced a few times before—the
> instant recognition that a technology is going to change my life in ways
> I can scarcely imagine. Since then, the practice of exchanging short text
> messages via mobile telephones has led to the eruption of subcultures in
> Europe and Asia. At least one government has fallen, in part because of
> the way people used text messaging.
>
> Adolescent mating rituals, political activism, and corporate manage-
> ment styles have mutated in unexpected ways.
>
> I've learned that "texting" is only a small harbinger of more profound
> changes to come over the next ten years. My media moment . . . was
> only my first encounter with a phenomenon I've come to call "smart
> mobs." When I learned to recognize the signs, I began to see them
> everywhere—from Napster to electronic bridge tolls.
>
> When you piece together these different technological, economic, and
> social components, the result is an infrastructure that makes certain kinds
> of human actions possible that were never possible before: The killer apps
> of tomorrow's mobile infocom industry won't be hardware devices or

software programs but social practices. The most far-reaching changes will come, as they often do, from the kinds of relationships, enterprises, communities and markets that the infrastructure makes possible.

So the cell phone, as Rheingold points out, may be used for much more than person-to-person communication and may have significant social and political impact.

Teenage Texters

Research indicates that some teenagers now send approximately 100 text messages a day to their friends and families. An article by Katie Hafner with the title "Texting May Be Taking a Toll" (in the May 25, 2009, *New York Times*) deals with the psychological impact of all this texting. She interviewed a pediatrician, Dr. Martin Joffe, who suggested that teenagers' texting late at night is depriving them of adequate sleep. She also interviewed Sherry Turkle, a psychologist who is director of the Initiative on Technology and Self at the Massachusetts Institute of Technology. Turkle believes that texting may be causing a change in the way adolescents develop. In a radio interview she gave about her new book on the subject, she pointed out that texting is quite a burden on young people, who have to be very careful about the texts they send to make sure they come off as sufficiently "cool." What texting does, Turkle suggests, is enable people to maintain contact with other but also keep a distance from them. In her book *Alone Together: Why We Expect More From Technology and Less from Each Other*, she writes (2011:15):

> A thirteen-year old tells me she "hates the phone and never listens to voice-mail." Texting offers her just the right amount of access, just the right amount of control. She is a modern Goldilocks: for her texting puts people not too close, not too far, just the right distance.

In her radio interview, Turkle said that she believes that the amount of texting by teenagers will eventually diminish as they become disenchanted with it and start thinking about the impact all this texting is having on their lives. "The phenomenon is beginning to worry physicians and psychologists," Haffner writes, "who say it is leading to anxiety, distraction in school, falling grades, repetitive stress injury and sleep deprivation." Texting, then, has complicated social and medical costs, and its impact upon young people is a cause for concern.

Now that I've dealt with the amount of new technology devices we own and the impact of cell phones on adolescents, let me turn to the social impact of other new technologies on other topics, such as computers and the Internet, the development of virtual communities, the video-game phenomenon, and new video and audio recording and playing devices.

Consider what has happened to the medium of television as the result of new technologies. At one time we had only three national television networks and some local stations; now there are countless cable and satellite channels available to people who subscribe to them. Some people have lamented that now "we have 500 channels but there's nothing on." By this they mean that the same genres that were carried by television networks are now found on the cable networks, except that some cable outlets are now very specialized and only carry programming devoted to specific genres such as music videos, sports, news, old films, or comedy.

To understand what is happening in this brave new mass-mediated digital world we live in, we must understand what *digital* means. It is to that subject I now turn. It is the world that has brought us iPods, iPads, digital cameras, video games, smart cell phones with digital cameras and the ability to play music, and many other devices.

THE DIGITAL WORLD

The first thing we must come to grips with is that the new media technologies involve the replacement of **analog** technologies with **digital** ones.

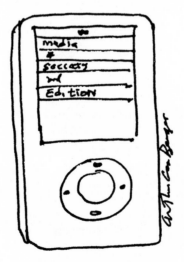

Consider what the watches everyone used to wear were like: they had a hand sweeping around the dial as the seconds passed, and they had a minute hand and an hour hand. These watches were analog watches, based on the notion that things are connected to one another, that time is continuous, that we live in a world in which there are many degrees of difference. The word *analog* is very similar to the word *analogy*, which means "similar to something," or "like something."

In the digital world, by contrast, everything is separated, and with digital watches and clocks time becomes a series of separate and discrete moments succeeding one another but not showing that any moment in time is related to any other one. With an analog watch, you can glance at your watch and say "it's a quarter to five," but with a digital watch you get a readout saying, in effect, it is now 4:45 PM and so many seconds.

Peter Lunenfeld, a scholar who has written a number of books on art and the new technologies, offers an excellent explanation of what the term *digital* means in his book *The Digital Dialectic: New Essays on New Media*. He writes:

> Digital systems do not use continuously variable representational relationships. Instead, they translate all input into binary structures of 0s and 1s, which can then be stored, transferred, or manipulated at the level or numbers of "digits" (so called because etymologically, the word descends from the digits on our hand with which we count out those numbers). Thus a phone call on a digital system will be encoded as a series of these 0s and 1s and sent over the wires as binary information to be reinterpreted as speech on the other end . . . It is the capacity of the electronic computer to encode a vast variety of information digitally that has given it such a central place within contemporary culture. As all manner of representational systems are recast as digital information, then all can be stored, accessed, and controlled by the same equipment. (1999:xv)

Lunenfeld offers the example of the digital photograph, which is composed of a number of *pixels*, cells that form "a grid of cells that have precise numerical attributes associated with them, a series of steps rather than a continuous slope." (1999:xvi). The new media technologies are digital, then, and are based on binary oppositions between various combinations of 0s and 1s—that is, ons and offs—and grids of separate cells with numerical attributes.

In the chart below I list some important devices and the date of their digitization.

Year	Medium
1962	Telephones
1967	Printers
1977	Films (segments of digitization in *Star Wars*)
1979	MP3 players
1993	Tablet computers (Apple Newton Message Pad)
1998	High-definition television (HDTV) sets
1998	Electronic book readers

We see, then, that we are in an age of digitalization and that our media are now almost completely digitized. The impact of this digitization has been enormous. For example, the MP3 player has revolutionized the music business, and electronic book readers are having a major impact on the book publishing industry. Scholars debate when the first tablet appeared, but there can be no debate about the impact of the Apple iPad, which was first introduced in 2010 and has spawned hundreds of imitators.

THE COMPUTER AND CULTURE

In the early days, when computers were just being developed, one businessman—I think he was at IBM—suggested that the entire United States could use, maybe, five computers. At that time, computers cost millions of dollars and filled up large rooms. Now, it isn't unusual to find families with five computers. Originally, people used computers because of so-called "killer applications" like spreadsheets and then word processing and, later, image manipulation. Now, of course, computers are ubiquitous and can be used to do all kinds of remarkable things.

The price of computers has gone down over the years. I bought my son a Commodore 64 (64K) for $900 around 1980, and $900 was worth a lot more then than it is worth now. Now, you can get powerful computers with huge hard drives for $500. Computer makers are now coming out with light laptops for $400 and very light ultra-books that cost around $1000, and you can get netbooks for around $300. It costs around $30 a month for Internet access, so the price of the computer isn't the only thing to be considered when dealing with the cost of having a computer.

Here is material from a 2012 advertisement for a computer and monitor package:

Asus Essentio CM1740-04 Desktop & 20" LCD Monitor Package $599.98 (CM1740-04, VE208N). Key features: AMD A8-3800

multicore processor; 8GB DDR3 memory; 1TB hard drive; Windows 7 Home Premium; HDMI output; 20" widescreen LCD monitor included

This computer is more powerful and thus more expensive than many other computers available to would-be purchasers of computers.

There is the matter of what has been called the knowledge gap to be considered. Those with access to computers and other new technologies quite obviously have an advantage over those who do not have access to them. In recent years, however, our schools and libraries have purchased computers, so they are more available than ever before. Nevertheless, there are many families at the bottom rungs of our socio-economic ladder that do not have the funds to purchase their own computers and to purchase access to the Internet, so children in these families are seriously disadvantaged.

With the development of the Internet, the computer now is seen as an important communication device and not just something that can be used for databases or spreadsheets or for word processing or manipulating images. In recent years, for example, computers have come to be used for playing video games. People send billions of e-mail messages to one another and are bothered by businesses sending billions of undesired e-mail advertising messages (known as spam). With the Internet, the world is open to us, but that also means that we are open to the world and vulnerable to all kinds of people who we will never meet and who don't know who we are—some of whom are criminals and others of whom are malicious.

The growth of the Internet also is changing our media-usage behavior. There are now millions of web sites that people visit for one reason or another. Many companies use web sites to sell products and services on the Internet. Many stores ("bricks") now also have elaborate web sites ("clicks") where they sell their merchandise.

The phenomenon of "cruising" or "browsing"—that is, looking around—the Internet is now worldwide, helped by powerful search engines such as Yahoo and **Google**. It's instructive to see how many sites Google found for searches on subjects involving media. A list of some of them follow (accessed on January 21, 2012):

Media	7,860,000,000
Media and children	1,380,000,000
Media and society	66,000,000
Media effects	53,300,000
Mass media	76,300,000
Social media	490,000,000
Facebook	22,930,000,000

We see, then, that search engines enable us to gain information about subjects in considerable depth and that there is a great deal of interest in various aspects of media on the Internet. (It's interesting to note that *Google* has now become a verb, as in "I Googled you.")

The number of sites on the Internet and the number of subjects they deal with are astounding—everything from sites with online books to fan sites dealing with video games or movie stars, from sites dealing with abstruse and esoteric philosophical movements (Google lists more than 13 million sites that have something about postmodernism in them) to sites dealing with medical problems or selling books or cameras or groceries or whatever.

The marriage of computers and printing devices has led to the development of digital printing presses that enable publishers to print books on demand and to print their covers and bind them. This **print-on-demand** phenomenon has revolutionized book publishing. In 2010, some 2.7 million self-published book titles (called non-traditional books by the book publishing industry) were produced. So the computer is having an incredible impact not only on publishing and television but in all kinds of other areas—from medical imaging to music.

The darker side of the computer is that it enables governments to store information about people—and some communications theorists worry that the power of the government to gather and to store information about people can lead to all kinds of abusive behavior by governmental agencies. And now that we live in an age of terrorism, some people are advocating that the government develop a national identity card with chips that would provide the government with data of all kinds about everyone in the country.

It is now possible, for example, to take photographs (digital, of course) of people's retinas and use these photographs in identity cards to enable airline passengers who purchase these cards (and pay a yearly fee) to check in and get to waiting rooms for departures very quickly. This technology could be used to warn off terrorists trying to board planes, but it could also be used to check on who is flying where, for whatever purposes the government might have in collecting this information.

The globalization of world communications means, also, that criminals and anti-social individuals with a knowledge of programming can use the Internet to spread destructive computer viruses that can disable millions of computers worldwide. Vandalism used to be local, but now, in the age of the Internet, it is global. There is now even "cyber-warfare," as countries battle by fighting one another, so to speak, on the Internet.

New devices for recording television programs or music are continually being developed. One of the fastest selling devices is the DVD (originally called the Digital Video Disk but now the Digital Versatile Disk). According to a *Video Business* article by Jennifer Netherby in January 2006, nearly 82 million U.S. households had switched from VHS (video home system) video cassette recorders to DVD by the end of 2005. DVD recording devices are on the market as well, and with economies of scale, the price of these recorders will continue to fall. Consumers can also watch DVDs on other devices such as video-game systems and computers, and some computers can record video on DVDs. As a result of the development of the DVD, sales of VHS plummeted, and more and more people are watching films or TV shows on their DVDs rather than VHS. The images are much sharper and the sound is better.

Now, a new technology for watching films has appeared on the scene—UltraViolet. It is explained by Robert Levine, a writer who specializes in new technologies:

> Consumers who recently purchased Warner Brothers' final *Harry Potter* film on DVD or Blu-ray found a surprise in the package: a digital copy of the movie in the new UltraViolet format. Although the name is not yet familiar, UltraViolet represents Hollywood's first step into the cloud—the much-hyped idea that media will be stored on remote servers and accessed by various devices.
>
> The idea behind UltraViolet is simple: The format allows buyers to own rights to films, which they can store in a "digital locker" and access

via various Internet services. It's potentially a huge convenience for consumers, who now have a dizzying number of devices (phones, tablets, computers) on which they can watch video content, and indeed, some 750,000 households in the U.S. and Britain have set up UltraViolet accounts, its backers say.

For the studios the stakes are high: DVD sales, which peaked at $15.5 billion in 2004, have stalled as consumers have turned to streaming services such as Netflix (NFLX) or, worse, illegal downloads. The studios that have announced releases in the UltraViolet format (Fox is expected to announce soon; Disney (DIS) remains a holdout) believe UltraViolet will help goose home video sales by enabling consumers to build a remotely stored library of movies. "We know consumers like collecting movies," says Mitch Singer, president of the Digital Entertainment Content Ecosystem, the consortium that controls UltraViolet. (http:// tech.fortune.cnn.com/tag/ultraviolet/)

Everywhere you look, new devices are being created, and technologies that were invented just a few years ago are being discarded. Smart phones now can take pictures, shoot videos, show television, hook up to the Internet, play music, be used to play games, and do all kinds of things that couldn't be imagined just a few years ago. These phones are really small computers and are incredibly powerful and sophisticated devices. The world is now wired, but we do not know, at this time, what changes and effects our new technologies will have on our everyday lives and on our societies.

Yet, despite all the new developments coming from our new technologies, people in America still spend an average of close to four hours per day watching television, and our networks and cable systems and newspapers and magazines are still controlled for the most part by media conglomerates. So while the new technologies and ethnic media outlets may have some role in countering the perspectives promulgated by the media conglomerates, they still are relatively minor voices in the scheme of things.

VIRTUAL COMMUNITIES

There is, I would suggest, something inherently alienating about the digital world that we now live in. The metaphor for digital devices is separation, representing a world of discrete moments and of binary oppositions—on or off, in or out, or yes or no. The digital devices we use are increasingly more powerful and are able to connect us to one another in remarkable ways, but, at the same time, they seem to be fostering a kind of hyperindividualism and a lack of a sense of community. We can say that *global* means you can be connected to everyone; the question is, *are* you connected to anyone? Are people less stressed in our new digital world or more stressed? Do they have less time for themselves, their loved ones, and their communities, or more time?

A student of American popular culture, John Fraim, has found something very interesting about this question of the decline of community in the United States. It involves the fact that gamblers now spend more and more time with slot machines and less time with "table" gambling. He writes:

> Does the long-range movement from tables to slots mirror a similar trend in America as a whole towards less sociability? Harvard professor Robert Putnam argues American culture as a whole has moved towards less sociability in his book *Bowling Alone*. The book argues that America faces a civic crisis in that once-social activities such as bowling leagues, dinner parties and community arts performances are slowly vanishing from the American landscape. Increasingly, argues Putnam, Americans are withdrawing from communal life, choosing to live and play alone. They are losing what Putnam calls "social capital" or the "glue" of trust in each other that is so essential to a democratic society.
>
> Does the decline of table gaming and the rise in slot machine gambling suggest that more and more people want to gamble alone? Rather than being a fantasy island set off from the rest of America, Las Vegas gaming trends might offer one of the best laboratories for investigation of large scale American social trends. (unpublished manuscript, 2002)

What Fraim has discovered about changes in gambling in America suggests that our sense of community may be declining—or, as some have suggested, taking new forms.

With the development of the Internet, new "virtual" kinds of community are evolving for people with shared interests. There are many people who belong, if that's the correct word, to such communities and who spend many hours each day online, communicating with other members of their virtual community. Within such communities there are often dozens of interest groups where people with mutual interests can send messages to one another. These virtual communities can be looked upon as **functional alternatives** to real communities, in which people know one another and there are many face-to-face interactions and shared activities.

The two most prominent virtual communities now are Facebook, which has an astounding 950 million active members, and Twitter, with 145 million registered users. I am a member of Twitter and Facebook and occasionally post messages and images on those sites. I have several hundred Facebook "friends," most of whom I do not know. The only interaction I have with these "friends" is that I occasionally get messages from the ones I know and several people "poke" me from time to time. If 950 million people belong to Facebook, it is an extremely powerful site, after its recent IPO, whose value is now estimated at approximately 100 billion. Quite obviously, social networking fills a need that many people have, but what long-term impact will it have?

An article by Patrick Wintour in the February 24, 2009, issue of the *Guardian* suggests that Facebook and other social sites may have deleterious effects on children:

> Social network sites risk infantilising the mid-21st century mind, leaving it characterised by short attention spans, sensationalism, inability to empathise and a shaky sense of identity, according to a leading neuroscientist.

> The startling warning from Lady Greenfield, professor of synaptic pharmacology at Lincoln College, Oxford, and director of the Royal Institution, has led members of the government to admit their work on internet regulation has not extended to broader issues, such as the psychological impact on children.

> Greenfield believes ministers have not yet looked at the broad cultural and psychological effect of on-screen friendships via Facebook, Bebo and Twitter.

> She told the House of Lords that children's experiences on social networking sites "are devoid of cohesive narrative and long-term significance. As a consequence, the mid-21st century mind might almost be infantilised, characterised by short attention spans, sensationalism, inability to empathise and a shaky sense of identity."

Lady Greenfield added that she believes Facebook and other similar sites should be studied carefully in terms of their impact on children and adults. While being a member of a virtual community does have some value, as far as helping people take care of their need for social interactions—we are, after all, social animals—I can only wonder whether the gratifications people get from being members of these communities are adequate to their needs for sociability.

Take the matter of our sexual needs. Howard Rheingold, in his book *Virtual Reality*, describes the possibilities for virtual sex in his chapter "Teledildonics and Beyond." He writes:

> The first fully functional teledildonics system will be a communication device, not a sex machine. You probably will not use erotic telepresence technology in order to have sexual experiences with machines. Thirty years from now, when portable telediddlers become ubiquitous, most people will use them to have sexual experiences with other people, at a distance, in combinations and configurations undreamed of by precybernetic voluptuaries. Through a marriage of virtual reality technology and telecommunications networks, you will be able to reach out and touch someone—or an entire population—in ways humans have never before experienced. Or so the scenario goes.

This telecommunicated sex would be made possible by people wearing close-fitting body suits full of sensory devices (not yet in existence) and having telesex with one another. Rheingold wrote his book in 1991, which means that this kind of sexual activity will be possible around 2021, if his timetable is correct. Woody Allen satirized the notion of mechanical devices providing sexual gratification in his film *Sleeper*, where people could use Orgasmatrons.

The question I ask is, why bother with virtual sex when real sex, between real people, is so much easier? Virtual sex, I would suggest, will probably be like virtual dining—you're still hungry after your virtual meal, or so I would imagine. Perhaps by 2021 we will have computers that eat food for us and relay sensations to our brains so we have the experience of having had a gourmet dinner without actually having had one.

Let me move on to a subject in which our participating in virtual realities of one kind or another is much more developed—video games.

VIDEO GAMES: A BIO-PSYCHO-SOCIAL PERSPECTIVE

According to the Entertainment Software Association, which tracks the sales of video games (www.theesa.com/facts/pdfs/ESA_EF_2011.pdf), consumers spent $25.1 billion on video games in 2101; approximately $16 billion was for games and the remainder was for accessories and hardware.

So we are dealing with a very important popular culture phenomenon. There are many different genres of video games: sports games, simulations, first-person shooters, and so on. Some games can be played on computers, but most dedicated video-game players purchase game-playing consoles such as the Sony PlayStation 2 or the Microsoft XBox. In recent years, video games moved to cell phones, and this is having a profound impact on the video-game industry. In 2011 a new Nintendo game player, the 3DS handheld player, "flopped," in part because many people now prefer to play video games on their cell phones. The games are inexpensive (sometimes free) and easy to access. In a sense, Nintendo was a victim of Apple's iPhone and various Android cell phones.

CRITICISMS OF VIDEO GAMES

It has been suggested that many costs—biological, psychological, and social— are connected with playing video games. Let me list some of them. You will notice similarities to the earlier arguments about the potential negative effects of television.

1. Damage to a player's muscles. This comes from repeating the same movements over and over again with joysticks and other input devices. These repetitive stress injuries often are quite serious and need expensive medical attention.
2. Obesity. This condition comes from a lack of exercise and from excessive snacking while playing games.
3. Related medical problems. Obesity leads to other medical problems, often involving heart disease (blocked arteries) and diabetes. Diabetes can affect kidney functions and cause many other serious medical problems that are very expensive to deal with.
4. Decrease in socialization with others. Some game playing is done with others, but even so, children don't have the experience of being with lots of other children and don't develop the ability to get along with them. This can lead to a sense of alienation from others and from society at large, especially with young people who become addicted to game playing.
5. Hyperactivity. This kind of behavior, manifested when not playing video games, is exacerbated, perhaps, by the incredible amount of excitement generated by some of these games and the instantaneous gratifications they provide.

6. Violence seen as a means of resolving problems. In many video games, an incredible amount of killing goes on—as players kill aliens, monsters, and other enemies. Even though players know they are playing games, some of them may conclude that violence is an effective tool for doing things they want to do. There are many video games full of violence and sex, such as *Mortal Kombat, Grand Theft Auto, Call of Duty, Halo, Red Dead Redemption, Assassin's Creed*, and countless others I could name.

7. Desensitization. In video games, players perform the actions that lead to virtual fighting, shooting, and killing. This is different from seeing others doing these things. It is possible that repeated experiences of being responsible for violence does desensitize some children, which then leads to their acting out and being violent in the real world. While video-game playing may not be the cause of this kind of behavior, it seems to be a contributing factor, especially in some youths who have psychological problems.

You can see from this list that while individuals (and their friends) may play video games privately, there are widespread public medical and psychological costs, which translate to social and political costs, involved with the video-game phenomenon. Private acts, we must realize, often have public consequences, and while much video-game playing is harmless, and some games provide wonderful and intellectually challenging entertainment, there are many negative aspects and social costs connected with this widespread phenomenon.

THE SUPREME COURT AND VIDEO-GAME VIOLENCE

What follows is the opinion of the Supreme Court delivered by Justice Scalia on June 27, 2011, which can be found on the court's website (www.supremecourt.gov):

> We consider whether a California law imposing restrictions on violent video games comports with the First Amendment.
>
> California Assembly Bill 1179 (2005), Cal. Civ. Code Ann. §§1746–1746.5 (West 2009) (Act), prohibits the sale or rental of "violent video games" to minors, and requires their packaging to be labeled "18." The Act covers games "in which the range of options available to a player

includes killing, maiming, dismembering, or sexually assaulting an image of a human being, if those acts are depicted" in a manner that "[a]
reasonable person, considering the game as a whole, would find appeals
to a deviant or morbid interest of minors," that is "patently offensive to
prevailing standards in the community as to what is suitable for minors,"
and that "causes the game, as a whole, to lack serious literary, artistic,
political, or scientific value for minors." §1746(d)(1)(A). Violation of the
Act is punishable by a civil fine of up to $1,000. §1746.3.

Opinion of the Court

Respondents, representing the video-game and software industries,
brought a pre-enforcement challenge to the Act in the United States
District Court for the Northern District of California. That court concluded that the Act violated the First Amendment and permanently
enjoined its enforcement. 2009), and we granted certiorari, 559 U. S.
_____ (2010).

Thus, video-game makers will be allowed to sell violent video games to minors, even though many scholars and representatives of child welfare groups
testified that these games can cause many psychological and adaptational
problems for young players, who should be prohibited from purchasing or
renting them.

Prohibiting young players from purchasing these games, the court
ruled in a split decision, would be a violation of the free speech rights of the
video-game makers. Judge Antonin Scalia wrote elsewhere in the decision:

Like the protected books, plays and movies that preceded them, video
games communicate ideas—and even social messages—through many
familiar literary devices (such as characters, dialogue, plot, and music)
and through features distinctive to the medium (such as the player's
interaction with the virtual world) . . . That suffices to confer First
Amendment protection.

One thing that emerged from Judge Scalia's ruling is that we can now classify video games as works of art—regardless of how sophisticated or crude
they may be.

POSITIVE ASPECTS OF VIDEO-GAME PLAYING

If there are problems and dangers connected to video-game playing, there
are also some benefits worth considering. James Paul Gee, a professor of
education at the University of Wisconsin, argues in his book, *What Video*

Games Have to Teach Us about Learning and Literacy, that video games help children learn a new kind of literacy. These games, Gee suggests, do several things for players, such as helping them learn how to establish an identity, how to choose between different ways of solving problems, and how to get information from nonverbal cues. So there are some positive attributes to video games, and Gee suggests they will play an important role in education in the future.

A psychologist at the University of California in Los Angels, Patricia Marks Greenfield, was one of the first scholars to see the beneficial effects of video-game playing. As she writes in her book *Mind and Media: The Effects of Television, Video Games, and Computers* "Pac-Man and other arcade computer games require the player to induce the rules from observation. Computer games therefore call up inductive skills much more than did games of the pre-computer era" (1984:111). The visual dynamism of video games and the fact that players actively participate in the outcomes of these games are the primary sources of their appeal, the author argues, and not the violence found in them. And, she adds, games can be developed that teach players how to cooperate rather than compete with one another.

One danger video games do pose, the author concludes, is that they are so responsive to the input of their players that they can lead to players becoming impatient with the slow and messy way things work in the real world. But this has to be weighed against the positive attributes of video-game playing, which involve developing a sense of competence and control as well as certain motor skills involving hand-eye coordination.

The explosive growth of the video-game industry in recent years—and it is a global phenomenon, we must understand—suggests that games provide numerous and powerful gratifications for video-game players. The dilemma these players face involves finding a way to navigate between the addictive and negative aspects of video games and their positive attributes, including their potential for developing new kinds of literacy and new modes of teaching.

THE TECHNOLOGICAL IMPERATIVE

One important question we must consider when dealing with technology is whether there is some kind of a *technological imperative*. Must all new technologies be allowed to develop as much as they can, regardless of the possible consequences to individuals and to societies? We can make bombs now that can kill millions of people; should we push ahead and make

The Cultural Significance of Pac Man

Pac-Man was one of the most popular video games in the 1980s. Let me offer some hypotheses about the hidden meanings found in this game. I do this to suggest that video games might have more cultural significance than we might imagine.

First, video games have auto-erotic aspects to them, as the term *joy stick* suggests. Marshall McLuhan argued that electronic media should be seen as extensions of ourselves, "outside of our bodies." Thus, when we play these games, we are, in a way, playing with ourselves. I don't think I'm stretching the truth too far to suggest that these games have aspects of them that can be seen as a disguised form of electronic masturbation.

In *Pac-Man*, the violence is feminized and is based on biting and ingestion rather than shooting guns and rockets and other masculine and phallic forms of violence and aggression. This gobbling of dots reflects a feminized form of aggression and is regressive. From a developmental standpoint, we have regressed from our phallic, gun-shooting stage (*Space Invaders*) to a more infantile oral stage. Freud suggested children go through four stages of development: oral, anal, phallic, and genital. *Pac-Man* and various other versions of the game are, quite obviously, at the oral stage

Games like *Space Invaders* involved scooting around the universe and zapping aliens with ray guns, rockets, and other phallic kinds of weapons. *Pac-Man*, however, takes place in a labyrinth, which suggests that we see ourselves as trapped and believe that our possibilities are now limited. We have to learn how to deal with being confined and having limited possibilities in the future. In a sense, the game suggests that we see ourselves as prisoners with few possibilities.

Pac-Man is a game in which dots eat dots, and this view of life is a metaphor for capitalist societies characterized by class conflict and a "dog-eat-dog" mentality. As captives of a labyrinth from which there is no escape, we can either work towards the collective good of everyone or, conversely, try to maximize things for ourselves, and it is this latter goal that is emphasized in *Pac-Man*. *Pac-Man* may reflect a paradigm shift in the American psyche; trapped in the labyrinth of America, people are suffering from a loss of nerve and a change of perspective, which makes them focus upon themselves (and how many dots they can gobble) and forget about their social obligations. So there's more to video games than fingering a joystick furiously and gobbling up dots or killing aliens.

bombs capable of destroying the whole earth? Or, on a less cataclysmic note, should we allow file-sharing programs to make it possible for people to download songs without paying for them? The U.S. Supreme Court has said this process is unlawful, but whether the Supreme Court's decision will have any practical impact remains to be seen.

Many philosophers have suggested that human beings must decide how far to let new technologies develop. For instance, we might be able to clone human beings, but most people think it is a bad idea to try to do so. Some technology theorists are worrying, now, that computers and robots will soon have enough "brain power" (if that's what you want to call it) to replicate themselves and may someday dominate human beings. We will all become, according to this scenario, *servo-proteins* that exist to service the new computers and robots that will create themselves. (The fact that Gary Kasparov tied an Israeli-programmed computer in a chess match in 2003 suggests there is hope, but Kasparov is probably the best chess player alive. An IBM computer called Watson beat Ken Jennings and Brad Rutter in 2011 playing Jeopardy, which suggests that all the theorists who worry about the problems humans will face when dealing with super-smart computers might be right.)

This matter of becoming servo-proteins is probably a far-fetched scenario, but it does pose the question very sharply: where do we draw the line and say technological development beyond a certain point is not to be allowed? Or can we? Ralph Waldo Emerson said, in a celebrated essay (*Ode to W. H. Channing*), "Things are in the saddle, and ride mankind." Perhaps, even as I write this, technology is in the driver's seat and mankind must go along for the ride. I would like to think that Emerson was pessimistic and not prescient. The technological imperative theory suggests that we cannot stop technology from developing to its logical conclusion, but many philosophers have argued that not only can we limit technology for pushing beyond certain points, we must. The various *Terminator* films deal with this matter in very vivid terms.

The American Academy of Pediatrics reports that by age 18, the average American child will have viewed about 200,000 acts of violence on television alone. For some, there is the concern that children who are inundated with the images of shootings, bombings and rapes will become desensitized to such violent acts and possibly learn to see them as valid responses to life's stresses. Some research has been done to support the idea that violent thoughts and behavior increase after exposure to violent films, music, television or video games. The argument of observational learning—that children learn by imitating what they see—is at the core of the majority of these studies. Some children are more able than others to tell the difference between make-believe and real-life events.

National Center for Children Exposed to Violence,
http://www.nccev.org/ (accessed June 5, 2012)

9

THE PROBLEM OF
MEDIA VIOLENCE

Many, and perhaps most, analyses of media violence don't pay attention to specific violent acts in specific texts, because researchers are looking for generalizations they can make and correlations they can find between the amount of exposure to media of selected populations and the amount of violence members of these populations commit.

There is a distinction between *causality* and *correlation* to be made.

Causality: X causes Y. Whenever you have X, you get Y.
Correlation: Y comes after X and is possibly connected to it.

We have not been able to do more than find strong relationships or correlations between the amount of television violence viewed and violent behavior in real life; we have had trouble proving that exposure to televised violence actually causes violent behavior. The evidence suggests that viewing television can and probably does lead to violent behavior in some people, but it doesn't seem possible to go beyond that assertion. This matter of the relationship between television violence and real-life violence has been of great interest to researchers.

In 1988, for example, Nancy Signorelli and George Gerbner published *Violence and Terror in the Mass Media: An Annotated Bibliography* (Greenwood Press), which deals with some 784 studies of television violence. It contains brief descriptions of articles from scholarly books and journals and articles from government reports, popular journals, and conference papers on violence in the media. The book covers areas such as media content, media effects, pornography and the media, and terrorism and the media.

Here are some web sites that deal with violence:

www.media-awareness.ca
www.nccev.org
www.lionlamb.org/media_violence.htm
web.mit.edu/comm-forum/papers/jenkins_ct.html

HOW IS MEDIA VIOLENCE DEFINED?

In their book, Signorelli and Gerbner offer the following definition of media violence:

> Reliable observation and systematic analysis usually requires limited and objective definitions. Most research studies have defined media violence as the depiction of overt physical action that hurts or kills or threatens to do so. A terroristic act is typically defined as one involving violence by, among, or against states or other authorities in order to spread fear and make a statement, usually political. Media violence and terror are closely related. They depict social relationships and the use of force to control, dominate, provoke, or annihilate. By demonstrating who can get away with what against whom, factual and fictional representations of violence or terror can intimidate people; provoke resistance, aggression, or repression; and cultivate a sense of relative strength and vulnerability as they portray the social "pecking order." (1988:xi)

Signorelli and Gerbner explain their understanding of cultivation, writing (1988:xviii) that "for most viewers, television's mean and dangerous world tends to cultivate a sense of relative danger, mistrust, dependence, and—despite its supposedly 'entertaining' nature—alienation and gloom." Other researchers, who worked independently of Gerbner and his associates, found the following things about media and violence (I have slightly modified the language of these reports for the sake of readability (Signorelli and Gerbner 1988:xviii):

1. Media exposure to violence boosts public estimates of crime and violence.
2. There is a significant relationship between exposure to crime shows and approval of police brutality and bias against civil liberties.

3. Television viewing is related to feelings of anxiety and fear of victimization.
4. Television viewing tends to cultivate the presumption of the guilt rather than the innocence of a suspect.

It is reasonable to argue, based on the above material, that television violence is not, as a number of theorists suggest, a harmless cathartic but instead has profound effects both upon individual viewers and society in general. Television may not be the direct and only cause of much of the violence that we find in American society, but it has to be considered a contributing factor. When Signorelli and Gerbner discussed terrorism, it seemed like just a minor aspect of the matter, but after the horrendous events of 9/11, terror has now become a major factor in analyses of violence. There is little question that people in the United States feel extremely vulnerable now as a result of the destruction by terrorists of the World Trade Center.

A LONGITUDINAL STUDY OF
TELEVISION VIEWING AND VIOLENCE

A 2002 study by the Center for Media and Public Affairs titled "TV Goes PG but Movies Are Still R Rated" shows that there was a 17 percent drop in prime-time violence on television between 1998 and 2001, broadcast violence decreased 11 percent, and violence on premium cable shows decreased 65 percent (http://www.cmpa.com/files/media_monitor/02marapr.pdf). This may represent a certain amount of progress, but a drop of 17 percent from a very high amount of violence may not be that important. We now have research that suggests that there is good reason to suggest that there is a strong connection—that is, correlation—between viewing television and aggressive acts.

An article by Nanette Asimov in the *San Francisco Chronicle* deals with an important longitudinal study on the relationship between television viewing and violence. It reports that young teenagers who watch more than an hour of television each day "are nearly four times as likely to commit aggressive acts in later years than those who watch less than an hour." She discusses the findings of a 17-year-long study on the relation between television viewing and violence. She writes (March 29, 2002:2):

> The 17-year study, to be published in today's issue of the journal *Science,*
> studied 707 children from adolescence to early adulthood. Researchers

found a "significant association" between television viewing and later violence by both boys and girls, although the effect was most striking in boys.

Jeffrey Johnson of Columbia University, one of the coauthors of the study, suggested that parents should not let children watch more than an hour of television a day during early adolescence. His study mentions that during an average hour of prime-time television, three to five violent acts are portrayed, and an hour of children's television has twenty to twenty-five violent acts. Most of the violent acts on children's television are comic, but that doesn't mean they don't predispose children towards violent behavior.

One of the more remarkable findings deals with youths who watched three or more hours of television per day at age 14 and acted in an aggressive manner at 16 or 20 years of age: it turns out that 45.2 percent of males and 12.7 percent of the females acted aggressively. Of the 14-year-olds who watched one hour or less per day, 8.9 percent of the males and 2.3 percent of the females acted aggressively. The authors of the study argue, also, that television viewing "remained significant" after they dealt with other factors that may generate violent behavior, such as neighborhood violence, neglect, and psychiatric disorders.

Children and Television Viewing

We saw the jump was between less than one hour and more than one hour a day. There was a four-fold increase. Parents should try not to let children watch more than one hour a day on the average.

We are social beings and we tend to want to try out things that we see other people doing, especially if we see the person rewarded for what they did or portrayed as a hero for it.

We found that teenagers who, at mean age 14, watched more than three hours a day of television were much more likely than those who watched less than one hour a day to commit subsequent acts of aggression against other people.

Jeffrey Johnson, Columbia University

In studies of television viewing and violence, the results are generally correlations between viewing television violence and violent behavior. This is because it is very difficult to establish causal relations between anything when dealing with human beings. But this does not mean that studies that establish correlations are of little interest. The study I have just cited, which dealt with children over a 17-year period, is the first that offers such a long-term view of the relationship between television viewing and violence. Defenders of television often argue that television may be a contributing factor in violence but it is not the sole factor or a causal one. The important question is—to what degree is television a contributing factor?

A 2009 analysis of the impact of violence in the media comes from the American Academy of Pediatrics' Council on Communications and Media. In a November 1, 2009, policy statement titled "Media Violence" that was published in the journal *Pediatrics* we find the following:

> Exposure to violence in media, including television, movies, music, and video games, represents a significant risk to the health of children and adolescents. Extensive research evidence indicates that media violence can contribute to aggressive behavior, desensitization to violence, nightmares, and fear of being harmed . . . Correlational and experimental studies have revealed that violent video games lead to increases in aggressive behavior and aggressive thinking and decreases in prosocial behavior. Recent longitudinal studies designed to isolate long-term violent video-game effects on American and Japanese school-aged children and adolescents have revealed that in as little as 3 months, high

exposure to violent video games increased physical aggression. Other recent longitudinal studies in Germany and Finland have revealed similar effects across 2 years. (http://videogames.procon.org/view.answers .php?questionID=1608)

With this discussion in mind, it is useful to consider the different kinds of violence one finds in the media and in life.

KINDS OF VIOLENCE

There are, let me suggest, any number of different aspects of violence. The following table lists a number of sets of paired opposites that summarize the various kinds of violence that exist in relation to the media, and shows how complicated a matter violence can be.

Violence, as this list suggests, is an incredibly complex matter. That helps explain why our responses to violence, as individuals and collectively, depend in certain cases on whether we see the violence as defensive (part of the scheme of things, as in sports) or as caused by hatred, or whether the violence is seen as just (by the police), or evil (violence used by murderers and terrorists). We feel differently about violence directed against machines or aliens than we do about violence directed against humans and about comic violence versus serious violence. I doubt that the typical television viewer has ever articulated all these different kinds and aspects of violence, but it is quite likely that viewers can differentiate between so-called good

Table 9.1.   Kinds of Violence Contrasted

Form of Violence	Opposite Form of Violence
mass-mediated violence	violence we see directly
real mediated violence (wars)	fictive mediated violence (stories)
comic violence (kids' TV shows)	serious violence (adult films)
violence to individuals	violence to groups and society
police violence (just)	criminal violence (unjust)
verbal violence (insults)	physical violence (hitting someone)
violence to humans	violence to aliens
"fake" violence (wrestling)	"true violence (bar brawls)
violence against heroes	violence against villains
violence against women	violence against men
visual images of violence	prose descriptions of violence
as sign of depravity	as cry for help

violence and bad violence and at the same time carry in their heads ideas about many of the aspects of violence listed above.

One problem, for example, involves comic violence. Young children are exposed to a great deal of comic violence on many of the television programs they see. We used to assume that because it was comic it had no serious effects. Now, a number of researchers have suggested that exposure to comic violence has negative effects on children.

VIOLENCE IN TEXTS:
QUANTITY VERSUS QUALITY

One problem with counting the number of violent incidents in a given time period is that it neglects the specific kinds of violence and the way violence is used in a particular text. One act of violence in a particular text may have a much more powerful impact than a number of other acts of violence in a different text. So merely counting the number of acts of violence on television in a given time period may not be very useful. Because there is no universally accepted way of scaling the impact of different acts of violence in a text, counting the number of acts of violence in a given time period is the best we can do. As the study cited above shows, there is a strong correlation between the amount of television viewing children and adolescents do and their tendency to be aggressive and commit violent acts, regardless of the role the violence might have played in a given text.

There is, of course, violence in many elite texts—that is, classics. Look at Shakespeare's *Hamlet*, for example. At the end of the play, the stage is littered with dead bodies. But the violence in *Hamlet* stems from the plot and is not gratuitous, like the violence in many contemporary films, where cars and buildings are blown up and people are killed one after another.

In many contemporary films and television programs, there is so much violence that we have, literally speaking, overkill. Violence loses its significance for the plots of these texts, though the impact of this violence on our psyches lingers on, I would suggest, long after we turn off our television sets or leave the theater. Many of these violence-filled films later are shown on television, which, even without these films, is permeated with violence. Consider, for example, local news show reports of violence, comic violence in children's programs, sports violence (especially in hockey and football), violence in cop shows and other dramatic pieces, and, of course, televised wrestling matches—which really should be seen as theatrical performances and not sport.

In some texts, as I suggested earlier, we may see a number of incidents of violence, but one particular incident may be much more important than others. In the classic western *Shane*, a pathological killer named Jack Wilson (played by Jack Palance) kills a hapless victim in a bar, but the most significant act of violence comes at the end of the film in which Shane (played by Alan Ladd) confronts Wilson in a shoot-out.

By the time this shoot-out occurs, the dramatic tension has built up, and violence in this scene has much more resonance and power than the other violent scenes in the film. And there is an incredible sense of relief in the audience as Wilson finally crumples to the ground, killed by Shane—a gunslinger even faster than Wilson. So some acts of violence in a text are much more powerful and meaningful than other acts of violence in the same text. In many contemporary films, which are permeated by violence—fights, exploding cars, killings, and so on—it is often difficult to see which violent scene or event is the most significant.

VIOLENCE IN NEWS BROADCASTS

If you watch a typical local television news show, you see stories about such things as murders, rapes, fires, and automobile accidents. Local television news shows, and to some extent national news shows, are filled with violence—in part because there is so much real violence in the world. In Oakland, California, for example, there were ninety-four murders during 2010. That meant that the ten o'clock news on KTVU, Channel 2, the hour-long local Fox news program from Oakland, had many news reports about murders in Oakland, as well as reports of rapes, kidnappings, and the like that took place in Oakland and elsewhere. The San Francisco local news broadcasts are similar, and the same applies to many other cities. A *USA Today* report shows that homicide rates are down remarkably in recent years:

> The long-term trend is particularly striking in the nation's three largest cities—New York, Chicago and Los Angeles. Homicides in New York have dropped 79% during the past two decades—from 2,245 in 1990 to 471 in 2009, the last full year measured. Chicago is down 46% during that period, from 850 to 458. Los Angeles is down 68%, from 983 to 312.
>
> Nevertheless, more than 14,000 people were murdered in the United States in 2010. This works out to 6.1 murders per 100,000 people.

Honduras has a murder rate of 57.9 people per hundred thousand and Germany has a murder rate of 0.98 murders per hundred thousand. These statistics suggest that . . . the United States has a very high murder rate for a first world country. (www.angelfire.com/rnb/y/homicide. htm#murd)

Television is an audio-visual medium, and television producers are looking for stories that have a strong visual element. Interviews with so-called talking heads don't have the visual power an image of a fire or a dead body has, even though these interviews may have more importance in that some talking heads have political power and their decisions can affect our lives in profound ways.

Because the violence shown in television news is real, because television news captures events that actually happened, news violence has a status different from violence in dramas and narratives that is not real. This real-world violence may affect viewers differently than the violence from dramatic fictions. It may convince viewers, as George Gerbner and others have suggested, that the world is a very dangerous place, generating feelings of anxiety and fear.

The question we must ask about local televised news is—are there other events, of more importance to the well-being of the community, that could be dealt with on the shows instead of the endless successions of murders, rapes, robberies, fires, and automobile crashes? It is important to remember that producers of local news programs select from a number of different possible stories to cover; they don't have to fill their newscasts with gossip and sensationalist stories, but they do so because they believe (and perhaps they are correct) that by doing this they attract a large audience. In other words, they claim to be giving their television viewers what they want.

This may or may not be true. But should television give people what they want or seem to want (in part because they have been brought up on a diet of sensationalistic news shows) or what they need—that is, information that will make them more informed and more responsible citizens? The question of whether what television audiences want (or say they want) is what they've been taught to want has not been resolved and is one that still troubles media researchers.

Many critics have suggested that news programs, which once were regarded as a public service to the community (and often lost money), now have become obsessed, like other kinds of television shows, with getting high ratings and making as much money as possible. Critics describe news as having undergone "tabloidization," by which they mean that news shows today have too many stories about celebrities, scandals, and other material of little real importance. In some cases, news shows feel forced to cover stories that have appeared in tabloid newspapers that are full of gossip, unsubstantiated reports on celebrities, and, in some cases, political scandal. News has become, to a considerable degree, an entertainment and as such it finds itself continually relying on the crutch found in many other entertainment genres—sensationalism and violence.

In his book *Going Live: Getting the News Right in a Real-time Online World*, Philip Seib offers a telling indictment of most radio and television news programs:

> Real-time journalism often delivers the news in easily consumable bites. But these are intellectual snacks, not meals; they satisfy only briefly and leave a hunger for more. There is not enough substance to be truly filling. This issue is not relevant to some news reports, since the story topics themselves—especially spot news items—are shallow and inconsequential. More substantive stories—those that have long-term importance—suffer from high-speed, quick-and-dirty coverage. (2002:58)

What people need to counter these stories, especially the ones found on local news shows that are full of murders and fires and similar material, is generally found in newspapers; they can offer context and in-depth coverage. Unfortunately, most Americans don't generally get this kind of material, since a high percentage of the American public relies on radio and television for all its news.

CHILDREN AND MEDIA VIOLENCE

There are a huge number of web sites devoted to media and violence, and a search on Google for the key phrase "media and violence" yields some 198,000,000 sites (on January 21, 2012). They offer their readers information discovered by the numerous psychologists and sociologists and other media scholars who have made serious studies of violence in the media. The findings of the preponderance of media scholars about violence follow (taken from the web sites of a number of pediatricians, media researchers, and other interested parties):

1. Media violence can lead to aggressive behavior in children. A study discussed in this book confirms this fact.

2. By age 18, the average American child will have seen more than 16,000 murders and viewed more than 200,000 acts of violence on television.

3. The level of violence during Saturday morning cartoons is higher than the level of violence during prime time. There are three to five violent acts per hour in prime time versus twenty to twenty-five acts per hour on Saturday morning.

4. Media violence is especially damaging to young children (under age 8) because they cannot easily tell the difference between real life and fantasy. Violent images on television and in movies may seem real to young children. They can be traumatized by viewing these images.

5. Media violence affects children by leading to increasing aggressiveness and anti-social behavior, by increasing their fear of becoming victims, by desensitizing them (making them less sensitive to violence and to victims of violence), and by increasing their appetite for more violence in entertainment and in real life.

6. Media violence often fails to show the consequences of violence. This is especially true of cartoons, toy commercials, and music videos. As a result, children learn that there are few if any repercussions for committing violent acts.

Many media researchers and pediatricians suggest that the amount of television children are permitted to watch should be limited to one and no more than two hours a day and that parents should monitor the television their children watch.

Experts also suggest that parents should not allow their children to watch violent television programs, videos, or films and should monitor the video games children are allowed to play. In addition, they suggest that parents must help children distinguish between fantasy and reality and explain to them that real-life violence has consequences. Unfortunately, a large percentage of parents do not monitor the television their children watch—in part because these parents use television as a babysitter and in part because many children (68 percent according to a Kaiser Family Foundation report, www.kff.org/entmedia/entmedia030905nr.cfm; see Chapter 1) have their own television set in their bedrooms. The semanticist S. I. Hayakawa once wrote an article entitled "Who's Bringing Up Your Children?" His answer was—television.

I consulted a neurologist about mediated violence, and he suggested that violent scenarios may affect us by modifying our neurological systems; violent acts may become a form of conditioning. That is, they may create certain pathways and circuits to the brain and affect its neurochemistry. The brain then is alerted by certain acts that function as "red flags," and this can lead to physical violence or other forms of antisocial behavior.

We know that children imitate others, so there is reason to fear that children will imitate the behavior of characters they identify with, often while not realizing what the outcome of their behavior will be. They may not realize that certain behaviors have very dire consequences. So there is reason to argue that young children, before the age of eight, should be shielded from mass-mediated violence. We should do the same for young adolescents, and actually for everyone, since watching portrayals of violence can have very negative consequences. Adults, also, as many scholars and researchers suggest, become fearful and anxiety ridden by being exposed to violence, even when they know that the violence is not real.

"KILL 'EM"

When I taught courses on media criticism, I used to ask my students to watch wrestling matches on television. It was not unusual during these matches to see some spectators, including little old ladies, run up to the ring and scream "kill him, kill him" to their favorite wrestler—usually a good-guy hero wrestler who was throwing a dirty, bad-guy wrestler around the ring, according to the script. These fans didn't want their hero to actually kill their opponent, but their behavior shows how violence—even scripted violence—can excite people. *There is a visceral, physiological effect from seeing violence, even fake violence,* that leads to people reacting in different ways—some get very excited, some scream and cheer, some tremble, some avert their eyes.

My point is that even if we think we are old and mature enough to handle violence, we may be fooling ourselves and we may be affected by it—traumatized, made anxious, and made fearful. The word *violence* is very close to the word *violate,* which has many negative denotations and connotations. When we watch violent acts in the media, we may be *violated,* or affected in ways we may not recognize.

The fact that we are probably exposed to 15,000 or more murders during the course of our television viewing as we grow up must have some effect on us. This is, perhaps, not true for most of us, but there are some of us who have psychological problems and other difficulties who will be more influenced by their exposure to television violence, film violence, and other mass-mediated violence (in music videos and rap music, for example). These individuals are much more likely to act out and be violent, sometimes in serious ways, as children, and they will continue to do so as they grow older.

There are several solutions that suggest themselves here. First, the people who make violent television shows and films and other texts must significantly reduce the amount of violence they inject into their works. There is even an aesthetic principle that makes this a reasonable course of action: the law of diminishing returns suggests that the continual use of violence dulls its impact, so producers, directors, and writers would serve their own interests—as well as those of society at large—in reducing the amount of violence in their texts. Second, we must reduce our exposure to violent texts, especially the exposure of our children to these works. As I've noted, during the aftermath of the 9/11 tragedy, a number of psychiatrists and mental health professionals suggested that it was a good idea for adults to cut down on the amount of news they were watching, since constant exposure to the horrendous images of the World Trade Center collapsing was having powerful and negative effects on viewers, both young and old.

It would also be a good idea if government or parental groups could find a way to induce the creators of television programs for children to reduce the comic violence in these shows. The airwaves, after all, are owned by the American people, and the networks and stations that use these networks are supposed to be doing so in the public interest. I recall seeing one interview with a television producer who said he won't let his children watch the shows he makes because they are too violent.

Nothing speaks more powerfully of the ascendance of the promotional system or the blurring of lines between consumers and citizens within market society, than advertising's role within contemporary democratic politics, particularly in the USA . . . Increasing amounts of party funds are directed at three strategic uses of political advertising for electioneering: acclaiming (branding) the candidates and their policies (61 percent), attacking the opposition and its policies (38 percent) and defending the candidates and their policies against the attacks of opponents (1 percent). By the time of the 1996 presidential campaign, over $200 million was spent on election advertising.

William Leiss, Stephen Kline, Sut Jhally, and
Jacqueline Botterill, *Social Communication in Advertising:
Consumption in the Mediated Marketplace* (2005:612)

What I am calling the Electronic Right comprises a broad alliance of elected officials, journalists, broadcasters and intellectuals, whose access to the media is supported by deep conservative reservoirs such as the Sarah Scaife and Carthage foundations (both controlled by Richard Mellon Scaife) and Olin, Smith-Richardson, J.M., and Bradly foundations. This policy-marketing machine sponsors an assortment of leading think tanks (such as the Heritage Foundation, American Enterprise Institute, Cato Institute, Hudson Institute, Manhattan Institute, and the Hoover Institution); various newspapers, magazines, journals and media pressure groups; conferences and seminars, books and articles, research studies, speaking engagements, editorial briefing sessions, and Internet projects; "astroturf" (fake grassroot) campaigns; radio and TV shows, including the public television programs of William F. Buckley, Peggy Noonan, Willaim Bennett, and Ben Wattenberg among others; and sundry antitax and antiregulatory organizations. Foundations on the left have vastly inferior resources . . .

Jeffrey Scheuer, *The Sound Bite Society:
Television and the American Mind* (1999:42–43)

10

MEDIA AND POLITICS

Earlier we examined the mass society thesis of certain social critics, who suggest that the mass media are leading to a society in which there is no sense of community and that mass culture will lead, inevitably, to a breakdown of democracy. This critique is, I suggested, a highly suspect one—and not based on convincing evidence. In this chapter I focus my attention on media and politics and will deal with topics such as media consolidation (and its possible consequences), the cultural imperialism hypothesis, the problem of pornography, and government regulation. In the 2012 presidential election, it has been estimated that the two candidates will spend approximately $2 billion on advertising. We can see that the media now play an increasingly important role in politics, which means that those who control the media have an important impact on American politics.

MEDIA CONSOLIDATION

Robert McChesney has argued, in an essay titled "The Global Media Giants," that there has been a continual and accelerated process of concentration in the media in the United States and globally as well. He writes (http://www.fair.org/index.php?page=1406):

> The global media system is now dominated by a first tier of nine giant firms. The five largest are Time Warner (1997 sales: $24 billion), Disney ($22 billion), Bertelsmann ($15 billion), Viacom ($13 billion), and Rupert Murdoch's News Corporation ($11 billion). Besides needing global scope to compete, the rules of thumb for global media giants are twofold: First, get bigger so you dominate markets and your competition can't buy you

out. Firms like Disney and Time Warner have almost tripled in size this decade. Second, have interests in numerous media industries, such as film production, book publishing, music, TV channels and networks, retail stores, amusement parks, magazines, newspapers and the like. The profit whole for the global media giant can be vastly greater than the sum of the media parts. A film, for example, should also generate a soundtrack, a book, and merchandise, and possibly spin-off TV shows, CD-ROMs, video games and amusement park rides. Firms that do not have conglomerated media holdings simply cannot compete in this market.

These media giants control an enormous amount of the media produced and spread throughout the world by the corporations they control. And they have numerous advantages over companies that cannot match their global reach.

In 2010, the top ten media conglomerates were:

Conglomerate	Revenues in Billions of Dollars
Comcast/NBC Universal	41.33
Walt Disney	28.71
Murdoch News Company	24.73
Viacom/CBS	20.54
Time Warner	20.28
Sony	16.09
Bertelsmann	15.79
Vivendi	12.45
Cox	11.01
Thomson Reuters	9.86

(www.grand-insolvency-show.com/2011/07/top-10-media-companies/)

Ben Bagdikian, the former dean of the School of Journalism at the University of California in Berkeley, was one of the first scholars to call our attention to this matter. As he explains (www.fair.org/extra/best-of-extra/corporate-ownership.html):

> In 1982, when I completed research for my book, 50 corporations controlled half or more of the media business. By December 1986, when I finished a revision for a second edition, the 50 had shrunk to 29. The last time I counted, it was down to 26. [When the latest edition of *The Media Monopoly* was published in 1993, the number was down to 20.] A number of serious Wall Street media analysts are predicting that by the 1990s, a half-dozen giant firms will control most of our media.

Of the 1,700 daily papers, 98 percent are local monopolies and *fewer than 15 corporations* control most of the country's daily circulation. A handful of firms have most of the magazine business, with **Time**, Inc. alone accounting for about 40 percent of that industry's revenues.

The **consolidation** of media companies that Bagdikian and McChesney talk about has taken place in other areas connected to the media. There are, for example, just four or five giant global advertising corporations that own most of the important advertising agencies. Companies that want to hire advertising agencies now demand, in many cases, that they be part of these global conglomerates so the advertisers can have a global reach.

The question that arises now is—what difference does it make? McChesney offers an answer (www.fair.org/extra/9711.gmg.html):

> On balance the system has minimal interest in journalism or public affairs except for that which serves the business and upper-middle classes, and it privileges just a few lucrative genres that it can do quite well—like sports, light entertainment and action movies—over other fare. Even at its best the entire system is saturated by a hyper-commercialism, a veritable commercial carpet bombing of every aspect of human life. As the CEO of Westinghouse put it (*Advertising Age*, 2/3/97), "We are here to serve advertisers. That is our raison d'etre."

McChesney mentions that the fifty corporations that control the media have connections with many other media organizations, which helps the media giants consolidate their power. The media giants also have political desires and interests that affect their programming and the editorial stances they take in their publications.

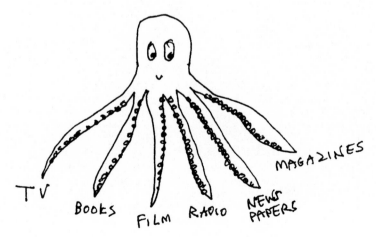

The Quality of Newscasts

Television stations owned by big, out-of-town companies tend to produce lower quality newscasts than those owned by smaller groups, a study by a journalism think tank has concluded. Newscasts at stations owned by large television networks fared poorly in the study. It was released Sunday by the Project for Excellence in Journalism, affiliated with the Columbia University School of Journalism . . . The five-year study, which examined roughly one-quarter of the nation's local TV stations, gave an "A" grade to only 11 percent of the stations owned by the 10 biggest media companies. Thirty-one percent of stations owned by small groups earned the top grade.

Associated Press, Monday, February 17, 2003.

It may be that the giant media organizations counter one another on certain political issues and that they do serve the public in certain areas—fighting racism and promoting safe sex to counter the AIDS epidemic, for example. It is also possible that their size makes it possible for them to take chances with artists and filmmakers that others cannot afford to take. For example, poetry books do not sell well, and if all publishers only put out books that had a good chance of making a profit, very few poetry books would be published. But publishing poetry books by serious poets can be looked upon as a public relations gesture by these companies, more than anything else.

ON CULTURAL IMPERIALISM: THE COCA-COLONIZATION HYPOTHESIS

The **cultural imperialism** theory, or Coca-colonization hypothesis, holds that the United States and a few other First World countries that export their films and television programs and other popular culture to the rest of the world are also exporting their capitalist ideologies and value systems with this material. It isn't that America is consciously trying to indoctrinate people in the Third World; what happens is that writers and film makers and television producers quite naturally make works that reflect their values—values they have learned while growing up in America. But these

values, such as the belief in the self-made man and woman and the importance of consumption, then, are spread all over the globe.

Most Third World countries can't afford to make films and television
programs. It is much cheaper to import works from First World countries,
and with these works they are also getting, without recognizing it, First
World ideologies and values. Thus, American and other First World cultures are not only dominating more fragile Third World cultures, they are
also destroying them. The spread of our films and television shows and our
McDonald's hamburger restaurants and Starbucks coffee shops is, according to this theory, leading to a kind of worldwide cultural homogenization.
Eventually, according to the logic of this argument, every place will look
like every other place: people everywhere will drink Coca-Cola or Pepsi,
eat at the same fast-food joints, dress the same, and watch the same films
and television shows.

The cultural imperialism theory assumes that the media are extremely
powerful; if they aren't, then the effects of our media will not be significant,
and American media will just be essentially a source of entertainment and
not a force for Americanizing and changing the fundamental value systems
of these cultures.

Herta Herzog-Massing dealt with this question in some research she
conducted on how people in Germany decoded or made sense of the
widely popular (at the time) television series *Dallas*. As she explained, in an
important article titled "Decoding *Dallas*,"

> Critics of popular culture, and of things American in particular, have
> concerned themselves with the question of whether the worldwide dif-
> fusion of programs such as "Dallas" made possible by the growth of the
> new media technologies may eventually result in worldwide cultural
> assimilation at the expense of indigenous diversity. (*Society*, 1986:74)

Massing's study of the way *Dallas* was interpreted in Germany led her to
write, "The answer to my initial question—do viewers in different countries read popular culture differently?—must be answered affirmatively"
(1988:77).

She was dealing with the way one First World country, Germany,
interpreted a text from another First World country, the United States.
But her finding, that people in different cultures interpret texts in different
ways, is a compelling reason to suggest that the media imperialism theory
may be a bit overblown and that the impact of our media and popular
culture on other cultures may be somewhat superficial. In recent years

many countries have been putting American television shows on in late hours, replacing them with their own shows that are more closely tied to the culture involved. But American movies still are dominant everywhere.

A NOTE ON IDEOLOGY AND THE MEDIA

What's really important, critics of the media argue, is the way these media giants can dominate political discourse and gain their ends—making further expansion and consolidation possible and shutting out competition. As the saying goes, "He who pays the piper, calls the tune." The owners of the media are the ones who call the tunes nowadays—they publish their "tunes" in the newspapers, magazines, and book publishers they own; they broadcast their "tunes" on their radio stations and television stations and cable networks; they make CDs of their "tunes"; they make video games of their "tunes"; and since we only hear their "tunes," for the most part, their "tunes" are the ones that stick in our minds and that we find ourselves humming.

By *tunes* I mean something much broader than songs, namely political viewpoints, ideological positions, attitudes, notions, and ideas. **Ideology** is generally defined as a system of logically coherent beliefs about the social and political order. The giant media conglomerates can help shape our ideologies in a number of different ways. First, their newspapers and radio and television stations function as **gatekeepers** and determine which stories they want to cover and which ones they will exclude or to which they will give scant attention. Second, the *way* the news media organizations cover stories also affects the opinions of readers and viewers and listeners of news programs. As I mentioned earlier, what we see on television is always something that someone has determined we will see (just as what we won't see has been determined for us).

The development of social media sites such as Facebook and Twitter has lessened the power of the media conglomerates, but since Americans still watch around four hours of television every day, the media conglomerates still have enormous power and impact.

THE PROBLEM OF PORNOGRAPHY

Beauty, as they say, is in the eye of the beholder, and so, it seems, is determining what is and what is not pornography. Where do we draw the line between the increasingly more explicit sexual content of the advertisements and commercials that flood our magazines, airwaves, and cable media and so-called soft-core pornography, and then between soft-core pornography and hard-core pornography?

There is also the question of whether pornography is harmful to children or others who are exposed to it and who, as is often the case, go seeking it. The Internet is full of pornographic sites, and older children and preteens, who are curious about sexual matters, often go searching for these pornographic sites. But, as I've suggested, one of the problems involved in dealing with pornography is that it is difficult to find a definition that everyone can agree upon. Pornography is, like many concepts, hard to pin down.

In a government paper, "US Media in the 1990s: III: The Media and Society," available on the Internet, Frederic A. Emmert writes:

> Although the courts have long held that media publishing or broad-casting obscenity and pornography do not enjoy First Amendment protection, it remains hard for a judge to define those terms. Consequently, in the 1973 "Miller versus California" and "Paris Adult Theater versus Slaton" cases, the U.S. Supreme Court rejected the notion of a national obscenity standard and left the definition and regulation of obscenity up to "contemporary community standards defined by the applicable state law." (www.4uth.gov.ua/usa/english/media/files/media1cd.htm)

The Supreme Court concluded, then, that there was no way to define obscenity in a manner that everyone could accept, and left the matter of defining pornography up to local communities. Obviously, cultural matters come into play, and in large, international cities such as New York and San Francisco, people may have a much different notion of what is obscene than in more conservative rural communities.

Emmert did explain how the Supreme Court believed communities could determine whether some text was obscene or not. He summarizes its findings as follows:

> The Court . . . proclaimed a general test for obscenity to be:
> 1) whether the "average person, applying contemporary community standards" would find that the work, taken as a whole, appeals to the prurient [sexually exciting] interest.
> 2) whether the work depicts or describes, in a patently offensive way, sexual conduct specifically defined by the applicable state law, and

3) whether the work, taken as a whole, lacks serious literary, artistic, political or scientific value.

As you can see, there are a great many loopholes here—which probably explains why the Supreme Court decided to let cities and states fight the matter out. For one thing, a text has to be prurient when "taken as a whole" and it also, as a whole, must lack "serious literary, artistic, political or scientific value." That means parts of texts may be prurient, but if the whole text isn't, or if the text is a serious work of art, the work cannot be considered pornographic. In addition, a text must depict or describe sexual conduct "in a patently offensive way," and the depicted or described conduct must be sexual conduct that is defined as illegal by state laws.

A SUPREME COURT DECISION ON VIRTUAL CHILD PORNOGRAPHY

On April 16, 2002, the U.S. Supreme Court rendered a verdict involving virtual child pornography and struck down a bill, the Child Pornography Prevention Act of 1996, as infringing on the First Amendment rights of artists and writers. This bill had made it criminal to create "virtual child pornography, distribute it or possess it." The Supreme Court, by a vote of six to three, argued that the bill was an infringement on the rights of free expression guaranteed by the First Amendment of the Constitution. The First Amendment reads, "Congress shall make no law . . . abridging the freedom of speech."

Justice Anthony Kennedy, who wrote the opinion for the majority, explained that the prohibition in the Child Pornography Prevention Act of 1996 involved "any visual depiction" and was not concerned about how an image was produced:

> The section [in the law] captures a range of depictions, sometimes called "virtual child pornography," which include computer-generated images, as well as images produced by more traditional means. For instance, the literal terms of the statute embrace a Renaissance painting depicting a scene from classical mythology, a "picture" that "appears to be of a minor engaging in sexually explicit conduct." The statute also prohibits Hollywood movies, filmed without any child actors, if a jury believes an actor "appears to be" a minor engaging in "actual or simulated . . . sexual intercourse."

Justice Kennedy's point, then, which he develops at length in his statement, is that the law could be used to prevent people from having access to great works of art or even lesser works that might have sexual content that some people find objectionable. He also wrote that "the government has shown no more than a remote connection between speech that might encourage thoughts or impulses and any resulting child abuse."

In another case, dealing with the French film *The Lovers*, the Supreme Court dealt with the problem of pornography and decided against attempts to censor the film. In that case Justice Potter Stewart said:

> I shall not today attempt further to define the kinds of material I un-
> derstand to be embraced within that shorthand description ["hard-core
> pornography"]; and perhaps I could never succeed in intelligibly doing
> so. But I know it when I see it, and the motion picture involved in this
> case is not that. (Justice Potter Stewart, concurring opinion in *Jacobellis
> v. Ohio* 378 U.S. 184 (1964), regarding possible obscenity in *The Lovers*)

We can see then that deciding what is obscene and pornographic is not an easy thing to do and that attempts by the government to protect children may, unwittingly, dampen free expression and have very negative consequences.

One of the problems legal experts face in dealing with artistic texts is that texts are often complicated, difficult to analyze, and elusive, and whether we are critics, moralists, or concerned citizens, we cannot easily reach consensus on them. As I pointed out earlier, there are all kinds of aesthetic factors involved in such texts, so it is hard for anyone to prove that a work is obscene, especially since in postmodern societies the barriers between everything seem to have been obliterated. We must remember that James Joyce's *Ulysses*, one of the greatest novels of the twentieth century, was once held to be obscene and only was brought into the country after a lawsuit brought by Bennett Cerf of Random House.

In 2002 a museum in New York City had an exhibit on contemporary art. In the exhibit was a "work of art" called *Cloaca*, which I heard about on a report on National Public Radio. *Cloaca* is, its creator says, a work of art. It is a machine that is fed food which it then grinds up, passes through its various tubes, and finally "defecates." I believe it was created in the Netherlands, where its "excrement" was packaged in plastic and sold to people—until it was found that the excrement could not be protected from bacteria and started putrifying. Some people consider *Cloaca* to be a cosmic joke and others think it is a wonderful work of art. In an art world in which almost anything goes, who is to say what is serious art and what isn't? And who is to say what is pornography and what isn't?

THE SPIRAL OF SILENCE:
PUBLIC OPINION AND POLITICAL IDEOLOGY

There is a theory of communication that helps us understand how certain ideas can become dominant in society. It was developed by a German scholar, Elizabeth Noelle-Neumann, who wrote, in an important article in *The Journal of Communication*, that people who believe—correctly or not—that they represent the majority opinion have a tendency to make their views known while those who believe they represent the minority opinion have a tendency to keep quiet. This is because people don't wish to be isolated and those who hold what they think is a minority view often convince themselves that their view is wrong. As she explains:

> He may find himself on one of two sides. He may discover that he agrees with the prevailing (or winning) view, which boosts his self-confidence and enables him to express himself with an untroubled mind and without any danger of isolation, in conversation, but cutting those who hold different views. Or he may find that the views he holds are losing ground: the more this appears to be so, the more uncertain he will become of himself, and the less he will be inclined to express his opinion. ("The Spiral of Silence: A Theory of Public Opinion," *Journal of Communication*, 24, 2 [1974], 44)

When some people speak up and others remain silent, there starts "a spiraling process which increasingly establishes one opinion as the prevailing one" (1974:44). This is exacerbated by the fact that people often underestimate the number of people who share their views and overestimate the number of people who oppose them.

It is quite obvious that the media play an important role in shaping public opinion, since what people read in the newspapers, hear on the radio, and see on television news programs (where many people in America get most of their news) has an effect on what people believe is the prevailing opinion on many different issues. Noelle-Neumann's theory suggests, then, that the media help shape public opinion rather than just reflecting it.

As we have seen, however, there is some question about how effective the media are in shaping public opinion. While there are a small number of giant corporations that control the media, countervailing forces often play an important role in shaping public opinion. We find, for example, that many groups aligned on important issues—based on race, ethnicity, gender, and religion—are increasingly making their voices heard, and their beliefs often are critical of the agendas and practices of the giant corporations and media conglomerates. These groups are often able to use and exploit the press for their own purposes, and now can use Twitter, Facebook, and blogs to make their arguments. In addition, the political parties have an important role in affecting public opinion, especially in regards to political and ideological issues.

Specific events often play an important role in shaping public opinion. For example, the collapse and bankruptcy of the Enron Corporation, at one time the seventh largest corporation in the United States, exposed the degree to which it and other energy producers had helped shape the government's energy policy. It also showed how a giant accounting firm, Arthur Anderson, wasn't correctly monitoring Enron and giving honest reports about its financial status. In February 2003, a congressional committee discovered that Enron had also found a way, in collusion with banks and other financial institutions, to avoid paying its fair share of taxes. This led to the suggestion by many politicians that we change our tax system so corporations cannot find ways to avoid paying taxes. Shaping public opinion isn't quite as simple as it might seem, and the spiral of silence might not always function the way Noelle-Neumann thought it would.

The terrible hurricanes in September of 2005, which were covered superbly and non-stop by the media, exposed the shocking degree to which the federal government was unprepared to deal with large, wide-scale emergencies. The television coverage also showed how much poverty there was in New Orleans, which was a blow to our belief that our economy was doing well and we were creating a just society in which poverty was being eliminated. Statistics revealed that poverty had been increasing in the United States in recent years, but statistics don't have much of an emotional impact. It was the power of the images of the poor people, mostly African Americans, and the desperate conditions in which they lived, that made the existence of this poverty much more real to Americans. Many residents of New Orleans hadn't left the city before hurricane Katrina devastated it because they didn't have cars and were too poor to leave. This media coverage severely damaged the reputation of the president and other high-ranking members of the government. The director of the Federal Emergency Management Agency (FEMA), who was a political appointee and not qualified for the job, was forced to resign.

The coverage of hurricane Katrina and of hurricane Rita, which followed closely after Katrina, exposed the inability of our government, at all levels, to cope with disasters. The media, in covering these disasters, played an important role in affecting public opinion. The television coverage of these storms had major political consequences.

GOVERNMENT REGULATION AND DEREGULATION OF BROADCASTING

Congress established an agency in 1934, the Federal Communications Commission (FCC), to regulate the broadcasting industry subject to the "public interest, convenience and necessity." The purpose of the agency was to promote diversity in broadcasting, and so it has issued, over the years, a number of different rules about how many radio and television stations a corporation could own in one city and rules about newspapers owning television stations in a city.

With the growth of cable, which does not use the public airwaves, the FCC has started relaxing its rules on ownership of radio and television stations by newspapers in a city, consolidation of ownership of radio and television stations, and the ownership of cable television systems by television networks and media organizations. The FCC also decided to stop enforcing the Fairness Doctrine, which mandated that broadcasters provide equal time for different points of view on issues of importance. Some members of Congress tried to reinstate the Fairness Doctrine but have been unable to do so.

In his book *The Sound Bite Society: Television and the American Mind*, Jeffrey Scheuer discusses recent developments in the broadcast industry relevant to the matter of deregulation:

> The modest balancing mechanism of the Fairness Doctrine was re-scinded in 1987; and the public interest standard, as a basis for relicensing stations, has become a national joke; the fox rules the chicken coop. Mark S. Fowler, the first FCC chairman under Reagan who theorized that television is just "a toaster with pictures," deregulated with a vengeance, even lifting rules prohibiting program-length commercials aimed at children . . . (1999:43)

He goes on to discuss the giveaway to the broadcasting industry of the new digital frequency spectrum, a resource also owned by the public, valued at $70 billion. This outraged some conservatives like Bob Dole, who called it "the biggest single gift of public property to an industry in this century." Schueur continues:

I should add that under the George W. Bush administration, deregulation is moving ahead very rapidly and it looks like the broadcasting industry and the media conglomerates will get just about everything that they want in the way of relaxed rules and regulations from the FCC. There are ideological implications to this relaxation of control over the media conglomerates, which we can see, for example, when it comes to television. (1999:45)

Scheuer then discusses the so-called "liberal bias" to the press and points out that, in reality, the networks and public television really have a conservative bias. He writes:

For all their alleged liberal bias, in recent decades, the networks and public television have been decidedly more hospitable to the showcasing of centrist and conservative voices. With rare exceptions, guests on public affairs programs are fonts of conventional wisdom, typically powerful Beltway insiders with views running the gamut from right to center. The fulcrum of debate on the talk shows is even further to the right: for every centrist or moderate liberal on the left side of the screen (e.g. Shields, Germond, Carlson, Clift, Caraville, Stephanopolous), there is a crown on the right and center-right: Barnes, Bay Buchanan, Pat Buchanan, Buckley, Gergen, Glassman, Kondracke, Krauthammer, Kristol, Limbaugh, McLaughlin, Matalin, Novak, Safire, Snow, Stassinopolous, Sununu, Wattenberg, Will, et al. (1999:47)

Scheuer points out also that the mainstream media tend to interview people from conservative and centrist think tanks more than from those on the left, and that newspaper opinion pages tend to be conservative as well. He cites an interesting statistic in this respect: Richard Nixon in the 1968 election and George W. Bush in the 2000 election received somewhere between 60 percent and 80 percent of the endorsements in daily newspapers We can see, then, that media conglomeration has social and political implications and is not just an economic matter. But we must remember that despite all the endorsements he received, George W. Bush received fewer votes than his opponent, Al Gore.

There are now some liberal talk shows on radio designed to counter the domination of the radio waves by conservative (and in some cases "right wing") talk show hosts. We have to realize these talk shows are political entertainments and the people working on the liberal talk shows have to demonstrate that they can be as entertaining as their conservative counterparts. Many young people now get their news from comedy news shows such as *The Colbert Report* and *The Daily Show* that have liberal hosts and help counter the conservative radio talk shows.

Fighting Media Conglomerates

There are many organizations that attempt to fight the power of the media conglomerates. What follows is a call for papers by an organization, the Union for Democratic Communications (UDC), for a conference on Democratic Communications and Global Justice. A list of the subjects they wish to have discussed will give you an idea of their interests:

> The Union for Democratic Communications invites the submission of paper and panel proposals, media projects, and workshops addressing the role of democratic communications in the struggle for global justice. We seek submissions with a critical take on existing media structures and practices, such as the continuing global concentration of the media, the commercialization of new media technologies, the creeping influence of advertising from the classroom to the newsroom, the distortion and suppression of news and information by the mainstream media. We also seek submissions that highlight struggles for global justice from the local to the global level; from preserving communities and cultures to protesting meetings of the world's rich and powerful.
>
> The Union for Democratic Communications is a group of communications researchers, theorists, educators, journalists, media producers, policy analysts, and activists. The UDC is dedicated to the critical study of communications establishments and policies; the production and distribution of democratically controlled media; the fostering of alternative, oppositional, independent, and experimental production; and the development of democratic communications systems at local, regional, national and international levels.

The term *critical* here means that the UDC is concerned with offering an ideological critique of the media and the government agencies and media conglomerates that control the media.

ETHNIC MEDIA: A COMPLICATING FACTOR

As America becomes ever more multi-cultural, with large numbers of people from Asia, Africa, Europe, and South and Central America moving here, we find that the power of ethnic media is growing. The notion that

America is a so-called melting pot in which ethnic groups quickly lose their ethnic identities and become Americanized, as I suggested earlier, doesn't seem to be working, at least in the short run. A better **metaphor** for the United States would be something like a beef stew, in which each component (that is, each ethnic group) retains its identity, while being part of something bigger than itself.

What has happened is that people from various ethnic groups move into areas where there are other people from their ethnic groups, establishing what a *Wall Street Journal* article on the growth of ethnic media called "islands of ethnic communities." The article "Ethnic Media Muy Popular in California," by Pui-Wing Tam, reports on a survey on ethnic media use in California:

> Ethnic media are pervasive: Fully 84% of the survey's Hispanic, Asian-American and African-American respondents say they get information through ethnic television, radio and publications. Ethnic-media consumers are loyal: 68% of respondents say they prefer ethnic TV stations over English channels for watching news. (April 23, 2002)

These various ethnic media outlets provide different perspectives from the major U.S. media outlets. But General Electric owns Telemundo, a major Hispanic network, and other media conglomerates either own or will probably purchase other ethnic media organizations lest these conglomerates not be able to reach increasingly large ethnic sectors of American society.

The relation between the media and society, we see, is a very complicated matter, and it is not easy to make generalizations about this relationship. There is, as I've pointed out, considerable evidence that there is increasing consolidation of control of the media by giant corporations, but it isn't easy to assess what impact this consolidation has had (and will have) on our culture, our political order, and our society in the long run—especially since the development of social media such as Facebook and Twitter.

We ought surely to look in the child for the first traces of imaginative activity. The child's best-loved and most absorbing occupation is play. Perhaps we may say that every child at play behaves like an imaginative writer, in that he creates a world of his own or, more truly, he rearranges the things of this world and orders it in a new way that pleases him better . . .

Now the writer does the same as the child at play; he creates a world of phantasy which he takes very seriously; that is, he invests it with a great deal of affect, while separating it sharply from reality. Language has preserved this relationship between children's play and poetic creation. It designates certain kinds of imaginative creation, concerned with tangible objects and capable of representation, as "plays"; the people who present them are called "players." The unreality of this poetic world of imagination, however, has very important consequences for literary technique; for many things which if they happened in real life could produce no pleasure can nevertheless give enjoyment in a play—many emotions which are essentially painful may become a source of enjoyment to the spectators and hearers of a poet's work.

Sigmund Freud, *The Relation of the Poet to Day-Dreaming* (1908)

11

MEDIA ARTISTS

B y *media artists* I mean all the people who create texts—either individually, as in the case of most non-fiction books or works of fiction by a novelist, or collectively, as in the case of a film or television show. In a typical film or television show, for example, we have:

Performance Artists: Actors and Actresses
Production Artists: Camera Operators, Musicians, Technicians, etc.
Creative Artists: Directors, Film Editors, Writers

We may add to these the producers, publicity people, and all those involved in the business side of television and filmmaking.

Most films involve an incredible number of different kinds of media artists and specialists. After a film concludes and as we get up from our seats in a theater, the credits roll, listing the large number of people who were involved in making that film, from the producer, director, actors, actresses, first assistant director, and second assistant director down to the grips and the makeup artists. Television programs, while usually not as complicated as films, still require many different kinds of artists. For example, there were a dozen writers on the writing team that created the situation comedy *Frasier*. The show that we see on television is just the tip of the creation and production iceberg, so to speak. A simple program, such as a cooking show, could easily have fifteen or twenty people involved in actually making the program.

There is a difference between writing books, which tends to be an individual effort, and making films and television shows, which is a collaborative effort. But writers of books, while they may write alone, still must take the wishes and desires of others—namely publishers and editors, and sometimes other people, such as marketing directors—into consideration. And of course writers, like anyone else doing creative work, must consider their audiences.

In order to show how complicated the process of creating media texts is, let me take a relatively simple kind of text—a scholarly book—as an example. For other kinds of texts, such as television programs, films, video games, and so on, you can assume that matters are even more difficult.

PUBLISHING A SCHOLARLY BOOK: A CASE STUDY

Let's say that someone writes a book on a scholarly subject—a book that may also be used in courses at colleges and universities. I make a distinction here between scholarly books that are written on some subject and may be used as texts in courses, and textbooks, which are written only for use in courses, and which generally have a great deal of teaching apparatus: study questions, extensive bibliographies, learning exercises, and so on. In some cases, the distinction between scholarly books and textbooks is hard to make.

Writers of scholarly books always face the problem of finding publishers who will agree to publish their books. In many cases, a writer must prepare a substantial proposal that describes the book, lists the chapters, discusses the competition, and offers a sample chapter or two. This is sent to editors at various publishers who publish the kind of book the author has written. Let us suppose an acquiring editor at XYZ Books likes a submitted proposal and asks to see the book manuscript. Generally speaking, scholars send off their proposals for books before they have actually written them, so they won't write a book that nobody will publish. Let us assume, now, that the scholar has written a book-length manuscript based on the proposal submitted earlier.

The acquiring editor, who is responsible for finding books to publish, must then convince an editorial committee at his or her publishing house—a committee made up of editors, marketing directors, and others—that the book (now in manuscript form) is worthwhile. By this I mean it is a good book—well-written and with sound scholarship—and it probably will find a suitable audience. It takes a considerable amount of money to publish a book, and publishers must make a profit if they are to survive. So every book published is, in a sense, a bet made by the publisher that a book will find enough of an audience to make publishing that book profitable. Publishers realize they can't win every bet, but if they don't win enough bets and sell enough books, they go out of business.

My experience has been that editors often have many useful suggestions to make about what is dealt with in a book—about how much weight should be given to certain subjects and about what might be added to the book or deleted from it. It is not unusual for an author to get a manuscript back with long notes, questions, and suggestions written on many pages of a manuscript. (Now, authors submit the text file of their manuscripts and editors often make comments right in the manuscript text file.)

Then, once the manuscript for the book is revised to the satisfaction of an editor, he or she often sends the manuscript to a number of scholars and professors who are thought to be experts in the subject, to see whether there are errors of fact and interpretation in the manuscript and whether there are topics that have been missed or not explained adequately. So it is not unusual for an author to receive several (sometimes four or five) anonymous reviews of the manuscript, each suggesting what should be done to make the book better, or, in some cases, even advising that the book not be published.

This means there is another step that must be taken—dealing with the scholarly and professorial reviews of a book, some of which are constructive and valuable and others of which can be mean-spirited and extremely hostile. Such reviews, even the negative ones, can be helpful, since they point out areas that might need work and problems readers might face in reading the book. So the author then must take the various suggestions into consideration and revise the manuscript again, where revisions are called for.

Let us suppose now that this is done to the satisfaction of the book's editor. Next, the book is sent to a copyeditor, who goes through the book doing things like checking for typing mistakes the author has made, smoothing the prose here and there, asking questions about facts, and checking footnotes and bibliographical citations. I have found copyeditors to be extremely helpful in the course of my career. In the old days, copyeditors wrote their questions on Post-it notes, and you'd get your manuscript back with three or four Post-it notes, with questions or suggestions on them, on some pages. Now copyeditors tend to ask their questions and make their suggested changes in colored typefaces right on the manuscript file from the author. Then they e-mail the file, with their questions, corrections and suggestions, back to the writer to consider. The writer, who responds to the questions the copyeditor asks, has to make sure the copyeditor hasn't changed the meaning of the text and approves any changes the copyeditor has made.

When the manuscript has been copyedited and revised by the author, it is then sent to a production editor, who is responsible for everything relating to its eventual production. The edited manuscript first goes to book designers, who decide on the typography of the book—what typefaces are to be used, what size the text block should be, how much spacing there should be between lines of type, where illustrations are to go, and how large or small they should be. The production editor generally tells the designer how many pages the book should be and the designer works within those guidelines. The production editor also must arrange to have a cover designed for the book. Sometimes the typography and cover design is done by artists who work for the publisher, and other times the typography and cover design are sent out to freelance book designers and cover artists.

When the manuscript has been typeset into what are often called page proofs, it is checked by a proofreader and the author, who look for errors made by the typesetter and for errors that the copyeditor and author missed earlier. The author then must make an index or have the page proofs sent to a professional index maker. Once the index is made, the page proofs can be sent to the printer and the book manufactured.

You can see, then, that while it only took one person to write the book, it took a number of people to move the book manuscript into production and actually publish the book. This process is less complicated with novels, but fiction editors often play an important role with novel writers—getting them to cut or expand their manuscripts and make various changes here and there, so novelists often work closely with their editors. One reason editors are important is that writers become so involved with their manuscripts that, in a sense, they can't see them clearly, and a person who is not so emotionally tied to a book can often see things that need to be done to it to make it better.

Writing scholarly books and novels is a lonely occupation. You sit in front of a computer (it used to be a typewriter) and spend hours putting words down, one after another. But once you have a manuscript that has been accepted by a publisher, you find yourself dealing with many book publishing professionals, with different areas of expertise, who work with you in turning your manuscript into a book.

THE BOOK BUSINESS

It's interesting to compare the audiences for books and other mass media, such as television programs. We can make distinctions between trade books, which are produced for the general public and sold in bookstores; scholarly books, which are written for scholars but often used in courses in universities;

and textbooks, which are produced for students and generally sold in university bookstores. Publishers sell scholarly books and textbooks by printing up catalogs describing their books and sending these catalogs to professors who may find a certain book of personal interest and also may want to use it in a course they are teaching. Most publishers now have sites on the Internet where their books are described and where buyers can arrange to purchase them. Trade books generally only have a three-month "window of opportunity." If they don't sell well during that period, they are typically remaindered, or sold to companies that grind them up and reuse the paper pulp.

A trade book that sells 100,000 copies is considered a great success, while a network television show that *only* attracts six or eight million viewers (and thus has poor ratings) is often considered a failure. Some trade books, of course, sell in the millions, but the average book is lucky if it sells five or ten thousand copies, and the average scholarly book doesn't sell anywhere near that number of copies. Textbooks are a different matter, and a good textbook in a core subject (such as an introduction to economics or a reader for freshman English) can sell tens of thousands, hundreds of thousands, or even millions of copies.

New technology has now come to the aid of the writers and publishers of scholarly books. The minimum press run for a scholarly book that makes economic sense is between five hundred and a thousand copies, though in many cases the press runs are much larger. But some scholarly books don't sell anywhere near a thousand copies, which means the publishers—usually university presses—often ended up with stacks and stacks of previously published scholarly books in their warehouses, which costs them money. Now, as a result of the development of new print-on-demand printers that can print a cover and the text of a book from a digital file in just a short period of time, scholarly book publishers can print their books on demand. That is, they can print books when they get orders for them and avoid large inventories of books, many of great scholarly importance, that may or may not find purchasers. And inventories of previously published books can be disposed of without the book going out of print.

Several commercial print-on-demand publishers, such as iUniverse and Xlibris, enable authors to "publish" (that is, self-publish) a book for a few hundred dollars or so. For this money authors get their book set into type (from a computer file the author must provide) with a cover designed for the book. When anyone orders one or more copies, they are printed up "on demand," so to speak.

A new competitor to iUniverse and Xlibris has appeared—a website called Lulu (www.lulu.com). Lulu allows writers to publish books at little cost. It provides a fully automated means of publishing books as long as the manuscript is written on a computer file and can be uploaded to the Lulu website. Authors only pay for the cost of printing copies of their books, which generally amounts to $8 to $10.

What this means is that anyone with a computer can now publish a book with companies such as Xlibris, iUniverse, and Lulu. These books are available to the general public, and many are described and listed at sites such as Amazon.com, BN.com (Barnes & Noble), and www.lulu.com. It isn't a way to make a great deal of money, but people who write books that may not be commercially viable can still publish them at very low cost. Before print-on-demand machines were developed, authors who couldn't find a regular publisher for their books had to use vanity publishers (in reality, printers who specialized in publishing books for authors who couldn't find regular publishers), and it generally cost thousands of dollars to have one's book manufactured.

THE KINDLE, THE NOOK, AND THE E-BOOK REVOLUTION

The book publishing industry is now in considerable flux with the incredible popularity of the Kindle, the Kindle Fire tablet, and numerous e-book readers and tablets made by other companies. What e-book companies call "dead tree books," that is books printed on paper, are losing ground, it would seem, to electronic editions of books that can be stored on e-readers. A typical e-reader can hold more than a thousand books.

Now, many publishers plan on publishing electronic versions of books that they are publishing in print. While middle-aged and older people are used to having print books, younger generations, raised on smart phones, tablets, and other devices, may not prefer printed books, so the future of the publishing industry is quite problematic—especially since some authors bypass traditional publishers and publish their books as e-books with Amazon.com or other companies.

An article by Carol Memmett in *USA Today* (September 6, 2011) offers some details:

> E-books, once considered the new kids in town, are shaking up the world of publishing with surging sales. The numbers tell the story:
>
> • Random House, the USA's largest publisher, says more than 20% of U.S. revenue in the first half of this year [2011] were from digital sales.

- Amazon recently announced that two more authors, Kathryn Stockett and Janet Evanovich, have reached the million mark in Kindle e-book sales.
- Eight of the top 20 titles on USA TODAY's Best-Selling Books list this week are e-books.
- Barnes & Noble's strong sales of digital content in the first quarter of its fiscal year 2012 (which ended July 30) helped make up for a decline in sales of printed books. The chain credits the Nook, its e-book reader, with strengthening its bottom line. Failure to jump more quickly into the digital frontier is blamed in part for the demise of Borders.

"It's been a watershed year for e-books," says Tina Jordan of the Association of American Publishers. "Any publisher will tell you that a best-selling title from a branded author can run upwards of 30% to 40% in digital sales."

We can see, then, that e-books and the devices people use to read them, such as the Kindle, the Nook, and tablets, are having a major impact on the book publishing industry.

SCRIPT WRITING AND ABERRANT DECODING

Let us move from books to television. Technically speaking—using communication jargon—we can say that writers of scripts for televised programs, such as sitcoms, dramas, or documentaries, encode a communication, assuming or hoping that their audiences will decode their communication correctly—that is, they will "get" what the writer wanted them to get and will interpret the text the way the writer wants them to interpret it. These terms—*encode* and *decode*—come from the linguist Jakobson's model of communication: a sender encodes a message and sends it, using some medium, to a receiver who decodes it. This also applies to films and all kinds of other mediated texts.

We sometimes find, in our everyday lives, that in our conversations we say something to someone who, for one reason or another, doesn't interpret what we said correctly. This misinterpretation could be caused by any number of things: our receiver didn't know some of the words we were using, couldn't hear everything we said, didn't notice the tone in which we said what we said, or wasn't paying attention and missed some of it.

When it comes to the mass media, where the sender is the writer of a film or television show (or a member of a team of writers), the opportunities for receivers (that is audiences) to misinterpret what's in a text grows exponentially. This misinterpretation is known as **aberrant decoding**. Umberto Eco, a novelist and semiotician who has written extensively on popular culture, has suggested that aberrant decoding tends to be the rule when it comes to the mass media. That is, people generally don't decode texts the way the media artists who create them expect them to be decoded. He writes in his article "Towards a Semiotic Inquiry into the Television Message":

> Codes and subcodes are applied to the message [text] in the light of a general framework of cultural references, which constitutes the receiver's patrimony of knowledge: his ideological, ethical, religious standpoints, his psychological attitudes, his tastes, his value systems, etc. (1972:115)

This problem becomes widespread with the development of the mass media, since there is often a considerable difference in class and educational levels between the writers of mass-mediated texts and those in the audiences for these texts. For example, writers may mention famous artists and philosophers or works of art that most members of their audience may never have heard of, or writers may make allusions to historical events that the members of the audience do not know about.

This means that writers for the mass media have to be very careful that they don't write material that's "over the heads" of their audiences. They must keep their target audience in mind, though this doesn't mean that everything on television has to be dumbed down so it can appeal to, and be understood by, the so-called lowest-common-denominator viewing public. In some cases, the target audience can be a relatively small (in percentage terms) number of people, such as those who watch elite programming on public television channels or on regular television networks or cable. These particular target audiences may not be large, but the people in these audiences tend to be affluent opinion makers whose influence is considerable and whose purchasing power is of interest to select advertisers.

MEDIA ETHICS AND JOURNALISTS

Ethics is that branch of philosophy that has to do with what might be described as right conduct. There are many different philosophical arguments that have been made about what is and what isn't ethical behavior, and what ethics should deal with. When we come to the media, there are a number of different areas involving ethics that suggest themselves.

Consider journalists. Journalists are supposed to work under a code of ethics that requires them to report the news honestly and accurately—by which we generally mean not putting their own interpretation or "spin" on what they cover. Some critics have suggested that all news involves interpretation, even when reporters wish to be accurate. Reporters are also expected to avoid even the appearance of any conflicts of interest. For example, a journalist who covers the stock market for a newspaper should not write an article praising a company in which he or she has an investment.

To give another example—in recent years, it was discovered that a number of reporters were being paid by the government and thus weren't being objective when they reported on certain topics. They had become, in effect, public relations workers and were not being honest with audiences and with their colleagues.

Journalists may face a different problem when reporting about events that cast a negative view on advertisers who spend a great deal of money in the newspaper or television station that employs them. This problem is often faced by news editors, who have to decide whether to run a big story that they know one of their important advertisers doesn't want them to run. Some editors deal with negative stories about such advertisers by burying them in newspapers or in news shows by just mentioning them in passing.

Journalists often face ethical dilemmas. Those who get information from people about some case being tried in the courts have often refused to give this information to prosecutors or even to reveal who gave them the information. Many journalists have spent time in jail for refusing to hand this kind of information over. That is because they have given their word to their informants that they wouldn't hand the information over or reveal who gave it to them. The notes a journalist has taken, for example, are considered private and privileged. The same applies to footage shot by television journalists in interviewing people for news programs.

Ideological and financial matters also generate ethical problems for journalists. The news editors at newspapers and radio and television stations have to decide what stories to run from all the stories they could run. Is a story about a murder-suicide more important than a story about a speech by a senator or congressperson? And how should that speech be characterized? What should be emphasized and what neglected? In many cases, ideological matters may be even more important than financial ones. Political partisanship often colors what stories are run and the perspective the reporter takes.

Newspapers and radio and television stations are generally owned nowadays by giant corporations, which have their own political agendas.

THE RUPERT MURDOCH SCANDAL

Rupert Murdoch is a press tycoon whose News Corporation owns many important newspapers, such as the *Wall Street Journal* and the *New York Post*; the Fox News network in the United States; and the *Sun*, the *Times of London*, the *Sunday Times*, and—until he shut it down in early July 2011—the *News of the World* in Britain. In order to get scoops and sell more newspapers, people who worked for *News of the World* illegally hacked into thousands of voice mails. Murdoch's activities were exposed by a rival newspaper in Britain, the *Guardian*. As a result of the scandal, Murdoch abandoned efforts to purchase full control of British Sky Broadcasting, which would have been very lucrative.

Investigations into News Corporation's activities led to the resignation of several high-ranking officers at Scotland Yard who were too close to Murdoch, and the arrest of a number of executives of News Corporation. Scandals like this should alert us to the dangerous power of people like Murdoch who control many newspapers and other media outlets, for they have a great deal of political influence.

It has been suggested that Murdoch and his News Corporation played an important role in helping the Conservative Party win the most recent election in Britain and get David Cameron chosen as prime minister. One of Cameron's first guests after he became prime minister was Rupert Murdoch. Now investigators in the United States are trying to find out whether Murdoch's employees hacked into the phones of victims of the 9/11 terrorist attack in New York.

ETHICS AND ADVERTISING 1: SELLING CANCER

Media artists (in advertising they are often called *creatives*) face ethical problems of all sorts. For example, think of the dilemma copywriters and art directors face in advertising agencies that have tobacco accounts. These artists and copywriters are asked to use their talents to sell a product, such as chewing tobacco, that medical evidence has proven leads to users of these products being stricken with illnesses or even cancer. It may be legal to purchase tobacco products, but for copywriters and artists it is not moral, I would suggest, to use their literary and artistic skills to convince people to purchase any tobacco product.

In other cases, copywriters are asked to sell products that don't work (such as diet remedies), aren't good for people (certain foods, chewing tobacco, and so on), or are dangerous (certain sport utility vehicles). On the other hand, people who work in advertising agencies often have families to support, and they may feel that they cannot put their job or the welfare of their families at risk. Advertising executives often argue that they are only providing people with information and it is up to each individual to decide what to do with the information the advertising agency has provided. Others say, less convincingly, "if we don't do tobacco ads, some other agency will, so we'll do these ads even though we really don't want to do them." There are, of course, some agencies that refuse to handle these kinds of accounts—especially tobacco accounts—which, I would argue, is the moral thing to do.

ETHICS AND ADVERTISING 2: PORTRAYAL OF WOMEN

Advertising agencies (and the companies that employ them) have frequently been attacked for the way they portray women in print advertisements and commercials. The overwhelming number of female models we see in the glossy advertisements in magazines and newspaper pages are unusual physical specimens, who look as if they are anorexic or close to being so. The images of these models give women the notion that they must be slender if they are to be glamorous and beautiful. These models also perpetrate the notion that women should define themselves as sex objects to be gazed at and lusted after by men and not as active, forceful individuals. Women are frequently portrayed in narrative texts as victims who are saved by male heroes, though in recent years strong women have been featured in many media texts.

As Anthony J. Cortese writes in *Provocateur: Images of Women and Minorities in Advertising*:

> Attraction is both socially constructed and biologically shaped to be an instantaneous decision. Whether a female is attracted to a male or vice versa is based on unconscious biological signals of sexual interest. Just as female animals are attracted to power and exhibitions of strength in males of the same species as signs of health and fertility, human females

are drawn toward displays of masculine power and strength . . . For females, a small waist . . . and a high-pitched voice are signs of vulnerability that appeal to a male's self-identification, through cultural transmission, as a protector.

Large pupils are sexually appealing and this dilation occurs unconsciously during arousal . . . Youth is also a sign of health and sex appeal . . . Women use foundation makeup to hide small wrinkles, because eliminating any signs of aging contributes toward a more desirable and attractive image. Skin tones are warmed up in order to project a healthy sexual glow.

An exaggerated leg length appears to be more adult and, therefore, more sexual . . . Hair grooming is also an important component of attraction and gender display . . . A smile symbolizes approval or attraction . . . Unconscious blushing is considered to be very sexual . . . How female breasts are displayed is a key part of sexual attraction. The cleavage area between the breasts is perhaps the epicenter and stimulation of interest. In fact, breast cleavage and the cleavage of the buttocks are considered to be very sexual. In truth, there is a great similarity between the appearance of the two types of cleavage. (1999:21, 22)

Cortese points out that our notions of what makes a woman beautiful are culturally and socially determined, though he reminds us that there is also a biological component to sexual attraction.

At different times through history, our notions of what makes a woman beautiful have changed; at one time we liked curvaceous and full-bodied women, but in recent years we have favored very slim, almost boyish-looking women. Attitudes about what makes a woman beautiful are also connected to socio-economic class, ethnicity, and a number of other variables. We just look at the average newspaper or magazine advertisement for two seconds, but those two seconds are enough, some theorists suggest, to register on our psyches and affect our behavior.

This exploitation of the female body has been attacked by feminist critics, social scientists, and others as having negative effects on both men and women. Men and women both are given unreal images of what an ideal woman is like—young, long-legged, glamorous, wasp-waisted, satin-skinned, and inflamed with sexual desire that is generally shown by their body language, display of cleavage, and facial expressions. In recent years, advertisers find that they can use extreme close-ups and show only parts of women to create the sexual tension and excitement they seek to generate, a device known technically as *synecdoche* (a part stands for the whole or vice versa).

ETHICS IN ADVERTISING 3:
POLITICAL COMMERCIALS

Over the past fifty years, the practice of running attack ads in political campaigns has grown considerably. In these highly negative commercials and print advertisements, candidates are attacked for something they supposedly did, something they said, some policy they supported, or some vote they cast. That is, the ad doesn't say what the politician responsible for it believes in but attacks his or her opponent. In many cases, the makers of these attack ads play fast and loose with facts and the truth for political advantage. The general public always says, when polled, that they hate these ads, but attack ads, especially commercials, have been shown to be very effective.

As Montague Kern writes in *30-Second Politics: Political Advertising in the Eighties* (1989:208)

> By 1986 negative advertising, which focuses on the opponent rather than a candidate in terms of both issues and character, was . . . considered to be a necessary evil by representatives of all the schools [of media consultants].

And negative advertising in attack commercials is with us today more than ever.

The danger in using these negative attack ads is that politicians who use them are thought to be mean-spirited and nasty; the danger in not responding to such ads with negative attack ads of one's own is that candidates allow these attack ads to give voters a picture of themselves that they can't live down. Politicians who use attack ads often find surrogates to do the attacking, and the same applies to politicians who respond to attack ads with their own counter-attack ads.

Those who are attacked in these negative political ads have learned to go on the offensive immediately, before the attack ad can take hold of people's imagination. The counter-attack ads often attack the credibility and truthfulness of the politician behind the attack ad. What this means is that political campaigns have become very negative in recent years, with politicians and parties attacking and counter-attacking one another.

Political scientists have suggested that one of the reasons politicians use attack ads is that they want to get voters who generally vote for Democrats so fed up with the process of voting that they don't vote. This means that conservative politicians will do better because a very high percentage of their constituents tend to vote.

One of the most famous negative attack ads was one known as "Re-volving Door," which was broadcast during the 1988 presidential campaign and suggested that Dukakis, the Democratic candidate, was "soft on crime." The title of the ad was "The Dukakis Prison Furlough Program," and it was made by Frankenberry, Laughlin, and Constable. The ad shows prison guards walking along a barbed wire fence. It then shows a close-up shot of prisoners going through a revolving door with a caption superimposed on the screen: "268 escaped." Next came a medium shot of the prisoners going through the revolving door. The next caption read: "And many are still at large." Then there was a dissolve to a wide shot of the prison wall, the guards, and the guard tower.

As the images of the prisoners in the revolving door and the guards show on the screen, the announcer in a voice-over read a dialogue that attacked Dukakis:

> As Governor, Michael Dukakis vetoed mandatory sentence for drug dealers. He vetoed the death penalty. His "revolving door" prison policy gave weekend furloughs to first degree murderers not eligible for parole. While out, many committed other crimes, like kidnapping, rape. And many are still at large. Now Michael Dukakis says he wants to do for America what he's done for Massachusetts. America can't afford that risk.

Dukakis didn't respond immediately to this commercial and as a result found himself on the defensive during the rest of his campaign. He had allowed the Bush campaign to define Dukakis as soft on crime by using these very gripping and, it turned out, long-lasting images that stuck in people's minds.

The people who make these attack ads—the political consultants, the copywriters, the art directors, and all the others involved in these activities—must realize that their behavior can be construed as highly questionable from an ethical point of view. Perhaps they justify it by thinking "all's fair in love and war"—and defining political campaigns as part of war.

Or perhaps they think that it is so important to get their candidate elected that other matters, like whether an attack is fair, are not important. But this seems very close to arguing that the ends justify the means, which is a philosophical position that says "Anything goes." Such a position is counter to the American belief that the means are implicitly tied to their ends and using immoral means for good ends corrupts those good ends.

A Questionable Republican TV Commercial

One of the most notorious television commercials of the 2000 presidential campaign was run by Republicans and referred to a drug prescription plan offered by the Democrats. In the commercial, there was one still, just on the screen for a brief moment, that used the word "RATS."

Some media critics have suggested that the Republicans did this to use **subliminal** suggestion and to connect, in the minds of those who were exposed to these commercials, Democrats and rats. The people who made this commercial denied that this was their intent. A neurologist I asked about subliminal suggestion said he thought it had been proven to be effective.

Jeffrey Scheuer makes an important point about political advertising in his book *The Sound Bite Society: Television and the American Mind*. He writes:

> It is a truism of our media-dominated age that television has largely usurped the traditional role of political parties. Power flows to those who control (or can afford to buy access to) the airwaves. The gatekeepers are the arbiters of visibility, such as Ted Koppel and Larry King, and their corporate media-masters; party bosses have been replaced by pollsters, media advisers, and direct-mail consultants. Virtually all political actions and communications—not just political ads but also floor speeches by legislators, news conferences, debates, and party conventions—are

designed expressly for consumption as sound bites by a TV audience. (1999:29)

In his book Scheuer describes the degree to which conservative political forces dominate television and other media.

We "sell" politicians and presidents the way we sell laundry detergent, and I can't help but think that this development has had very negative consequences for the country—as shown, for instance, in the relatively small percentage of eligible voters who actually vote. When people don't vote in large numbers, small and highly disciplined minorities, often organized around a single issue, can have a great impact on the political process, far beyond what their numbers would suggest.

THE CITIZENS UNITED SUPREME COURT DECISION

The impact of the Citizens United decision of the Supreme Court is discussed by Kent Greenfield, a professor of law at Boston College. He writes in his article "How to Make the 'Citizens United' Decision Worse" (*Washington Post*, January 19, 2012, Opinion page), discussing the importance of **super PACS** (political action committees):

> *Citizens United v. Federal Election Commission* overturned long-standing campaign finance laws restricting corporate political expenditures, reasoning that the political speech of corporations was as important to the marketplace of ideas as the voices of human citizens. As is well known, denunciations of the opinion, which allowed groups to raise and spend unlimited amounts supporting or opposing candidates, were loud and widespread. President Obama even took the rare step of criticizing the court while delivering his *2010 State of the Union address*—while some of the justices sat before him. As the rise of *super PACs* has already shown in the Republican primaries, the coming presidential election will be swamped with cash, and our democracy will not be better for it.

In the Iowa caucus, a super PAC allied to Mitt Romney attacked Newt Gingrich, and the negative commercials put out by this super PAC led to Gingrich's defeat. Gingrich made an appeal to a wealthy friend, who sent $5 million to a super PAC allied to Gingrich, which it used to attack Romney in South Carolina. Romney, though ahead by double digits a few days before the primaries, lost to Gingrich, who received 40 percent of the votes compared to Romney's 28 percent. Gingrich's performance in the

Republican debates in South Carolina also helped his cause enormously. Nobody knows what impact these super PACs will have on our presidential elections, and elections at other levels as well, but many law professors and others involved in politics think the decision was a bad one that opens the door for corporations and wealthy individuals to have a major impact on American politics.

Media artists, we see, have tremendous power; their words, their images, the narratives they create, the songs they write have audiences that often number in the millions. The same, of course, applies to those who perform the works that media artists create. With this power comes a great responsibility—one that too many writers and artists (and all the others connected with creating and performing texts in the various media) do not, so it seems, want to accept.

GLOSSARY

Aberrant Decoding: When audiences decode, make sense of, or interpret texts in ways that differ from the ways the creators of these texts expect them to be decoded, we have aberrant decoding. Aberrant decoding is the rule, rather than the exception, when it comes to the mass media, according to the semiotician Umberto Eco.

Aesthetics: When applied to the media, aesthetics refers to the use of sound, lighting, music, camera work, and editing that have an emotional impact on audiences of mass-mediated texts.

Analog: This term is the opposite of digital and refers to technologies that permit a focus on relationships and similarities (the term analog is derived from the same Greek word as analogy). The watches we used to wear, with hour, minute, and second hands, were analogy devices. Digital devices are based on binary structures: on or off. They don't show you that it is fifteen minutes before three o'clock but that it is 2:45 PM.

Artist: For our purposes an artist is not only someone who does paintings or sculptures or plays musical instruments, but is anyone involved in the creation or performance of any kind of text—especially mass-mediated texts.

Attitudes: Social psychologists use the term to refer to a relatively enduring state of mind in a person about some phenomenon or aspect of experience. Attitudes usually are either positive or negative, have direction, and involve thoughts, feelings, and behaviors tied to these attitudes.

Audience: When we deal with audiences of the mass media, we mean people who watch a television program, listen to a radio program, or attend a film or some kind of artistic performance (symphony, rock band, etc.) The members of an audience may be together in one room or in many different places. In the case of television, we often have families in which each member of the family watches a different program from his or her own set. In technical terms, audiences are addressees who receive mediated texts sent by some addresser.

Broadcasting: We use the term *broadcasting* to deal with texts that are made available over wide areas by using radio or television signals. Broadcasting differs from other forms of distributing texts such as cable casting, which uses cables, and satellite transmission, which requires "dishes" to capture signals sent by the satellites.

Class: A class, from a linguistic standpoint, is any group of things that has something in common. We use the term *class* to refer to social classes, or, more literally, socio-economic classes: groups of people who differ in terms of income and lifestyle. Marxist theorists argue that there is a ruling class which shapes the ideas of the proletariat, the working classes.

Clutter: When viewers are exposed to numerous commercials, one after the other, they get mixed up about what they have seen and often can't differentiate the commercials from one another. Clutter can be seen as a kind of information overload for commercials and advertising.

Codes: By *codes* we mean systems of symbols (letters, words, sounds, or whatever) that generate meaning. Language is a code. It uses combinations of letters that we call words to mean certain things. The relation between the word and the thing the word stands for is arbitrary, based on convention. In some cases, the term *code* is used to describe hidden meanings and disguised communications.

Cognitive Dissonance: *Dissonance* refers to sounds that clash with one another, are unpleasant, and cause pain and anxiety in listeners. According to social scientists, people wish to avoid ideas that challenge the ones they hold—ideas which create conflict and other disagreeable feelings. Cognitive dissonance refers, then, to ideas that conflict with ones people hold and generate psychological anxiety and displeasure. People seek to avoid cognitive dissonance.

Communication: For our purposes, communication is a process that involves the transmission of messages from senders to receivers. We often make a distinction between communication using language (verbal communication) and communication using facial expressions, body language, and other means (non-verbal communication).

Communications: Communications, the plural of the term *communication*, refers to messages, to what is communicated, in contrast to the process of communication, just described.

Concept: We will understand *concept* to be a general idea or notion that explains or helps us understand some phenomenon or phenomena. For example, Freud uses the concepts "id," "ego," and "superego" in his psychoanalytic theory to explain the way the human psyche operates.

Consolidation: This refers to the fact that most of the media companies are now controlled by an increasingly smaller number of corporations.

Critical Research: Critical approaches to media are essentially ideological; they focus on the social, economic, and political dimensions of the mass media and the way they are used by organizations and others allegedly to maintain the status quo rather than to enhance equality. This contrasts with administrative research.

Cultural Homogenization: *Cultural homogenization* is used to suggest that the media of mass communication are destroying Third World cultures and regional cultures in specific countries, leading to a cultural sameness, standardization, or homogenization.

Cultural Imperialism (also Media Imperialism): Supporters of this theory, sometimes known as "Coca-colonization," argue that the flow of media products (such as films and television programs) and popular culture from the United States and a few other capitalist countries in Western Europe to the Third World is colonizing people in these countries. Along with these texts and popular culture, it is alleged that values and beliefs (and, most importantly, bourgeois capitalist ideology) are also being transmitted, leading to the domination of people in Third World countries.

Culture: From an anthropological perspective, culture involves the transmission from generation to generation of specific ideas, arts, customary beliefs, ways of living, behavior patterns, institutions, and values. When the term *culture* is applied to the arts, it generally is used to specify "elite" kinds of art works, such as operas, poetry, classical music, serious novels, and so on.

Demographics: *Demographics* refers to similarities found in selected groups of people in terms of characteristics such as religion, gender, social class, ethnicity, occupation, place of residence, and age.

Digital: "Digital systems," as Peter Lunenfeld explains things, "translate all input into binary structures of 0s and 1s, which can then be stored, transferred, or manipulated at the level of numbers or "digits" (so called because etymologically, the word descends from the digits on our hand with which we count out those numbers)."

Ethnocentrism: This refers to the notion that some members of ethnic groups have that their ideas, their customs, their beliefs, and their way of life are better that those held by other ethnic groups.

Expressive Theories of Art: The expressive theory of art holds that the principle function of art is to express the feelings, beliefs, and emotions of the creator of texts and works of art.

Facebook: The most important social media site with an estimated 950 million users in 2012 and growing rapidly. It is one of the most valuable media companies in the world.

Focal Points: *Focal points* refer to the five general topics or subject areas we can concentrate upon in dealing with mass communication. These are: the work of art or text, the artist, the audience, America or the society, and the media.

Formula: In narrative theory, a formulaic text refers to a text with conventional characters and actions that audiences are familiar with. Genre texts, such as westerns, sitcoms, detective stories, science fiction adventures, and romances are highly formulaic.

Functional: In sociological theory, the term *functional* refers, broadly speaking, to the contribution an institution makes to the maintenance of society. Something is functional if it helps maintain the system in which it is found.

Functional Alternative: The term *functional alternative* refers to an entity that can be used as an alternative to something—that is, it takes the place of something else. For example, professional football games can be seen as a functional alternative to religious services on Sundays.

Gatekeepers: In the news world, gatekeepers are editors and others who determine what stories are used in newspapers or news programs on the electronic media. Literally speaking, gatekeepers stand at some gate and determine who or what goes through it. Thus, these gatekeepers determine what news stories we get, but in a broader sense, gatekeepers decide what programs and films we see, what songs we hear, and so on.

Gender: *Gender* refers to the sexual category of an individual, masculine or feminine, and to behavioral traits customarily connected with each category.

Genre: *Genre* is a French term that means "kind" or "class." In this book it refers to the kind of formulaic texts found in the mass media: soap operas, news shows, sport programs, horror shows, detective programs, and so on.

Google: Google, possibly named after a comic strip character, "Barney Google," is the dominant search engine in the United States and many other countries. Google also has a popular e-mail program, Gmail; a site for storing images, Picasa; and a social networking site, Google+, that it uses to compete with Facebook.

Hegemonial Ideological Domination: This refers to the way the ruling classes dominate the thinking of the masses, who cannot locate the source of their beliefs because they are so widespread as to seem to be "that which goes without saying." It is a form of domination more subtle than ideological manipulation or indoctrination.

Hypodermic Needle Theory of Media: The hypodermic theory, generally discredited now, holds that all members of an audience "read" a text the same way and get the same things out of it. Media are seen as like a hypodermic needle, injecting their message to one and all. Some theorists talk about interpretive communities, which suggests that groups of people can get similar messages from texts.

Hypothesis: A hypothesis is a notion that is assumed to be true for the purposes of discussion or argument or further investigation. It is, in a sense, a guess or supposition that is used to explain some phenomenon.

Ideology: An ideology can be understood to mean a logically coherent, integrated explanation of social, economic, and political matters that helps establish the goals and direct the actions of some group or political entity. People act (and vote or don't vote) on the basis of some ideology they hold, even though they may not have articulated it or thought much about it.

Image: Defining images is extremely complicated. I define an image as a combination of signs and symbols—what we find when we look at a photograph, a film still, a shot of a television screen, a print advertisement, or just about anything. The term is also used for mental as well as physical representations of things. Images often have powerful emotional effects on people and historical significance, as my discussion of 9/11 demonstrates. Two books that deal with images in some detail are Kiku Adato's *Picture Perfect: The Art and Artifice of Public Image Making* and Paul Messaris's *Visual Literacy: Image, Mind and Reality*.

Incidental Learning: This is the kind of learning we do outside of the classroom, when we learn from experiences we have, of one kind or another. Much of the learning we do in the course of our lives is incidental.

Intertextuality: The term involves alluding to, imitating, adapting, and modifying previously created texts, styles of expression, or genres.

Latent Functions: Latent functions are understood to be hidden, unrecognized, and unintended functions of some activity, entity, or institution. They are contrasted by social scientists with manifest functions, which are recognized and intended.

Lifestyles: This term, which means literally style of life, refers loosely to the way people live—to the decisions they make about such matters as how to decorate their apartment or home (and where it is located), what kind of car to drive, what kind of clothes to wear, what kinds of foods to eat (and which restaurants to dine at), where to go for vacations, and so on.

Limited Effects (of Media): Some mass communication theorists argue that the mass media have limited or relatively minor effects in the scheme of things. They cite research which shows, for example, that effects from media don't tend to be long lasting and argue that the notion that mass media have strong effects has not been demonstrated. This notion is no longer as prominent as it once was.

Manifest Functions: The manifest functions of some activity, entity or institution are those that are obvious and intended. Manifest functions contrast with latent functions, which are hidden and unintended. The manifest function of television viewing may be for entertainment while the latent function might involve becoming more materialistic.

Mass: For our purposes, *mass* as in "mass communication" refers to a large number of people who are the audience for some communication. There is considerable disagreement about how to understand the term *mass*. In earlier years, theorists said a "mass" is comprised of individuals who are heterogeneous, do not know one another, are alienated, and do not have a leader. Others attack these notions, saying they are not based on fact or evidence but on speculative theories that have not been verified.

Mass Communication: *Mass communication* refers to the transfer of messages, information, texts, and so forth for a sender of some kind to a large number of people, a mass audience. This transfer is done through the technologies of the mass media—newspapers, magazines, television programs, films, records, computers and CD-ROMs, and so on. The sender often is a person in some large media organization, the messages are public, and the audience tends to be large and varied.

Mass Culture: This term refers to theories, popular in the 1950s, about the impact of the mass media on societies. Some mass culture theorists argued that the media are dehumanizing us and turning us into kitsch loving cretins, so-called mass men and mass women, who are ripe targets for totalitarian belief systems in homogenized cultures. This theory is not very well accepted now.

Mass-mediated violence: This term refers to violent acts found in mass-mediated texts. The acts are found in media such as films, television programs, comic strips and video games.

Media Aesthetics: When applied to the media, aesthetics involves the way technical matters such lighting, sound, music, kinds of shots and camera work, editing, and related matters in texts affect the way members of audiences react to these texts.

Media Violence: According to Gerbner and Signorelli, *media violence* can be described as "the depiction of overt physical action that hurts or kills or threatens to do so" (1988:xi). In my discussion of violence, I offer varying kinds and aspects of violence that have to be considered in dealing with media portrayals of violence.

Medium (plural: media): A *medium* is understood to be a means of delivering messages, information, and texts to audiences. There are different ways of classifying the media. One of the most common is print (newspapers, magazines, books, billboards), electronic (radio, television, computers, CD-ROMS), and photographic (photographs, films, videos). But there are other ways of classifying them that are described in this book.

Metaphor: A metaphor is a figure of speech which conveys meaning by analogy. We must realize that metaphors are not confined to poetry and literary works but, according to some linguists, are the fundamental way in which we make sense of things and find meaning in the world. A simile is a weak form of metaphor that uses either "like" or "as" in making an analogy. Metaphors can be communicated by visual images; they aren't dependent upon language.

Mimetic Theory of Art: This theory, dating from Aristotle's time, suggests that art is an *imitation* of reality. Art, then, is a "mirror" of life, which explains why we can find so much about society and people in texts. Some theorists claim that art is not a mirror but a lamp that projects the reality of the creators behind texts.

Model: In the social sciences, models are abstract representations that show how some phenomenon functions. Theories are typically expressed in language, but models tend to be represented graphically and often use statistics or mathematics. Denis McQuail and Sven Windahl define *model* in *Communication Models for the Study of Mass Communication* as (1993:2) "a consciously simplified description in graphic form of a piece of reality. A model seeks to show the main elements of any structure or process and the relationships between these elements."

Modernism: *Modernism* is the term is used by critics to deal with the arts (architecture, literature, visual arts, dance, music, and so on) in the period from approximately the turn of the twentieth century until the around the sixties. The modernists rejected narrative structure for simultaneity and montage and explored the paradoxical nature of reality. Some of the more important modernists were T. S. Eliot, Franz Kafka, James Joyce, Pablo Picasso, Henri Matisse, and Eugene Ionesco. The period after Modernism is called Postmodernism.

Multi-tasking: This terms deals with the way many people do a number of things at the same time, such as listening to the radio while writing on a computer or watching television and also sending text messages to friends. Numerous research studies have shown that when people multi-task, they don't do any of their tasks as well as they would if they just did the single task.

Narrative: A narrative is a story—a sequence of events that deal with the activities of heroes, villains and all kinds of other people. There are numerous theories about what narratives are and how they work. The Russian theorist Vladimir Propp's theory is discussed in some detail in this book. A syntagmatic analysis of narratives tells you what happens in a story. A paradigmatic analysis tells you what the story means.

Narrowcasting: A medium like radio, which has stations that tend to focus on discrete groups of people, is said to be narrowcasting. This contrasts with broadcasting media, like television, which try to reach as large an audience as possible.

Non-verbal Communication: A great deal of communication comes from non-verbal phenomena. Our body language, facial expressions, style of dress, style of wearing our hair, and so on are examples of our communicating feelings and attitudes (and a sense of who we are) without using words. Even in conversations, a great deal of the communication comes from our body language.

Objective Theory of Art: This theory suggests that artists create their own realities in their works of art. Art, then, projects its own reality and we enjoy film, novels, and others kinds of art because we can enter into the world projected by the artist.

Para-social Relationships: People who watch a great deal of television develop the illusory belief that they actually know the actors and actresses they see all the time. These feelings they have lead to what we describe as para-social relationships.

Popular: The term *popular* is one of the most difficult terms used in discourse about the arts and the media. Literally speaking, *popular* means appealing to large numbers of people. It comes from the Latin term *popularis*, "of the people."

Popular Culture: *Popular culture* is a term that identifies certain kinds of mass-mediated texts that appeal to large number of people—that is, that are popular. But mass communication theorists often identify (or should we say confuse) "popular" with "mass" and suggest that if something is popular, it must, by necessity, be of poor quality, appealing to the mythical "lowest common denominator." Popular culture is generally held to be the opposite of "elite" culture—arts which require certain levels of sophistication and refinement to be appreciated, such as ballet, opera, poetry, classical music, and so on. Postmodern theorists reject this popular culture/elite culture polarity.

Pornography: This term is almost impossible to define. Generally speaking, pornography is held to be material that is sexually explicit and is meant to arouse sexual excitement. The root of the term, *porne*, means "prostitute" in Greek.

Postmodernism: We Americans are, some theorists suggest, living in a postmodern era—and have been doing this since the 1960s, more or less. Literally speaking, the term *postmodernism* (sometimes written as post-modernism) means "after modernism," the period from approximately 1900 to the 1960s. Postmodernism is characterized by, as a leading theorist of the subject, Jean-François Lyotard, put it, "incredulity toward metanarratives" (*The Postmodern_Condition: A Report on Knowledge*, 1984:xxiv). By this he means that the old philosophical belief systems or metanarratives that had helped people order their lives and societies no longer are accepted or given credulity. This leads to a period in which, some have suggested, anything goes.

Power: Power is, politically speaking, the ability to implement one's wishes as far as policy in some entity is concerned. When we use the term to discuss texts, we use it to describe their ability to have an emotional impact upon people—readers, viewers, or listeners—and sometimes to have social, economic and political consequences.

Pragmatic Theory of Art: This theory of arts focuses on the functional quality of art—its ability to do things to people, such as persuade them to purchase products and services they see in commercials. This theory is different from objective, expressive, and mimetic theories of art. The pragmatic theory of art argues that art should do something and have consequences that are desirable, such as teaching people or, in some cases, indoctrinating them.

Print-on-Demand: As a result of recent technological developments in printing, it is now possible to publish books using computers and printers that can print a book and its cover in a short period of time. Now, some books are being published only as print on demand books, by companies like www.Lulu.com, which will publish a book when someone pays the cost of printing the book and mailing it.

Product Placement: Advertising agencies now pay to have products they wish to advertise used or "placed" in television programs and movies as a way of getting to viewers of these texts.

Psychographics: In marketing, *psychographics* is used to deal with groups of people who have similar psychological characteristics or profiles. The VALS (Values and Life Styles) typology is an example of a marketing system based on psychographics. Psychographics differs from demographics that marketers use to focus upon social and economic characteristics that some people have in common.

Public: Instead of the term *popular culture*, some theorists use phrases such as "the public arts" or "public communication" to avoid the negative connotations of the terms *mass* and *popular*. A public is a group of people, a community. We can contrast public acts—those meant to be known to the community—with private acts, which are not meant to be known to others. But private acts often have social and public consequences.

Ratings: Ratings refer to the percentage of people or households in an area who are tuned in to a specific program, station, or network. Ratings conventionally drop the percentage sign and just use numbers. If 250 families out of a sample of 1000 families are listing to a given program, it will be given a rating of 25.

Reader Response Theory (also Reception Theory): Reader response theory suggests that readers (a term used very broadly to cover people who read books, watch television programs, go to films, and listen to texts on the radio) play an important role in the realization of texts. Texts, then, function as sites for the creation of meaning by readers, and different readers interpret a given text differently. How differently is a matter of considerable conjecture.

Reality Television: These television shows are not scripted and do not employ actors and actresses, but rely on "ordinary individuals" who are placed in difficult situations, such as *Survivor*, or compete in singing and dancing shows, such as *Dancing With Stars*. Although they are not scripted, the editing is used to generate drama and provide a narrative line to the shows.

Reinforcement: In psychoanalytic theory, individuals seek to avoid cognitive dissonance—ideas that conflict with their belief systems—and search for reinforcement—theories that support their values and beliefs and thus make them feel comfortable. We can see this desire for reinforcement in the choices people make about which programs to watch on television. They generally watch programs that reinforce their values and beliefs.

Relativism: In philosophical thought, relativism refers to the belief that truth is relative and not absolute, that there are no universally accepted objective standards. In ethical thought, relativism suggests there are no absolutes of morality and ethics. Thus, for relativists, different cultures have different ways of living and practices that are as valid as any others. That is, morality and ethical behavior are relative to particular groups and cannot be generalized to include all human beings. This contrasts with the notion that there are ethical absolutes or universals which can and should be applied to everyone.

Responsive Chord: This theory suggests that the best way to understand the impact of the media is to recognize that the primary function of the media is to provide texts that resonate with the knowledge base of audiences and use it to generate certain responses. This theory suggests we are like tuning forks that resonate when hit the right way.

Semiotics: Literally, *semiotics* means "the science of signs." *Semeion* is the Greek term for sign. A sign is anything that can be used to stand for anything else. According to C. S. Peirce, one of the founders of the science, a sign "is something which stands to somebody for something in some respect or capacity."

Shares: Using television as our topic, this term refers to the percentage of people or households tuned into a program, station, or network with sets in use. Because there are always more television sets in a market than the number of sets being used, the share figure is always higher than the rating. If 250 families are listening to a program in a market of 1000 families, but only 750 families are watching television, the share will be 33.

Sign: In semiotic theory, *a sign* is a combination of a *signifier* (sound, object) and a *signified* (concept). The relationship between the signifier and signified is arbitrary, based on convention. Signs are anything that can be used to stand for something else.

Socio-economic Class: *Socio-economic class* is a categorization of people according to their incomes and related social status and lifestyles. In Marxist thought, there are ruling classes that shape the consciousness of the working classes, and history is, in essence, a record of class conflict.

Socialization: *Socialization* refers to the processes by which societies teach individuals how to behave: what rules to obey, what roles to assume, and what values to hold. Socialization was traditionally done by the family, by educators, by religious figures, and by peers. The mass media seem to have usurped this function to a considerable degree nowadays, with consequences that are not always positive. Anthropologists use the term *enculturation* for the process by which an individual is taught cultural values and practices.

Social Media: Sites like Facebook, LinkedIn, and Twitter are described as social media—using the web and mobile phones to facilitate social interaction. They allow people to send words, images, and videos to others and interact with them.

Spiral of Silence: This theory, developed by a German scholar, Elizabeth Noelle-Neuman, argues that people who hold views that they think are not widely held (whether this is correct or not) tend to keep quiet while those who hold views that they believe are widely accepted tend to state their views strongly, leading to a spiral in which certain views tend to be suppressed while others gain increased prominence.

Stereotypes: Commonly held, simplistic and inaccurate group portraits of categories of people are called *stereotypes*. These stereotypes can have a positive, negative, or mixed viewpoint, but they usually are negative. Stereotyping always involves making gross over-generalizations. (For instance, all Mexicans, Chinese, Jews, African Americans, WASPs, Muslims, Americans, lawyers, doctors, professors, and so on are held to have certain characteristics.)

Subculture: Subcultures are cultural subgroups whose religious practices, ethnicity, sexual orientation, beliefs, values, behaviors, and lifestyles vary in certain ways from those of the dominant, mainstream culture. In any complex society, it is normal to have a considerable number of subcultures.

Subliminal: This theory suggests that images shown on television or film screens for only a small fraction of a second, and generally not consciously recognized by viewers, can have effects on people exposed to these images.

Super PACs: A Supreme Court decision made it possible for corporations, unions, or any group to spend money in behalf of a political candidate they like. They cannot coordinate with the candidate, but since Super PACs are run by political operatives who used to work for the candidate or support the candidate, the inability to coordinate with a political candidate is irrelevant.

Text: The term *text* is used in academic discourse to refer to, broadly speaking, any work of art in any medium. The term *text* is used by critics as a convenience so they don't have to name a given work all the time or use various synonyms. There are problems involved in deciding what the text is when we deal with serial texts, such as soap operas or comics.

Texting: Some teenagers now send 100 or more text messages a day to their friends. This phenomenon is of great interest to psychologists and other media scholars who are concerned about the effects of all this texting on the individuals who are doing the texting and upon society at large.

Theory: A *theory*, as the term is conventionally understood, is expressed in language and systematically and logically attempts to explain and predict phenomena being studied. Theories differ from concepts, which define phenomena that are being studied, and from models, which are abstract, usually graphic in nature, and explicit about what is being studied.

Time Shifting: Using various kinds of recording devices, we can now record shows when they are aired but view them whenever we want—a practice known as time shifting.

Typology: A typology is a classification scheme or system of categories that someone uses to make sense of some phenomena. Classification schemes are important because the way we classify things affects the way we think about them.

Twitter: Twitter is a micro-blogging site that allows members to send 140-word "tweets" or messages. Some sites now allow people to add images to their tweets. Twitter users develop lists of "followers" who get their tweets.

Ur Text: An Ur Text is a template for other texts, a foundational model from which other texts are derived.

Uses and Gratifications: The uses and gratification theory argues that researchers should pay attention to the way members of audiences use the media (or certain texts or genres of texts) and the gratifications they get from their use of these texts and the media. Uses and gratification researchers focus, then, on how audiences use the media and not how the media affect audiences.

Values: Values are understood to be abstract and general beliefs or judgments about what is right and wrong, what is good and bad, that have implications for individual behavior and for social, cultural, and political entities. There are a number of problems with values from a philosophical point of view. First, how does one determine which values are correct or good and which aren't? That is, how do we justify values? Are values objective or subjective? Second, what happens when there is a conflict between groups, each of which holds a central value that conflicts with that of a different group?

Video Games: Video games are electronic games that are interactive—that is, they allow players to participate in the action of the game. They are played, generally speaking, on specialized consoles that have very powerful graphic and sound capabilities, though many video games can also be played on computers.

Violence (Mass-Mediated): *See* media violence.

Vicious Cycles: This theory argues that if young children are exposed to content on television that is too adult and too stressful, their development is impaired. They become locked into a vicious cycle in which, because they are stunted in their development, they become alienated from others and cannot have successful relationships with others. They then end up relying on television, the medium that had such a terrible effect on them, to amuse and entertain themselves.

Youth Culture: Youth cultures are subcultures formed by young people around some area of interest, usually connected with leisure and entertainment, such as, for example, surfing, skateboarding, rock music, or some aspect of computers: games, hacking, and so on. Typically youth cultures adopt distinctive ways of dressing and develop institutions that cater to their needs.

SELECTED BIBLIOGRAPHY

Abrams, M. H. 1958. *The Mirror and the Lamp: Romantic Theory and the Critical Tradition*. New York: W. W. Norton.

Adatto, Kiku. 1993. *Picture Perfect: The Art and Artifice of Public Image Making*. New York: Basic Books.

Adorno, Theodor W. 1967. *Prisms* (Transl. by Samuel and Sherry Weber). Cambridge, MA: MIT Press.

Adorno, Theodor W. 1991. *The Culture Industry: Selected Essays on Mass Culture*. London: Routledge.

Aronowitz, Stanley. 1992. *The Politics of Identity*. New York: Routledge.

Aronowitz, Stanley. 1993. *Dead Artists, Live Theories and Other Cultural Problems*. New York: Routledge.

Armstrong, Nancy. 1987. *Desire and Domestic Fiction: A Political History of the Novel*. New York: Oxford University Press.

Bakhtin, M. M. 1981. *The Dialogic Imagination*. (Transl. by Caryl Emerson and Michael Holquist, ed. by Michael Holmquist). Austin, TX: University of Texas Press.

Bakhtin, Mikhail. 1984. *Rabelais and His World* (Transl. by Helene Iswolsky). Bloomington, IN: Indiana University Press.

Bal, Mieke. 1985. *Narratology: Introduction to the Theory of Narrative*. Toronto: University of Toronto Press.

Barker, Martin, and Ann Beezer. 1992. *Reading into Cultural Studies*. London: Routledge.

Barthes, Roland. 1970. *Writing Degree Zero and Elements of Semiology* (Transl. by Annette Lavers and Colin Smith). Boston: Beacon Press.

Barthes, Roland. 1972. *Mythologies* (Transl. by Annette Lavers). New York: Hill and Wang.

Barthes, Roland. 1977. *Empire of Signs* (Transl. by Stephen Heath). New York: Hill & Wang.

Barthes, Roland. 1988. *The Semiotic Challenge* (Transl. by Richard Howard). New York: Hill & Wang.

Bateson, Gregory. 1972. *Steps to an Ecology of Mind*. New York: Ballantine Books.

Baudrillard, Jean. 1983. *Simulations* (Transl. by Paul Foss et al.). New York: Semiotext.

Baudrillard, Jean. 1996. *The System of Objects* (Transl. by James Benedict). London: Verso.

Beilharz, Peter, Gillian Robinson, and John Rundell. 1992. *Between Totalitarianism and Postmodernity: A Thesis Eleven Reader*. Cambridge, MA: MIT Press.

Bennett, Tony, and Janet Woollacott. 1987. *Bond and Beyond: The Political Career of a Popular Hero*. New York: Methuen.

Berger, Arthur Asa. 1973. *The Comic-Stripped American*. New York: Walker & Co.

Berger, Arthur Asa. 1975. *The TV-Guided American*. New York: Walker & Co.

Berger, Arthur Asa. 1984. *Signs in Contemporary Culture: An Introduction to Semiotics*. New York: Annenberg-Longman.

Berger, Arthur Asa. 1989. *Seeing Is Believing: An Introduction to Visual Communication*. Mountain View, CA: Mayfield Publishing Co.

Berger, Arthur Asa. 1990. *Agitpop: Political Culture and Communication Theory*. New Brunswick, NJ: Transaction.

Berger, Arthur Asa. 1991. *Media USA*. 2nd Edition. New York: Longman.

Berger, Arthur Asa. 1993. *An Anatomy of Humor*. New Brunswick, NJ: Transaction.

Berger, Arthur Asa. 1994. *Blind Men and Elephants: Perspectives on Humor*. New Brunswick, NJ: Transaction.

Berger, Arthur Asa. 1994. *Cultural Criticism: A Primer of Key Concepts*. Thousand Oaks, CA: Sage Publications.

Berger, Arthur Asa. 1997. *Postmortem for a Postmodernist*. Walnut Creek, CA: AltaMira Press.

Berger, Arthur Asa (ed.). 1998. *The Postmodern Presence: Readings on Postmodernism in American Culture and Society*. Walnut Creek, CA: AltaMira Press.

Berger, Arthur Asa. 1998. *Media Analysis Techniques* (2nd ed.). Thousand Oaks, CA: Sage Publications.

Berger, Arthur Asa. 2000. *Ads, Fads and Consumer Culture*. Boulder, CO: Rowman & Littlefield.

Berger, Arthur Asa. 2001. *Jewish Jesters*. Cresskill, NJ: Hampton Press.

Berger, Arthur Asa. 2002. *The Mass Comm Murders: Five Media Theorists Self-Destruct*. Lanham, MD: Rowman & Littlefield.

Berger, Arthur Asa. 2002. *Video Games: A Popular Culture Phenomenon*. New Brunswick, NJ: Transaction Publishers.

Berman, Marshall. 1982. *All That Is Solid Melts into Air: The Experience of Modernity*. New York: Touchstone Books.

Best, Steven, and Douglas Kellner. 1991. *Postmodern Theory*. New York: Guilford.

Bettelheim, Bruno. 1976. *The Uses of Enchantment*. New York: Knopf.

Blau, Herbert. 1992. *To All Appearances: Ideology and Performance*. London: Routledge.

Bogart, Leo. 1985. *Polls and the Awareness of Public Opinion*. New Brunswick, NJ: Transaction.

Bolter, Jay David, and Richard Grusin. 2000. *Remediation: Understanding New Media*. Cambridge, MA: MIT Press.

Boorstin, Daniel. 1975. *The Image: A Guide to Pseudo-Events in America*. New York: Atheneum

Bowlby, Rachel. 1993. *Shopping with Freud: Items on Consumerism, Feminism and Psychoanalysis*. London: Routledge.

Brenkman. 1993. *Straight Male Modern: A Cultural Critique of Psychoanalysis*. New York: Routledge.

Brenner, Charles. 1974. *An Elementary Textbook of Psychoanalysis*. Garden City, NY: Anchor Books.

Brown, Mary Ellen (ed.). 1990. *Television and Women's Culture: The Politics of the Popular*. Newbury Park, CA: Sage Publications.

Brown, Mary Ellen. 1994. *Soap Opera and Woman's Talk: The Pleasure of Resistance*. Thousand Oaks, CA: Sage Publications.

Buck-Morss, Susan. 1989. *The Dialectics of Seeing: Walter Benjamin and the Arcades Project*. Minneapolis, MN: University of Minnesota Press.

Burton, Graeme. 1990. *More Than Meets the Eye: An Introduction to Media Studies*. London: Arnold.

Butler, Judith. 1993. *Bodies That Matter*. New York: Routledge.

Cantor, Muriel G., and Joel M. Cantor. 1991. *Prime-Time Television: Content and Control*. Thousand Oaks, CA: Sage Publications.

Cantor, Muriel G. 1988. *The Hollywood TV Producer*. New Brunswick, NJ: Transaction.

Carey, James (ed.). *Media, Myths and Narratives: Television and the Press*. Newbury Park, CA: Sage Publications.

Certeau, Michel de. 1984. *The Practice of Everyday Life* (Transl. by Steven Rendall). Berkeley, CA: University of California Press.

Certeau, Michel de. 1986. *Heterologies: Discourse on the Other* (Transl. by Brian Massumi). Minneapolis, MN: University of Minnesota Press.

Clarke, John. 1992. *New Times and Old Enemies: Essays on Cultural Studies and America*. London: Routledge.

Collins, Richard, James Curran, Nicholas Garnham, and Paddy Scannell (eds.). 1986. *Media, Culture & Society: A Critical Reader*. Newbury Park, CA: Sage Publications.

Coward, Rosalind, and John Ellis. 1977. *Language and Materialism: Developments in Semiology and the Theory of the Subject*. London: Routledge & Kegan Paul.

Crane, Diane. 1992. *The Production of Culture: Media and the Urban Arts*. Newbury Park, CA: Sage Publications.

Creed, Barbara. 1993. *The Monstrous-Feminine: Film, Feminism, Psychoanalysis*, London: Routledge.

Creedon, Pamela J. 1993. *Women in Mass Communication* (2nd ed.). Thousand Oaks, CA: Sage Publications.

Crook, Stephen, Jan Pakulski, and Malcolm Waters (eds.). 1992. *Postmodernization: Change in Advanced Society*. London: Sage Publications.

Cross, Gary. 1993. *Time and Money: The Making of a Consumer Culture*. London: Routledge.

Culler, Jonathan. 1976. *Structuralist Poetics: Structuralism, Linguistics and the Study of Literature*. Ithaca, NY: Cornell University Press.

Culler, Jonathan. 1977. *Ferdinand de Saussure*. New York: Penguin Books.

Culler, Jonathan. 1981. *The Pursuit of Signs*. Ithaca, NY: Cornell University Press.

Culler, Jonathan. 1982. *On Deconstruction*. Ithaca, NY: Cornell University Press.

Danesi, Marcel, and Donato Santeramo (eds.). 1992. *Introducing Semiotics: An Anthology of Readings*. Toronto: Canadian Scholars Press.

Danesi, Marcel. 1994. *Messages and Meanings: An Introduction to Semiotics*. Toronto: Canadian Scholars Press.

Danesi, Marcel. 2002. *Understanding Media Semiotics*. London: Arnold.

Davis, Robert Con, and Ronald Schleifer. 1991. *Criticism & Culture*. London: Longman.

Denney, Reuel. 1989. *The Astonished Muse*. New Brunswick, NJ: Transaction.

Denzin, Norman K. 1991. *Images of Postmodern Society: Social Theory and Contemporary Cinema*. London: Sage Publications.

Doane, Mary Ann. 1991. *Femmes Fatales*. New York: Routledge.

Donald, James, and Stuart Hall (eds.). 1985. *Politics and Ideology*. Bristol, PA: Taylor & Francis.

Douglas, Mary. 1975. *Implicit Meanings: Essays in Anthropology*. London: Routledge & Kegan Paul.

Douglas, Mary. 1992. *Risk and Blame: Essays in Cultural Theory*. London: Routledge.

Douglas, Mary. 1997. "In Defence of Shopping." In *The Shopping Experience*. Edited by Pasi Falk and Colin Campbell. London: Sage Publications.

Duncan, Hugh Dalziel. 1985. *Communication and the Social Order*. New Brunswick, NJ: Transaction.

Dundes, Alan. 1987. *Cracking Jokes: Studies in Sick Humor Cycles and Stereotypes*. Berkeley, CA: Ten Speed Press.

Durkheim, Emile. 1967. *The Elementary Forms of the Religious Life*. New York: The Free Press.

Dyer, Richard. 1993. *The Matter of Images: Essays on Representations*. London: Routledge.

Eagleton, Terry. 1976. *Marxism and Literary Criticism*. Berkeley, CA: University of California Press.

Eagleton, Terry. 1983. *Literary Theory: An Introduction*. Minneapolis, MN: University of Minnesota Press.

Easthope, Antony. 1991. *Literary into Cultural Studies*. London: Routledge.

Eco, Umberto. 1972. "Towards a Semiotic Inquiry into the Television Message." *Working Papers in Cultural Studies*. Autumn, no. 3.

Eco, Umberto. 1976. *A Theory of Semiotics*. Bloomington: Indiana University Press.

Eco, Umberto. 1984. *The Role of the Reader*. Bloomington, IN: Indiana University Press.

Elam, Keir. 1980. *The Semiotics of Theatre and Drama*. London: Methuen.

Ettema, James S., and D. Charles Whitney (eds.). 1994. *Audiencemaking: How the Media Create the Audience*. Thousand Oaks, CA: Sage Publications.

Ewen, Stuart. 1976. *Captains of Consciousness*. New York: McGraw-Hill.

Ewen, Stuart, and Elizabeth Ewen. 1982. *Channels of Desire: Mass Images and the Shaping of American Consciousness*. New York: McGraw-Hill.

Featherstone, Mike. 1991. *Consumer Culture & Postmodernism*. London: Sage Publications.

Fiske, John, and John Hartley. 1978. *Reading Television*. London: Methuen & Co.

Fiske, John. 1989. *Reading the Popular*. London: Routledge.

Fiske, John. 1989. *Understanding Popular Culture*. London: Routledge.

Fjellman, Stephen M. 1992. *Vinyl Leaves: Walt Disney World and America*. Boulder, CO: Westview.

Franklin, Sarah, Celia Lury, and Jackie Stacey. 1992. *Off-Centre: Feminism and Cultural Studies*. London: Routledge.

Freud, Sigmund. 1960. *A General Introduction to Psychoanalysis* (Transl. by Joan Riviere). New York: Washington Square Press.

Freud, Sigmund. 1963. *Jokes and Their Relation to the Unconscious* (Transl. by James Strachey). New York: W.W. Norton.

Freud, Sigmund. 1965. *The Interpretation of Dreams* (Transl. by James Strachey). New York: Avon.

Frith, Simon. 1981. *Sound Effects: Youth, Leisure and the Politics of Rock and Roll*. New York: Pantheon.

Fry, William F. 1968. *Sweet Madness: A Study of Humor*. Palo Alto, CA: Pacific Books.

Gandelman, Claude. 1991. *Reading Pictures, Viewing Texts*. Bloomington, IN: Indiana University Press.

Garber, Marjorie, Jann Matlock, and Rebecca Walkowtiz (eds.). 1993. *Media Spectacles*. New York: Routledge.

Garber, Marjorie, Pratibha Parmar, and John Greyson (eds.). 1993. *Queer Looks: Perspectives on Lesbian and Gay Film and Video*. New York: Routledge.

Garber, Marjorie. 1993. *Vested Interests: Cross-Dressing and Cultural Anxiety*. New York: HarperPerennial.

Gitlin, Todd. 1985. *Inside Prime Time*. New York: Pantheon.

Goldstein, Ann, Mary Jane Jacob, Anne Rorimer, and Howard Singerman. *A Forest of Signs: Art in the Crisis of Representation*. Cambridge, MA: MIT Press.

Gowans, Alan. 1971. *The Unchanging Arts: New Forms for the Traditional Functions of Art in Society*. Philadelphia: J. B. Lippincott

Greenblatt, Stephen J. 1992. *Learning to Curse: Essays in Early Modern Culture*. New York: Routledge.

Greenfield, Kent. "How to Make the 'Citizens United' Decision Worse." *The Washington Post*, January 19, 2012.

Greenfield, Lauren. 2002. *Girl Culture*. San Francisco: Chronicle Books.

Grossberg, Lawrence, Cary Nelson, and Paula Treicher. 1991. *Cultural Studies*. New York: Routledge.

Grossberg, Lawrence. 1992. *We Gotta Get Out of This Place: Popular Conservatism and Postmodern Culture*. New York: Routledge.

Grotjahn, Martin. 1966. *Beyond Laughter: Humor and the Subconscious*. New York: McGraw-Hill.

Guiraud, Pierre. 1975. *Semiology*. London: Routledge & Kegan Paul.

Gumbrecht, Hansl Ulrich. 1992. *Making Sense in Life and Literature* (Transl. by Glen Burns). Minneapllis, MN: University of Minnesota Press.

Habermas, Jurgen. 1987. *The Philosophical Discourse of Modernity: Twelve Lectures* (Transl. by Frederick G. Lawrence). Minneapolis, MN: University of Minnesota Press.

Habermas, Jurgen. 1989. *The New Conservatism: Cultural Criticism and the Historians' Debate* (Transl. by Shierry Weber Nicholsen). Minneapolis, MN: University of Minnesota Press.

Hall, Stuart, and Paddy Whannel. 1967. *The Popular Arts: A Critical Guide to the Mass Media*. Boston: Beacon Press.

Hall, Stuart. 1988. *The Hard Road to Renewal*. London: Verso.

Hall, Stuart. 1991. *New Times: The Changing Face of Politics in the 1990s*. London: Routledge.

Hall, Stuart, and Tony Jefferson (eds.). 1990. *Resistance through Rituals: Youth Subcultures in Postwar Britain*. London: Routledge. (This was originally published as *Working Papers in Cultural Studies* 7/8 from the Centre for Contemporary Cultural Studies at the University of Birmingham. For an in-depth study of Stuart Hall's work, see *Journal of Communication Inquiry*, Summer 1986, which is devoted to him.)

Hartley, John. 1992. *The Politics of Pictures: The Creation of the Public in the Age of Popular Media*. London: Routledge.

Hartley, John. 1992. *Tele-ology: Studies in Television*. London: Routledge.

Haug, W. F. 1971. *Critique of Commodity Aesthetics: Appearance, Sexuality and Advertising in Capitalist Society* (Transl. by Robert Bock). Minneapolis, MN: University of Minnesota Press.

Haug, W. F. 1987. *Commodity Aesthetics, Ideology & Culture*. New York: International General.

Herzog-Massing, Herta. 1986. "Decoding *Dallas*." *Society* 24, no. 1, 74–77.

Hoggart, Richard. 1992. *The Uses of Literacy*. New Brunswick, NJ: Transaction Books.

Hoover, Stewart M. 1988. *Mass Media Religion: The Social Sources of the Electronic Church*. Newbury Park, CA: Sage Publications.

Hutcheon, Linda. 1989. *The Politics of Postmodernism*. London: Routledge.

Iser, W. 1988. "The Reading Process: A Phenomenological approach." In D. Lodge (Ed.) *Modern Criticism and Theory: A Reader*. New York: Longman. (Original work published in 1972.)

Jacobs, Norman (ed.) 1992. *Mass Media in Modern Society*. New Brunswick, NJ: Transaction.

Jakobson, Roman. 1985. *Verbal Art, Verbal Sign, Verbal Time* (ed. by Krystyna Pomorska and Stephen Rudy). Minneapolis, MN: University of Minnesota Press.

Jally, Sut, and Justin Lewis. 1992. *Enlightened Racism: The Cosby Show, Audiences and the Myth of the American Dream*. Boulder, CO: Westview.

Jameson, Frederic. 1981. *The Political Unconscious*. Ithaca, NY: Cornell University Press.

Jameson, Frederic. 1991. *Postmodernism: Or the Cultural Logic of Late Capitalism*. Durham, NC: Duke University Press.

Jameson, Frederic. 1992. *The Geopolitical Aesthetic: Cinema and Space in the World System*. Bloomington, IN: Indiana University Press.

Jameson, Frederic. 1992. *Signatures of the Visible*. New York: Routledge.

Jauss, Hans Robert. 1982. *Toward an Aesthetic of Reception* (Transl. by Timothy Bahti). Minneapolis, MN: University of Minnesota Press.

Jensen, Joli. 1990. *Redeeming Modernity: Contradictions in Media Criticism*. Newbury Park, CA: Sage Publications.

Jones, Steve. 1992. *Rock Formation: Music, Technology and Mass Communication*. Thousand Oaks, CA: Sage Publications.

Jones, Steven G. (ed.). 1994. *Cybersociety: Computer-Mediated Communication and Community*. Thousand Oaks, CA: Sage Publications.

Jowett, Garth, and James M. Linton. 1989. *Movies as Mass Communication*. Newbury Park, CA: Sage Publications.

Jowett, Garth S., and Victoria O'Donnell. 1992. *Propaganda and Persuasion* (2nd ed.). Thousand Oaks, CA: Sage Publications.

Jung, Carl G. (ed.). 1968. *Man and His Symbols*. New York: Dell.

Kamalipour, Yahya R., and Kuldip R. Rampal (eds.). 2001. *Media, Sex, Violence, and Drugs in the Global Village*. Lanham, MD: Rowman & Littlefield.

Kellner, Douglas. 1992. *The Persian Gulf TV War*. Boulder, CO: Westview.

Korzenny, Felix, and Stella Ting-Toomey (eds.). 1992. *Mass Media Effects Across Cultures*. Newbury Park, CA: Sage Publications.

Lacan, Jacques. 1966. *Ecrits: A Selection* (Transl. by Alan Sheridan). New York: Norton.

Laurentis, Teresa de. 1984. *Alice Doesn't: Feminism, Semiotics, Cinema.* Blooming-ton, IN: Indiana University Press.

Laurentis, Teresa de. 1987. *Technologies of Gender: Essays on Theory, Film and Fiction.* Bloomington, IN: Indiana University Press.

Lazere, Donald (ed.). 1987. *American Media and Mass Culture: Left Perspectives.* Berkeley, CA: University of California Press.

Lefebvre, Henri. 1984. *Everyday Life in the Modern World* (Transl. by Sacha Rabi-novitch). New Brunswick, NJ: Transaction.

Levine, Robert. "The Cloud Goes to Hollywood." http://tech.fortune.cnn.com/tag/ultraviolet/

Lévi-Strauss, Claude. 1967. *Structural Anthropology.* Garden City, NY: Doubleday.

Levy, Mark R., and Michael Gurevitch (eds.) 1994. *Defining Media Studies: Reflec-tions on the Future of the Field.* New York: Oxford University Press.

Lipsitz, George. 1989. *Time Passages: Collective Memory and American Popular Culture.* Minneapolis, MN: University of Minnesota Press.

Lotman, Yuri M. 1976. *Semiotics of Cinema.* Ann Arbor, MI: Michigan Slavic Contributions.

Lotman, Yuri M. 1977. *The Structure of the Artistic Text* (Transl. by Gail Lenhoff and Ronald Vroon). Ann Arbor, MI: Michigan Slavic Contributions.

Lotman, Yuri M. 1991. *Universe of the Mind: A Semiotic Theory of Culture.* Bloom-ington, IN: Indiana University Press.

Lull, James. 1991. *Popular Music and Communication.* Thousand Oaks, CA: Sage Publications.

Lunenfeld, Peter (ed.). 1999. *The Digital Dialectic: New Essays on New Media.* Cam-bridge, MA: The MIT Press.

Lyotard, Jean-François. 1984. *The Postmodern Condition: A Report on Knowledge.* Minneapolis, MN: University of Minnesota Press.

MacCannell, Dean, and Juliet Flower MacCannell. 1982. *The Time of the Sign: A Semiotic Interpretation of Modern Culture.* Bloomington, IN: Indiana University Press.

MacDonald, J. Fred. 1994. *One Nation Under Television.* Chicago: Nelson-Hall.

Mandel, Ernest. 1985. *Delightful Murder: A Social History of the Crime Story.* Min-neapolis, MN: University of Minnesota Press.

Mattelart, Armand, and Michele Mattelart. 1992. *Rethinking Media Theory* (Transl. by James A. Cohen and Marina Urquidi). Minneapolis, MN: University of Min-nesota Press.

McCarthy, Thomas. 1991. *Ideals and Illusions: On Reconstruction and Deconstruction in Contemporary Critical Theory.* Cambridge, MA: MIT Press.

McCue, Greg, with Clive Bloom. 1993. *Dark Knights: The New Comics in Context.* Boulder, CO: Westview.

McLuhan, Marshall. 1965. *Understanding Media: The Extensions of Man.* New York: McGraw-Hill.

McLuhan, Marshall, and Quentin Fiore. 1967. *The Medium Is the Message.* New York: Bantam Books.

McLuhan, Marshall. 1970. *Culture Is Our Business.* New York: McGraw-Hill.

McQuail, Denis. 1992. *Media Performance: Mass Communication and the Public Interest.* Thousand Oaks, CA: Sage Publications.

McQuail, Denis. 1994. *Mass Communication Theory: An Introduction* (3rd ed.). Thousand Oaks, CA: Sage Publications.

Mellencamp, Patricia. 1990. *Indiscretions: Avant-Garde Film, Video and Feminism.* Bloomington, IN: Indiana University Press.

Mellencamp, Patricia (ed.). 1990. *Logics of Television: Essays in Cultural Criticism.* Bloomington, IN: Indiana University Press.

Memmett, Carol. "E-book Popularity Is Rewriting the Sales Story," *USA Today,* September 6, 2011.

Messaris, Paul. 1994. *Visual Literacy: Image, Mind & Reality.* Boulder, CO: Westview Press.

Metz, Christian. 1982. *The Imaginary Signifier: Psychoanalysis and the Cinema* (Transl. by Celia Britton et al.). Bloomington, IN: Indiana University Press.

Mindess, Harvey. 1971. *Laughter and Liberation.* Los Angeles: Nash Publishing.

Modleski, Tania. 1984. *Loving with a Vengeance: Mass-Produced Fantasies for Women.* New York: Routledge.

Modleski, Tania (ed.). 1986. *Studies in Entertainment: Critical Approaches to Mass Culture.* Bloomington, IN: Indiana University Press.

Modleski, Tania. 1988. *The Women Who Knew Too Much: Hitchcock and Feminist Theory.* New York: Routledge.

Moores, Shaun. 1994. *Interpreting Audiences: The Ethnography of Media Consumption.* Thousand Oaks, CA: Sage Publications.

Morley, David. 1988. *Family Television: Cultural Power and Domestic Leisure.* London: Routledge.

Morley, David. 1993. *Television Audiences and Cultural Studies.* London: Routledge.

Mulvey, Laura. 1989. *Visual and Other Pleasures.* Bloomington, IN: Indiana University Press.

Nash, Christopher (ed.). 1990. *Narrative in Culture.* London: Routledge.

Nichols, Bill. 1981. *Ideology and the Image: Social Representation in the Cinema and Other Media.* Bloomington, IN: Indiana University Press.

Nichols, Bill. 1992. *Representing Reality: Issues and Concepts in Documentary.* Bloomington, IN: Indiana University Press.

O'Shaughnessy, Michael. (2002) *Media and Society: An Introduction.* New York: Oxford University Press.

Penley, Constance. 1989. *The Future of an Illusion: Film, Feminism and Psychoanalysis.* Minneapolis, MN: University of Minnesota Press.

Phelan, James (ed.). 1989. *Reading Narrative: Form, Ethics, Ideology.* Columbus, OH: Ohio State University Press.

Potter, W. James. 1998. *Media Literacy.* Thousand Oaks, CA: Sage Publications.

Powell, Chris, and George E. C. Paton (eds.). 1988. *Humour in Society: Resistance and Control.* New York: St. Martin's Press.

Prindle, David. F. 1993. *Risky Business: The Political Economy of Hollywood*. Boulder, CO: Westview.

Propp, Vladimir. 1973. *Morphology of the Folk Tale* (2nd ed.) Austin, TX: University of Texas Press.

Propp, Vladimir. 1984. *Theory and History of Folklore* (Transl. by Ariadna Y. Martin and Richard P. Martin). Minneapolis, MN: University of Minnesota Press.

Ramet, Sabrina Petra (ed.). 1993. *Rocking the State: Rock Music and Politics in Eastern Europe and the Soviet Union*. Boulder, CO: Westview.

Real, Michael R. 1989. *Supermedia: A Cultural Studies Approach*. Newbury Park, CA: Sage Publications.

Reinelt, Janelle G., and Joseph R. Roach (eds.) 1993. *Critical Theory and Performance*. Ann Arbor, MI: University of Michigan Press.

Richardson, Glenn W., Jr. 2003. *Pulp Politics: How Political Advertising Tells the Stories of American Politics*. Lanham, MD: Rowman & Littlefield.

Richter, Mischa, and Harald Bakken. 1992. *The Cartoonist's Muse: A Guide to Generating and Developing Creative Ideas*. Chicago: Contemporary Books.

Ryan, John, and William M. Wentworth. 1998. *Media and Society: The Production of Culture in the Mass Media*. New York: Allyn & Bacon.

Ryan, Michael, and Douglas Kellner. 1988. *Camera Politica: The Politics and Ideology and Contemporary Hollywood Film*. Bloomington, IN: Indiana University Press.

Sabin, Roger. 1993. *Adult Comics: An Introduction*. London: Routledge.

Saussure, Ferdinand de. 1966. *Course in General Linguistics* (Transl. by Wade Baskin). New York: McGraw-Hill.

Schechner, Richard. 1993. *The Future of Ritual: Writings on Culture and Performance*. London: Routledge.

Scheuer, Jeffrey. 1999. *The Sound Bite Society: Television and the American Mind*. New York: Four Walls Eight Windows.

Schwichtenberg, Cathy (ed.). 1993. *The Madonna Collection*. Boulder, CO: Westview.

Schneider, Cynthia, and Brian Wallis (eds.). 1989. *Global Television*. Cambridge, MA: MIT Press.

Schostak, John. 1993. *Dirty Marks: The Education of Self, Media and Popular Culture*. Boulder, CO: Westview.

Seig, Philip. 2002. *Going Live: Getting the News Right in a Real-Time Online World*. Lanham, MD: Rowman & Littlefield.

Sebeok, Thomas (ed.). 1978. *Sight, Sound and Sense*. Bloomington, IN: Indiana University Press

Seldes, Gilbert. 1994. *The Public Arts*. New Brunswick, NJ: Transaction.

Shukman, Ann. 1977. *Literature and Semiotics: A Study of the Writings of Yuri M. Lotman*. Amsterdam: North-Holland Publishing.

Silverman, Kaja. 1983. *The Subject of Semiotics*. New York: Oxford University Press.

Skovman, Michael (ed.). Undated. *Media Fictions*. Aarhus, DK: Aarhus University Press.

Smith, Gary (ed.). *On Walter Benjamin: Critical Essays and Recollections*. Cambridge, MA: MIT Press.

Steidman, Steven. 1993. *Romantic Longings: Love in America 1830–1980*. New York: Routledge.

Stephenson, William. 1988. *The Play Theory of Mass Communication*. New Brunswick, NJ: Transaction.

Stetler, Brian. "8 Hours a Day Spent on Screens." *The New York Times*, March 16, 2009.

Szondi, Peter. 1986. *On Textual Understanding* (Transl. by Harvey Mendelsohn). Minneapolis, MN: University of Minnesota Press.

Theall, Donald F. 2001. *The Virtual Marshall McLuhan*. Montreal & Kingston: McGill-Queen's University Press.

Todorov, Tzvetan. 1975. *The Fantastic: A Structural Approach to a Literary Genre* (Transl. by Richard Howard). Ithaca, NY: Cornell University Press.

Todorov, Tzvetan. 1981. *Introduction to Poetics* (Transl. by Richard Howard). Minneapolis, MN: University of Minnesota Press.

Traube, Elizabeth G. 1992. *Dreaming Identities: Class, Gender, and Generation in the 1980s Hollywood Movies*. Boulder, CO: Westview.

Turkle, Sherry. 2011. *Alone Together: Why We Expect More from Technology and Less from Each Other*. New York: Basic Books.

Turner, Bryan S. 1990. *Theories of Modernity and Postmodernity*. London: Sage Publications

Van Zoonen, Liesbet. 1994. *Feminist Media Studies*. Thousand Oaks, CA: Sage Publications.

Volosinov, V. N. 1987. *Freudianism: A Critical Sketch* (Transl. by I. R. Titunik). Bloomington, IN: Indiana University Press.

Weibel, Kathryn. 1977. *Mirror Mirror: Images of Women Reflected in Popular Culture*. Garden City, NY: Anchor Books.

Wernick, Andrew. 1991. *Promotional Culture*. London: Sage Publications.

Willemen, Paul. 1993. *Looks and Frictions: Essays in Cultural Studies and Film Theory*. Bloomington, IN: Indiana University Press.

Williams, Raymond. 1958. *Culture and Society: 1780–1950*. New York: Columbia University Press.

Williams, Raymond. 1976. *Keywords*. New York: Oxford University Press.

Williams, Raymond. 1977. *Marxism and Literature*. New York: Oxford University Press.

Williams, Rosalind. 1990. *Notes on the Underground: An Essay on Technology, Society and the Imagination*. Cambridge, MA: MIT Press.

Williamson, Judith. 1978. *Decoding Advertisements: Ideology and Meaning in Advertising*. London: Marion Boyars.

Willis, Paul. 1990. *Common Culture: Symbolic Work at Play in the Everyday Cultures of the Young*. Boulder, CO: Westview.

Wilson, Clint C., and Felix Gutierrez. 1985. *Minorities and Media: Diversity and the End of Mass Communication*. Thousand Oaks, CA: Sage Publications.

Winick, Charles. 1994. *Desexualization in American Life: The New People*. New Brunswick, NJ: Transaction.

Wintour, Patrick. "Facebook and Bebo Risk 'Infantilizing' the Human Mind" *The Guardian*, February 24, 2009.

Wollen, Peter. 1972. *Signs and Meaning in the Cinema*. Bloomington, IN: Indiana University Press.

Wollen, Peter. 1993. *Raiding the Icebox: Reflections on Twentieth-Century Culture*. Bloomington, IN: Indiana University Press.

Wright, Will. 1975. *Sixguns and Society: A Structural Study of the Western*. Berkeley, CA: University of California Press.

Zettl, Herbert. 1973. *Sight, Sound, Motion*. Belmont, CA: Wadsworth.

Zizek, Slavoi. 1991. *Looking Awry: An Introduction to Jacques Lacan through Popular Culture*. Cambridge, MA: MIT Press.

INDEX

ABOUT THE AUTHOR

Arthur Asa Berger is professor emeritus of Broadcast and Electronic Communication Arts at San Francisco State University, where he taught from 1965 until 2003. He was a Fulbright Scholar at the University of Milan in 1963 and a visiting professor at the Annenberg School for Communication at the University of Southern California in 1984. He taught a short course on advertising and American culture at the Heinrich Heine University in Dusseldorf in 2002 as a Fulbright Senior Specialist and lectured on semiotics and media analysis at the University of Buenos Aires and other institutions of higher learning in Argentina as a Fulbright Senior Specialist in 2012. He has lectured at more than twenty universities in countries such as England, France, Finland, Brazil, Turkey, Morocco, Tunisia, Thailand, Cambodia, and Vietnam. His books have been translated into Italian, Swedish, German, Korean, Chinese, Turkish, Indonesian, and Arabic.

Berger has been writing about media and popular culture for more than fifty years. His MA thesis in 1956 was on the reception of the historian Arnold Toynbee in the American magazine press, and his doctoral dissertation, in 1965, was on Al Capp's comic strip *Li'l Abner*. His dissertation was published as *Li'l Abner: A Study in American Satire*. He has published more than sixty books and more than one hundred articles and countless book reviews over the course of his career. He was in the Army from 1956 to 1958 and wrote high school sports for the *Washington Post* during this period.

In recent years, Berger has written a number of comic academic novels that also function as textbooks: *Postmortem for a Postmodernist* (AltaMira Press), *The Mass Comm Murders: Five Media Theorists Self-Destruct* (Rowman & Littlefield), *Durkheim Is Dead: Sherlock Holmes Is Introduced to Social Theory* (AltaMira Press), and *The Hamlet Case* (XLibris). These four mysteries have also been translated into Chinese.

235

Berger is married to a former philosophy professor, Phyllis Wolfson Berger, and has two children and four grandchildren. He lives in Mill Valley, California, and can be reached at arthurasaberger@gmail.com or arthurasaberger@yahoo.com.